PHILLIPSBURG LIBRARY

6748 9100 055 711 2

THIS BOOK IS NO LONGER THE
PROPERTY OF THE PHILLIPSBURG
FREE PUBLIC LIBRARY

DATE DUE

6 9 04

D1502311

The FASTEST TRAINS in the World

FREE PUBLIC LIBRARY
PHILLIPSBURG, N. J.

The
FASTEST TRAINS
in the World

G. Freeman Allen

THIS BOOK IS NO LONGER THE
PROPERTY OF THE PHILLIPSBURG
FREE PUBLIC LIBRARY

Charles Scribner's Sons
New York

385.22
Allen

Copyright © G. Freeman Allen 1978

Copyright under the Berne Convention

All rights reserved. No part of this book
may be reproduced in any form without the
permission of Charles Scribner's Sons

1 3 5 7 9 11 13 15 17 19 I/C 20 18 16 14 12 10 8 6 4 2

Printed in Great Britain
Library of Congress Catalog Card Number 78-64377
ISBN 0-684-16075-7

By the same author
Modern Railways the World Over
British Railways Today and Tomorrow
British Rail After Beeching
The Last Years of British Steam
Salute to the LNER

Contents

Introduction

This book is deliberately titled. It is about the 'Fastest Trains' rather than the 'Fastest Railways' because, for me, a train in the world of transport has only one connotation. I concede that the term 'railway' might be stretched to cover any form of track to guide vehicles, but a 'train' is a steel-wheeled vehicle or vehicles on steel rails and nothing else. So this is a book about proper trains. It has nothing to do with air-cushions, Maglev, or any other of the guided transport exotica for which so much has been promised in recent years, so little as yet realised.

Nor is it a book for the dedicated engineering student. I have dealt only in such basic technical detail as seems essential to an understanding of the practical and economic barriers to rapid advance of everyday inter-city speed on rails.

Practical social value apart, speed on rail has fascinated more people of all ages, I fancy, than the pace of any public transport. Is even Concorde as riveting as a hundred-mile-an-hour train? From a starting-point around 1900, when railways were first reaching for the 'ton', I have tried to relive all the nail-biting excitements in assembling a narrative of the major high-speed exploits of the past around the world. That leavens, I hope, the main substance of the book, which aims to enlighten on the countless factors with which railway managements and engineers must reckon before they can significantly accelerate today's inter-city trains. It has been no easier to translate the remarkable French test exploits at 200mph of 1955 into everyday passenger performance at tolerable cost than to transmute supersonic military aircraft design into a viable passenger jetliner format. Researching this book, I have been forcibly reminded of the way so many euphoric speed forecasts of the late 1960s and early 1970s have collapsed under fuller appreciation of all the problems. In those days there was scarcely a major railway in the West which wasn't confident of running 150mph or 250kmph trains before the decade was out. (And by the 1980s, of course, we were sure to be flitting about the countryside at 300mph or 500kmph in tracked hovercraft, Maglev cars or whatever.) By the late 1970s, in contrast, only the French sound certain of running 150mph (250kmph) trains intensively before the 1980s recede.

I should add that, so far as future high-speed prospects are concerned, I have dealt only with trains and equipment that have already had their potential publicly proved at the time of writing. Thus, for instance, I have not felt able to discuss the Russian prototype equipment — the Riga-built ER200 electric multiple-unit and Czech-built CH200 electric locomotive prototype to work with Russian RT200 'Troika' coaches — which in early 1978 were starting trials with a view to 125mph (200kmph) operation on the Moscow-Leningrad line.

Finally, my warm thanks to the many agencies and individuals around the high-speed railway world who have helped gild the text with illustrations. Each is appropriately credited on the pages concerned.

Laleham-on-Thames
January, 1978

G. Freeman Allen

1. Steam's Quest for the Hundred

Nowadays no one is quite sure of the ultimate practical limit of speed on rail. Ever since the French suddenly burst through the 200 miles-an-hour and 300 kilometres an hour barrier in a carefully planned series of test runs in 1955, the crunch has been cost, not technological capability. No doubt about it, the rapid advance in rail traction and vehicle technology since the 1950s have made trains to standardise the peak French speeds of 1955 perfectly feasible. But can 200mph or 300kmph be run day in, day out economically, without intolerably expensive wear and tear on track and vehicles — or without enormous cost in technical innovation or track rebuilding to avoid it?

There are almost as many theoretical answers to that question as there are rail engineering chiefs around the world's major rail systems. And according to which of them you believe, the rail speed horizon today for practical purposes of day-to-day operation is anything from 150 to 300 miles an hour or 250 to 500 kilometres an hour.

In the second half of the last century and the first half of this there was only one speed mark that counted. It was the same worldwide, except that if you dealt in traditional Anglo-Saxon terms it was 100 miles an hour and if you worked in metrics, 160 kilometres an hour. One didn't have to be an experienced technologist to deduce that the orthodox steam locomotive could not be pushed much faster.

The 100mph-160kmph barrier was probably broken for the first time around the turn of the century. One has to write 'probably' because, *pace* the chauvinists on both sides of the Atlantic, scarcely any of the early claims are backed by watertight evidence that defies analysis. None of the American exploits was scientifically timed. The solitary British 'hundred' was certainly timed by a respected recorder on the train, but subsequent dissection of his statistics has suggested that he may have been momentarily distracted and jotted down an exaggerated peak speed.

Some of the records alleged were plainly incredible. For instance, there was the ludicrous tale of a freight engine, commandeered to replace a failed locomotive on the 'Florida Mail' of the onetime Plant system, later the US Atlantic Coast line, which was supposed to have hurtled over the final five miles (8.04km) of its run to a dead stand at Jacksonville, Fla, in just 2½ minutes. Allowing for deceleration, that would have meant the engine careering into this stretch at a peak of around 140mph (225kmph)!

Even the two runs that are revered as authentic in all North American record books (if not in Europe, because fully timed data in support is lacking) are open to question in the hindsight of latter-day steam locomotive science. That the late 19th Century techniques of steam passage layout and valve-setting were advanced enough to allow an engine to apply and exhaust steam at anywhere near the rapidity essential to hold the 120mph (193.08kmph) claimed is hard to credit. Obviously, though, speeds exceptional for the period were attained.

Left: *Buchanan's 4-4-0 No 999, claimed to have worked the New York Central's 'Empire State Express' up to a peak of 112.5mph (181kmph) on 11 May 1893.* / Locomotive Publishing Co

The first of the two earliest American record claims that are most widely accepted was posted in May 1893. In that last decade of the 19th Century the New York Central was effectively run by the dynamic diarchy of its General Passenger Agent, a patent medicine salesman-turned-railroader named George H. Daniels, and its Superintendent of Motive Power & Rolling Stock, a Scot named William Buchanan who had started on the railroad workshop floor at 17 and then without a day of formal training worked his way up via both engine cab and lathe to the top engineering spot on Vanderbilt's railroad. Daniels was a born showman with a flair for promotion way ahead of his time. His was the authorship, for instance, of one of the world's most striking train names, 'Twentieth Century Limited', to epitomise the great historical step forward of the faster luxury trains he and Buchanan were engineering on the Central's route from New York to Chicago at the turn of the century. Another of Daniels' publicity strokes was the pioneering of free redcap baggage service for passengers, which won the Central immediate and widespread public kudos.

Intent on revolutionising the New York-Chicago rail service, Daniels seized on the 1893 staging of the Columbian Exhibition in Chicago as the opportunity for a short-term proving of equipment potential. That summer and autumn he put on the 'Empire State Express' to run New York Fair visitors to the Chicago fair in a hitherto unheard-of 20 hours for the 980 miles via Central's Lake Shore route. A splendorous overnight train-set was turned out for the service by the Wagner Palace Car Company, the last-surviving Pullman rival. Webster Wagner, a sometime politician as well as engineer, had so enthused Vanderbilt with the sleeping cars which he built for the Commodore's Hudson River Railroad in 1868 that Vanderbilt organised a company under Wagner's presidency which managed to evade the Pullman takeover maw until the turn of the century.

To front the 'Empire State Express' Buchanan turned out, expectedly, a 4-4-0. For Buchanan was the supreme advocate of this, the so-called 'American' wheel arrangement. Long after other American roads had stepped up to 4-4-2s and 4-6-0s, he clung to simply engineered and laid-out 4-4-0s as the ideal horses for speed over distance; and for quite a time the performance of his 4-4-0s confounded every critic — and they were many — who slated him for conservatism.

For Daniels' brainchild Buchanan had his West Albany shops build a one-off that was especially styled for pace. No 999's driving wheels were a striking 7ft 2in (2.184m) in diameter, so that the leading one had — unusually for an American engine — to be modestly splashered above the running plate; and she was air-braked on every wheel, those of her bogie tender included. Since engine and train were to be exhibited at Chicago between trips, she was elegantly finished, too; her injector pipes were nickel-plated, her cab was nicely done in black walnut and the legend 'Empire State Express' was boldly traced on her tender in silver-leaf script.

The first surge through the rail speed barrier was claimed for No 999 on 9 May 1893. The 'Empire State Express' was lagging behind the tight schedule — for those days — of 8 hours 40 minutes for the 440 miles (708km) from New York to Buffalo, four stops en route included. In an energetic time-recovery effort, so the conductor claimed, No 999 had whipped its four-car train up to a peak of 102.8mph (165.4kmph) in the course of covering 69 miles (111km) in 68 minutes.

Only two days later, on 11 May, the conductor maintained he had timed No 999's driver, Charlie Hogan, to do better still. As they stormed down a gentle 1 in 350 grade to Buffalo in the region of Batavia, NY, he had reckoned Hogan to cover a measured mile in 32 seconds flat by his watch. That was 112.5mph (181kmph). However vulnerable the evidence, on the strength of it the ebullient Daniels managed to persuade the US Postmaster General to display No 999 and train on a bi-coloured two-cent postage stamp. No 999 won herself eventual preservation and permanent display in Chicago's Museum of Science and Industry, even though some years later the New York Cental management itself conceded to sceptical foreign critics that the top speed on 11 May might have been no higher than 81mph.

In June 1902 George Daniels inaugurated his 'Twentieth Century Limited' and crystallised the 20 hour New York-Chicago timing as a daily service all year round. 'Surely', editorialised one incredulous English newspaper, 'it is only a experiment? There are over 900 miles between the two American cities. Can so high a rate of speed as will be necessary to accomplish the feat be maintained daily without injury to the engine, the rails and the coaches? The operators will soon find that they are wasting fortunes in keeping their property in condition and then, loving money better than notoriety, the 20 hour project will be abandoned.' It wasn't, of course; even with steam, whole hours were to be cut from the timing before diesels reduced the schedule to an ultimate 16 hours.

'America's Greatest Railroad' was Daniels' cherished tag for his New York Central. But the Pennsylvania topped that with the boast that it was 'The Standard Railroad of the World'. By the dawn of this century they were in fierce contention, above all in the long-haul New York-Chicago passenger business. Pennsylvania's route between the two cities was shorter, 908 miles (1,461km) against Central's 960 miles (1,545km), but west of Philadelphia its grading was severe, whereas the Central made much promotionally of its easier 'Water Level Route.' But if Central could make Chicago in 20 hours so could Pennsylvania, even though the latter's best train was dragging out as much as 28 hours on the run before the premiere of Central's 'Twentieth Century Limited'.

Americans were astounded when the Pennsylvania announced that from 15 June 1902, the very day of the rival 'Century's' debut, it would lop a whole eight hours from its New York-Chicago schedule and run a new 'Pennsylvania Special' between the two cities in 20 hours. The press blazoned a 'Great Speed War' in banner headlines and the public lapped it up as avidly as a World Series. Pennsylvania's 'Red Rippers', as they were popularly dubbed in the Eastern US by virtue of their traditional Pennsylvania Tuscan red livery, ran for just over a year and a half, until February 1904, when they were written out of the timetables because rising freight traffic in the Pittsburgh area was choking the layout and making hay of the 'Special's' timekeeping day after day.

But in 1905 the Pennsylvania swung back into attack. Since mid-1902 it had been steadily modifying its layout in the Pittsburgh area, creating new freight cut-off routes and switching traffic flows. Now it could dare even bolder schedules.

On 8 June 1905 the eastern US was astounded by a display advertisement in the New York Daily Tribune proclaiming: '18 Hours to Chicago — The Fastest Long Distance Train in the World — "The Pennsylvania Special".' Just three days later the 'Red Rippers' were to be dashingly reincarnated, an incredible two hours faster than before.

The gauntlet was scarcely grounded before Central grabbed it. The same two hours were slashed from the 'Century's' timecard; and Central, too, brazenly splashed its train with the identical slogan to Pennsylvania's 'Fastest Long Distance Train in the World', though granted they had possibly more right to the title in view of the Water Level Route's greater mileage. The speed war had been rejoined *con brio* and the public was enthralled. In those pre-airliner days, of course, rail was the fastest travel medium and excited as much press attention as the airlines do today; it wasn't only small-town American newspapers that thought even a modestly schedule-beating run worthwhile copy for its news pages.

Four cars made up the 'Pennsylvania Special': a combination baggage car and Pullman smoking saloon, draped with ornate tapestries and furnished with deep leather armchairs; a diner decked out in fine linen and gleaming silver where the catering was sumptuously elaborate; a 12-section Pullman sleeper that included a drawing room and a state room, staffed by both porter and maid; and a combined six-compartment and observation Pullman car, the saloon staff including a shorthand-typist whose services were free.

At the head end would be one of Pennsylvania's latest Class E2 Atlantics. The Pennsylvania had started to build 4-4-2s in 1899, beginning with centre-cab 'camelbacks' but soon switching to several series of orthodox engines. With these handsome machines Pennsylvania could at last match up to the neighbouring Philadelphia & Reading, with which it was in strenuous contention for the lucrative short-haul New Jersey passenger business from Camden to Atlantic City. In the last few years of the 19th Century the pacey exploits of Reading's Baldwin-built four-cylinder Vauclain compound 4-4-2s, vigorously publicised by the Reading management and happily rehearsed by the press, had badly scarred Pennsylvania pride. Mind you, the most striking feats claimed for the Reading Atlantics at this time lack any data to encourage credulity. On its booked times the Reading's Camden-Atlantic City 'Seashore Flyer' was certainly the world's fastest daily scheduled train in the late 1890s. Whether its Atlantic No 1027 did once, as alleged, reel off the 55.5 miles (89.3km) in 44¾ minutes with six cars and

285 passengers, or on another occasion hit a top speed of 106mph (170.6kmph) is something else.

But back to the 'Pennsylvania Special'. Among the engrossed travellers on the inaugural eastbound trip of the train's 1905 revival was a *Chicago Tribune* reporter. Wrote he:

'Had it been a circus train it would not have attracted any larger crowds along the way... Farmers from the country miles around drove their biggest wagons, loaded to the guards with their wives and children and their neighbours' children, to see the 18 hour train go by. They did not see much. The cry of the whistle and a cloud of smoke warned them of its coming. Then a flash of red, and in another second their straining eyes were gazing at the spot where the train had been... At Englewood, where a stop of one minute was made, the station platform was thronged with people, and their handkerchiefs made it look as if a cloud of white butterflies was just settling down upon them... At Fort Wayne, which was reached two minutes ahead of schedule, nearly 1,500 curiosity seekers were on hand to watch the progress of changing engines. Many a baseball game in progress along the way was halted as spectators and players alike gathered along the roadside to cheer the speeding train.'

It was the inaugural day's westbound 'Pennsylvania Special', though, which took posterity's headlines. Some 20 miles east of Mansfield, Ohio, the 'Special's' 4-4-2 was

Below: Another early American speed record claimant: four-cylinder Vauclain compound 4-4-2 No 1027 of the Philadelphia & Reading Railroad, with 'camelback' cab. It was said to have reached 106mph on the tightly-scheduled Camden-Atlantic City 'Seashore Flyer' in the late 1890s. / Locomotive Publishing Co

Above: *A Pennsylvania Atlantic on the Schuylkill River Bridge at Philadelphia; this 1907 scene pictures a Class E3a engine with a heavy consist of vintage wooden Pullmans.*

Right: *Heroine of the westbound 'Pennsylvania Special' run on 11 June 1905, when a speed record of 127.1mph (204.5kmph) was claimed between AY Tower and Elida, O., on the basis of recorded passing times: Class E2 4-4-2 No 7002 on display at the Chicago Railroad Fair of 1948-9.*

Below right: *The 'Pennsylvania Special' on the onetime steel truss bridge over the Schuylkill River at Philadelphia, headed by a Pennsylvania Class E2 4-4-2. / Locomotive Publishing Co*

lamed by a hot box. The engine of a freight train in the vicinity was hurriedly coupled in the cripple's place and trundled the 'Special' the next 30 miles or so to Crestline. There Engineer Jerry McCarthy and 4-4-2 No 7002 had been readied to take over, McCarthy under orders to recoup as much as possible of the 26 minutes deficit on schedule — and of the Pennsylvania's threatened reputation.

He drove like Jehu. From Crestline to Fort Wayne is 131.4 miles (211.4km) and they were gobbled up, according to the day's operating records, in 115 minutes. That alone, representing a start to stop average speed of 68.56mph (110.31kmph), was way above contemporary par for such a distance in any part of the world. But over the three miles (4.83km) from AY Tower to Elida in Ohio, they asserted, McCarthy had whipped his engine up to 127.1mph (204.5kmph).

A fantastic achievement — but perhaps literally so. What was the evidence? Just the passing times recorded by operating staff at each end of the section as the train flashed by them. The gulf between average speeds over the whole Crestline-Fort Wayne distance is so wide and the timing data so rudimentary that, taking into account the technological considerations I outlined earlier, one can only record that famously equivocal verdict of Scottish jurisprudence: not proven.

As a postscript it's worth adding that despite the public excitement generated by the 'Special's' sprint, it was Central's 'Century' that took and held the major share of the New York-Chicago passenger business. Pennsylvania had no counter to Daniels' flamboyant salesmanship — not least to his inspired choice of train name. Pennsylvania's passengers, in contrast, could seldom distinguish between the 'Pennsylvania Special' and the 'Pennsylvania Limited', another all-Pullman train on the same itinerary. So in November 1912 the 'Specials' were re-christened, at first 'Broad Way Limited' in recognition of Pennsylvania's six-track layout between New York and Philadelphia, but soon as the more familiar 'Broadway Limited'. With the renaming came deceleration of the now heavier train to a 20 hour New York-Chicago time.

A year ahead of these North American excitements the first 100mph had been claimed for European steam traction (as will be recounted in a later chapter, the first European 'hundreds' by any form of power are credited to German electric traction). As with the New York-Chicago exploit, this early European steam feat was the direct outcome of inter-railway rivalry.

At the turn of the century England's Great Western and London & South Western Railways were battling it out for transatlantic liner traffic from Plymouth to London. In 1903 the North German Lloyd and Hamburg-America lines, then the fastest on the North Atlantic route, elected to make Plymouth their English port. Although Plymouth was served by both GWR and LSWR, the GWR was far better prepared to pick the new plum; and initially it monopolised both passenger and mail traffic off the transatlantic ships.

But the LSWR, licking its lips at the income from its fine new Ocean Terminal at Southampton, was not about to be shut out of another lucrative-looking maritime business. It hastened to establish another new marine terminal at Plymouth, which was ready in 1904. That was the starting gun. True, both railways made the ensuing contest something of a 'friendly' by mutual agreement that the LSWR should carry the passengers, the GWR the mails: but even so it was a weighty matter of prestige whether passengers or mails reached London first.

With its fiery locomotive superintendent Dugald Drummond riding the passenger boat trains to screw endeavour up to the tightest pitch, the LSWR wasn't long in overtaking the GWR's headstart. By the end of April 1904, in fact, the LSWR train showed a very neat pair of heels to the Great Western mail. They would have been cleaner still but for the GWR's ace in the hole — the intersection of GWR and LSWR routes at Exeter, where the LSWR had to use GWR tracks for over a mile through Exeter St Davids station (but in the converse direction to GWR trains, as the LSWR route traced an inverted 'S' through the cathedral city).

When the LSWR's Class S11 4-4-0 came bounding down to the Exeter Cowley Bridge Junction with the GWR route on 23 April 1904, having negotiated the twisting, sharply graded 56¼ miles (90.5km) round the northern edge of Dartmoor in just over the hour, its crew were sanguinely expecting the GWR to forego its statutory right to halt every LSWR train in St Davids station. But not so. The LSWR driver and fireman were congratulating each other that they were on terms with the enemy, for the GWR mail train was at that moment bearing down on them in the opposite direction, when they caught the signals against them. Fuming, they ground the S11 to a halt, tugging the whistle chord furiously. For a whole half-minute the flinty-hearted GWR staff at Exeter let them stand and shriek their whistle before they were allowed to storm off up the hill on to their own route to London. Despite the enemy's sabotage, the LSWR managed to make their Waterloo terminus in London that day in a record 4 hours 3 minutes from Plymouth, well clear of the GWR mail train's arrival in the capital.

But exactly seven days later the mail train reached the GWR's Paddington terminus in London just 3 hours 54 minutes after departing Plymouth — and that with two engine changes en route, against the LSWR's one. But it was just a trailer for 9 May 1904. Not only was every Great Western man on the ground involved in the mail train operation keyed up, but also the mighty George Jackson Chuchward, the railway's revered locomotive chief. The track was in fine fettle and the operating organisation finely tuned, he told his enginemen: so let them go forth and 'break their bloody necks'. And what better pretext than a goodly cargo of gold, due to be transhipped to the mail train connecting with the German liner docking at Plymouth on 9 May?

Both railways from Plymouth to Exeter, the LSWR round the northern fringe and the GWR skirting the south of bleak Dartmoor, were nastily curved as the original engineers fought to take advantage of every contour of the hilly terrain and keep gradients in check. Even so, gradients were — and still are, in the case of the GWR line; much of the LSWR route has been closed in recent times — extremely severe. On the outskirts of Plymouth the GWR line soon strikes the steady 1 in 41 of Hemerdon bank. Beyond that it still climbs, but not so steeply, to Wrangaton, then dips, easily at first until at Rattery signalbox the slope sharpens to a precipitate 1 in 46-57 into the delightful valley town of Totnes. From Totnes a train curves into the famous climb to Dainton summit, which steepens eventually to 1 in 37 before the tunnel crowning the summit. Then follows an equally swift downhill descent to Newton Abbot, after which it is level pegging along the sea wall from Teignmouth to Starcross and up the Exe Valley to Exeter. Because of the curvature the whole Plymouth-Exeter section is stringently speed-restricted and there is little scope to exploit the down grades. Even with modern diesel traction an engine crew respecting the rules would be unlikely to better today's non-stop schedule of 45 minutes for the 31.85 miles (51.25km) by much.

Yet on 9 May 1904 Driver Clements thrashed his elegant inside-cylinder 4-4-0 *City of Truro* up the slopes and round the curves with such abandon that the gold-bearing GWR mail train was into Exeter in an extraordinary 33½ minutes from Plymouth. Risking an average of nearly 70mph (112.6kmph) down the winding track from Wrangaton to

Above: *Europe's first steam claimant to 100mph honours: the Great Western 4-4-0* City of Truro, *for which 102.3mph was claimed on 9 May 1904. This action photo was taken when she was resurrected from her museum home for special duty in 1957.* / M. Mensing

Above right: *Scene of* City of Truro's *exploit: the gradient is obvious and the sharpness of the curvature can be discerned in the background of this September 1955 view of Dainton bank, between Plymouth and Exeter. BR Western Region 'County' 4-6-0 No 1012* County of Denbigh *heads westward.* / R. O. Tuck

Right: *Another view of the revived* City of Truro, *piloting the similarly resuscitated Midland Railway compound 4-4-0 No 1000 out of Doncaster to London's Kings Cross with a special in April 1960.* / Eric Oldham

Totnes, he gave his five-coach, 150 tonnes train such a flying start up Dainton bank that they negotiated its serpentine curves at an overall average of 57.5mph (92.5kmph), despite grades steeper than 1 in 100 the whole way.

Thus far, though, the buccaneering Clements had just been flexing his muscles. The other side of Exeter he flogged *City of Truro* so remorselessly up the 20miles of almost unbroken grind to Whiteball summit, which finishes at 1 in 115, that they were still making a mile a minute at the top. And when the track began to fall away on the initial 1 in 80-90 of the descent to Taunton he left the throttle alone. Exhaust still roaring, *City of Truro* steadily accelerated until, three miles (4.8km) below the summit, a dedicated recorder of locomotive performance in the train who had been specially invited by the GWR to observe the run claimed his stopwatch had clicked on a peak speed of 102.3mph (164.6kmph).

But at that instant Clements had to throw out the anchors. A track gang was on nonchalant patrol right in his path. A rapid succession of frantic whistles didn't budge them, so there was nothing for it but to yank the throttle shut and slam on the brakes until at last the gang realised a train was bearing down on them and ambled out of the way.

Clements had been baulked only a third of the way down the hill. Unchecked he may well have established a peak speed proof against any critical analysis. But although the record claimed by the respected observer on the train, Charles Rous-Marten, is widely accepted and *City of Truro* is honourably preserved in Britain's Swindon Railway Museum on the strength of it, some experts subsequently ran a meticulous rule over the timings and alleged inconsistencies. Rous-Marten, they suggested, may have been distracted by the violent braking and Clements' petrifying whistles into misreading his watch by a few seconds. Give or take those disputed seconds, Clements had certainly come close enough to 100mph to make this an epic

run for the times. Incidentally, although no more sensational peak speeds were attained on the remaining stages of that day's mail train run, one should add that GWR single-driver inside-cylinder 4-2-2 *Duke of Connaught* rounded off Clements' work by wheeling the gold from Bristol to London in a time not bettered in regular daily service until the latter-day advent of British Rail's 125mph High Speed Diesel Trains.

The race from Plymouth was ended by abrupt tragedy. That might so easily have come that same year of 1904, when it was common gossip that both contenders were grossly exceeding speed restrictions and taking extravagant risks. Knowledgeable Americans off the transatlantic liners, it was said, were frequently pressing a fistful of dollars on the LSWR drivers in hopes of a record sprint to London; and the enginemen were giving the visitors value by such hectic excesses as hitting the sharp curves through Salisbury at twice the stipulated speed limit. Within a month or two, however, LSWR chiefs had stamped on the recklessness with some strongly-worded injunctions against any attempt to improve on the already exacting boat train schedules. For two years thereafter little was heard of the boat trains. Then on 1 July 1906 Britain awoke to disaster.

The previous evening a five-coach LSWR boat train had set off uneventfully from Plymouth to its usual engine-

changing point in the heart of England's West Country at Templecombe. Here Driver Robins and 4-4-0 No 421 backed on for the second stage of the journey. Robins was an experienced man who knew the road perfectly. What's more, he clearly had no dreams of glory that night: quite the reverse, talking to one of the station staff before he coupled on, he was worried that he might he carpeted if he gained any time on the schedule to London.

The subsequent catastrophe is therefore inexplicable for certain. It happened on the sharp curve at the London end of Salisbury station, long restricted to a maximum speed of 30mph (48.3kmph).

The few railwaymen about just before 02.00 reckoned No 421 was making about 70mph (112.6kmph) as she came careering downhill towards Salisbury. Her whistle was shrilling, her throttle well open — and the dumbfounded bystanders gradually realised it was going the stay that way. Though the station she stormed, lurching crazily as she hit the opening of the curve, then keeling right over at the sharpest pitch. She caught the rear of an empty milk train on the next track, cannoned off and rammed into an aged 0-6-0 goods engine in a bay platform. At that instant No 421's tender jack-knifed upwards, crushing the crew to instant death, while the following coaches strewed themselves about the layout, splintering to matchwood. In all 24 passengers and four railwaymen were killed.

The only conceivable explanation, since it was a clear summer's night and Robins was a seasoned engineman with nothing intemperate in mind, is that he unaccountably mistook his whereabouts as he approached Salisbury. Whatever the real reason, the newspaper-reading public had theirs quickly cut and dried. It could only be the whole business of railway racing, which must cease forthwith. So, although LSWR and GWR continued to contend for the Plymouth business for some years thereafter, high speed was never again the weapon. The ghosts of Salisbury haunted both companies for a long time.

15

2. The Golden Age of Steam Speed

Below: *A Pennsylvania Class E6 4-4-2 of the type that headed the Lindbergh film special of May 1927. In this picture No 61 is believed to be fronting the 'Broadway Limited'.* / Ian Allan Library

The First World War over, the railways did not resume their chase for 100mph in earnest until the 1930s. By then the automobile was really challenging for their passenger business and there was menace in the sound of an aeroplane engine.

There was one historic occasion in the late 1920s, though, when a train rubbed an airplane's prop in the dirt. In May 1927 air-mail pilot Charles Lindbergh had engrossed the world as well as his native Americans by piloting his 200hp Ryan monoplane *Spirit of St Louis* non-stop and solo from Roosevelt Field, Long Island, to Le Bourget, Paris in 33 hours 8 minutes. Lindbergh had intended to stay in Europe awhile, but President Coolidge had him promptly shipped home in state on the US Navy cruiser *Memphis* to a rapturous welcome from the President in person at the Washington Navy Yard on the Potomac. Just about everything the President could bestow he lavished on the national hero — Distinguished Flying Cross, Congressional Medal of Honor and promotion from captain to colonel on the spot, to the ecstasy of what looked like all Washington crowding the riverside and the base of the Washington Monument.

Now film of the epoch-making affair had to be rushed off for processing, much of it to New York. Most of the agencies had hired airplanes: one even contracted a popular stunt pilot of the day to parachute film straight into laboratories at Long Island City. But the International News Reel Co had reason to know train could beat plane if a railroad car were rigged up to process its film en route to New York.

It wasn't the first time the Pennsylvania had been asked to take on an airplane in a straight fight. In those days railroads were used to coping with emergency charters. Already that spring of 1925, for instance, Pennsylvania had rustled up an E6 Atlantic and three coaches to rush a noted Jewish tenor and his retinue the 92.6 miles (149km) from Philadelphia in 90 minutes so that he could cover two same-night engagements; and the selfsame night another special had been improvised to allow a politician to harangue all-but consecutive meetings in Jersey City and Philadelphia. Then, on Coolidge's Inauguration Day, 4 March 1925, International and Pennsylvania had laid on their first mobile film laboratory exercise — and succeeded: International's film of the ceremony was unfolding on New York cinema screens well before any that had been flown out of Washington.

For the Lindbergh operation Pennsylvania mobilised 1914-built Class E6s Atlantic No 460, a standard baggage van fitted out as a darkroom and a standard day coach, the last hooked on more to add weight and braking power than anything else. No sooner had the automobile convoy with the film wheeled into Union station and its photographers literally run their precious film to the train than she was off.

The Pennsylvania had clearly determined to steal some of the day's glory. Despatchers down the track to New York had been bidden to keep freight clear; certain local authorities en route had been contacted and persuaded to relax speed restrictions imposed in their population zones; and an elite four-man engine crew had been mustered, with Assistant Road Foreman James Warren at the throttle as far

as Baltimore, Assistant Road Foreman Aleck Sentman from there on to New York.

From the first pull of his throttle Warren hammered the Atlantic relentlessly. So much so that they took the first water troughs too fast and the air-operated tender scoop picked up precious little, ploughing out a fierce spray about the train wheels instead. To make good they would have to call an unscheduled halt for water.

The footplate party decided to make the water stop at Wilmington. Already they had averaged 80mph (128.7kmph) for long stretches and beyond Baltimore someone — posterity does not record who — claimed a mile had been tossed off in 33 seconds, which meant 110mph (177kmph). Hereabouts the hurtling train was briefly paced by one of the rival agencies' planes, which powered down to hedgehop on the same course for a short while, setting up for real the kind of picture often faked by railroad publicists at the time.

The scurrying footplate crew topped up their tank at Wilmington in less than a minute and three-quarters, then stormed off towards Philadelphia, 23.3 miles (37.5km) away. They were through Philadelphia in 17½ minutes, which represented an average of 79.9mph (128.6kmph) from a standing start, so if the passing time was accurate they must certainly have been close to 100mph (160kmph). Foreman Anderson reckoned they'd touched 115mph (185kmph). Anderson himself took over the throttle again after Philadelphia and coaxed the Atlantic up to its highest sustained speed of the whole remarkable run. Despite a slowing for another water pick-up from troughs, he ran 66.6 miles (107.2km) off the reel to the outskirts of Newark in 47 minutes flat for an average of almost precisely 85mph (136.8kmph). When the special halted at Manhattan Transfer for the mandatory switch to electric traction over the last 8.6 miles through the Hudson River Tunnel to New York's Pennsylvania Station, the 216 miles (347.5km) from Washington were shown to have been covered in only 175 minutes, the Wilmington water stop included, for an overall average speed of 74.05mph (119.1kmph). Sirens screaming, a police escort convoyed the fully processed newsreels off to Broadway cinemas; and within 15 minutes of the train's coming to rest in the city New Yorkers had the day's rapture in Washington on their screens. It was more than an hour later before any of the rival airborne film was ready for showing. Whether or not the Atlantic's speed did peak as high as 115 or even 110mph, it was unquestionably a ranking run in the rail speed annals.

As the 1920s dissolved into the 1930s, the rail speed focus was taken by Britain's Great Western Railway yet again. Ever since 1923 the GWR had been steadily screwing up the Swindon-London time of its 'Cheltenham Spa Express'. This was a fairly humdrum service until it had threaded the Cotswold Hills to join Brunel's superbly engineered Bristol main line at Swindon for the final 77.3 miles of near-level track to London's Paddington terminus. By 1929 the GWR had cut the time for this stretch back to 70 minutes, average 66.2mph (106.5kmph), and could justifiably lay claim to operate 'The World's Fastest Daily Train'. In the public timetables the train's title was the prosaic same as ever; but to the public at large it was now the 'Cheltenham Flyer'.

The GWR was briefly robbed of its crown in 1931 by a bitter contest between Canadian National and Canadian Pacific for the Montreal-Toronto passenger business. This climaxed in a Canadian Pacific booking of 108 minutes for the 124 miles (199.5km) from Montreal West to Smith's Falls, which on average bettered the GWR by some 2.7mph. Within months, the GWR had taken time out of its 'Flyer's' schedule sufficiently to regain the world title. Eventually, by September 1932, the GWR was timing the 'Flyer' at an average of 71.4mph (114.9kmph) from Swindon to London.

Above: *The Great Western Railway's 'Cheltenham Flyer' speeds up the Thames Valley behind 'Castle' 4-6-0 No 5000* Launceston Castle *in November 1934. The headboard proclaims that it is the 'World's Fastest Train'.* / British Rail, Oxford Publishing Co

Above right: *Another shot of the 'Cheltenham Flyer', this time in the Thames Valley near Pangbourne headed by 4-6-0 No 5005* Manorbier Castle, *one of two GWR engines that were semi-streamlined in 1935. Some GWR directors were far keener to take up the new fashion than the railway's engineering chief, Collett, who is said to have done their bidding by impatiently applying plasticine to a model and ordering the result to be translated into engineering drawings. The various excrescences were gradually removed from the engines over subsequent years, beginning with the cylinder fairings later in 1935, because they caused overheating.*

Right: *The GWR 'King' that was similarly streamlined in 1935, No 6014* King Henry VII, *poses with the new 'Cornish Riviera Express' train-set of that year near Swindon.* / British Rail, Oxford Publishing Co

The highpoint of the 'Cheltenham Flyer's' career, though, was a deliberate attempt at record-breaking on 6 June 1932. That day one of the Great Western's four-cylinder 'Castle' 4-6-0s, standard power for the 'Flyer' as for the backbone of the railway's express passenger traffic, streamed up the 77.3 miles from Swindon to Paddington in 56¾ minutes at a start to stop average of 81.7mph (131.5kmph). No 5006 Tregenna Castle was the engine, on a six-coach rake of some 198 tonnes. For 28 miles (45.1kmph) on end she was making never less than 90-92mph (145-148kmph). To the end of British steam the start-to-stop average speed registered that afternoon was never excelled by any regular service train.

But the diesel was already growling at steam's heels when Tregenna Castle made the record books in the early summer of 1932. The Germans were just unveiling the prototype of the streamlined diesel multiple-units with which, from 1933 onwards, they were to weave a high-speed web interlacing every major population centre in the country. With these units 100mph (160kmph) became for the first time scheduled

Right: *Typical of the 'rail-paces-air' shots beloved of (and often crudely faked by) railroad sales and publicity departments in the late 1920s and early 1930s are these 1929 photos of Canadian National's Montreal-Chicago 'International Limited' and New York Central's 'Twentieth Century Limited', the latter overflown by a Fokker monoplane with the brand 'Universal Air Lines'.*

Below: *In March 1935 Gresley's LNER Class A3 4-6-2 No 2750* Papyrus, *seen here on everyday express work at the time emerging from Hadley Wood Tunnel, was whipped up to 108mph on a pre-streamliner trial from Kings Cross to Newcastle and back.* / James R. Clark

routine in daily passenger operation. Across the Atlantic diesel traction was to begin its conquest of North American railroads a year later. With these new tools, plus developments in electric traction, the upsurge of world rail speed was to be such that the 'Cheltenham Flyer' would slide to well below one-hundredth place in the world table of fastest trains by 1939.

Steam was not to yield the pass without its own fling at regular 100mph operation, though.

In Britain the London North Eastern Railway was keen to set new speed standards on its East Coast main line from London to the North. The newborn German diesel train-sets looked heaven-sent for the purpose, but when the Germans put in their assessment of feasible schedules for the London-Newcastle route of 268.3 miles (431.7km) the LNER was not altogether impressed. Its management had a feeling steam could improve on the Germans' 4¼ hour end-to-end estimate. Moreover, the German train-set's seating was cramped by comparison with that of orthodox locomotive-hauled coaches and its catering limited to a cold buffet; wouldn't this be off-putting to a businessmen's clientele that now took full trainboard meal service and roomy first-class comfort for granted?

So Nigel Gresley, the LNER's Chief Mechanical Engineer, was bidden to draft a steam alternative. As a preliminary, he tested the sustained speed potential of his existing 4-6-2 types. On 30 November 1934 his Class A1 4-6-2 No 4472 *Flying Scotsman* (still alive today as an active museum-piece in private ownership) was coupled to a four-coach train and despatched on a speed test from London's King Cross to Leeds and back. Schedule was so comfortably kept going north that the load was stiffened by two coaches to 208 tonnes for the return. Descending the eight mile (12.9km) Stoke bank south of Grantham, Britain's ideal rail racetrack in steam days, on this leg *Flying Scotsman* was coaxed up to 100mph (160kmph). This time the peak was incontravertible, because the test train included a dynamometer car. More significant, though, was that of the day's out-and-home round of 371½ miles (597.7km), no less than 250 miles (402.3km) had been covered at an average of 80mph (128.7kmph) or more.

And that was with Gresley's original Pacific design. On 5 March 1935 one of his Class A3s with higher boiler pressure and superheating and improved valve and cylinder design, No 2750 *Papyrus*, was set at the full Kings Cross-Newcastle course with a six-coach train and ridiculed the diesel men's prospectus by reaching the Tyneside city in 3 hours 57 minutes: then after a 2¾ hours' servicing pause, sweeping back to London in just under 3 hours 52 minutes. The driver, a firebrand named Sparshatt, was the same as for the 1934 trial, specially selected for the job in both instances. This time he urged *Papyrus* up to a fully authenticated peak of 108mph (173.8kmph) down Stoke bank and had her averaging 100mph (160kmph) for 12 miles (19.3kmph) on end. At the end of the day they had torn off around 300 miles (483km) at an average of 80mph (128.7kmph).

By the date of *Papyrus's* run, however, the LNER management had already made up its mind. A new breed of streamlined Pacific with train-sets to match had been ordered in March 1935.

Britain's first essay in specific high-speed train design emerged in September 1935, named 'Silver Jubilee' to mark the contemporaneous royal event and liveried to match in silver-grey from end to end. Up front was Gresley's new Class A4 Pacific, the familiar upperworks of a steam locomotive shrouded in a smooth streamlined casing — and not for meretricious publicity effect, as was the case with a good many of the frills and furbelows draped about passenger engines around the world in the late 1930s and 1940s. Laboratory tests had persuaded Gresley that in the 70-100mph (112-160kmph) speed range the air resistance of a conventionally-outlined train doubled, until at 100mph it was absorbing as much as 85% of the traction power. Not only did he streamline his A4 Pacific, therefore, but also its train as effectively as he could, by blocking off the gaps between coach ends with rubber sheeting and dipping underframe panels between the coach bogies almost to rail level.

Below: *The first LNER Pacific to be taken up to 100mph was Gresley's Class A1 No 4472* Flying Scotsman, *seen in this 1930s picture heading its namesake train up the bank out of London's Kings Cross terminal.* / Ian Allan Library

Above: The record-breaking 'Silver Jubilee' demonstration run of 27 September 1935: Gresley's Class A4 4-6-2 No 2509 Silver Link storms past grandstanders at the top of Potters Bar bank, on its way out of the London suburbs to a British speed record of 112.5mph (181kmph).
/ E. R. Wethersett, Ian Allan Library

Right: First-class travel in the LNER streamliners of the 1930s was like this.

On 27 September 1935, three days before the 'Silver Jubilee' was opened to the public, the LNER staged an inforgettable demonstration run. The flagship of the A4 Pacifics, No 2509 *Silver Link*, was the engine, coupled to the standard seven-coach train-set of two articulated twin-sets and a restaurant-kitchen articulated triplet grossing 224 tonnes. *Silver Link's* enginemen had been instructed to give the Pacific her head, so as to persuade the guests the planned London-Newcastle schedule of four hours lay comfortably within the A4's range; but Gresley himself, one now believes, did not fully realise before they set out that afternoon what a thoroughbred he had created.

It might have been less thrilling if the track and vehicle suspension art of the day had been on a par with Gresley's steam locomotive science. Before *Silver Link* had cleared the London suburbs she was closing on 100mph and ripping into curves and pointwork previously negotiated at not more than three-quarters of the new train's speed. The articulated suspension swung the coach bodies about and inside the train it felt like riding a caterpillar at the steady trot. Faces paled, though not Gresley's: he was jovially unmoved as on a downgrade of 1 in 200-264 some 30 miles (48.3km) out from Kings Cross his Pacific stormed up to a peak of 112.5mph (181kmph). For 25 miles continuously *Silver Link's* pace was above 100mph (160kmph) and the average for that distance was 107.5mph (173kmph).

It is worth adding that the 27 September 1935 demonstration was *Silver Link's* only full-dress trial before tackling daily service on the 'Silver Jubilee'. She went all but straight from the Doncaster works assembly line to head the streamliner each way for the train's inaugural fortnight — in other words to cover just over 4,500 miles (7,240km) at an average of 70mph (112.6kmph). In fact none of the first quartet of Gresley's A4 Pacifics had a minute of lost time booked against them in the streamliner's first 100,000 miles (160,000km) of operation.

From launch to its death in the Second World War's immediate castration of Britain's crack passenger services the 'Silver Jubilee' attracted a near-capacity trainload every working day. By 1937 suspension modification had smoothed the ride somewhat, but it could still be boisterous where track was less than perfect by contemporary standards. Not that its regular clientele seemed to care. Even in the early years when some of the diner crews would discreetly clear flower vases from the tables as the 'Jubilee' powered out of Kings Cross, a thoroughly sickening lurch would have the hardened passengers just lift an eyebrow above the evening paper's financial page to exchange a 'Lively tonight, what?'

Whether the streamliner can be accounted a strictly commercial success is something else. Her own direct operating costs she may have covered with a margin to spare and her value to the LNER's overall public image was immense. But she was a one-off in speed. The track had to be swept of other traffic long before she was due; and in her wake she left another sizeable vacuum. In other words, when she was about track usage of the LNER main line was a long way below the economic optimum. Since the Second World War, with cost-consciousness an enforced obsession, railway managements have become increasingly disinclined to single out trains for exceptional acceleration. Around the world the drive is to keep the speed of all traffic on a trunk route, freight as well as passenger, within the narrowest possible band of maximum and minimum average speed so as to maximise track occupation and spread direct operating and fixed asset costs over as many services as possible. As we shall see, where very high passenger train speeds are sought, it may even be economically sensible to segregate passenger and freight trains to their own dedicated routes.

Below: A 'grainy' photo typical of miniature camera photography in the 1930s, but a striking impression of the third and last pre-war LNER streamlined express, the 'West Riding Limited', heading through Retford for London behind Class A4 4-6-2 No 4495 Golden Fleece. / Cecil J. Allen collection

Right: *There were several French essays in steam streamlining in the mid-1930s. This PLM Railway experiment was conducted with a 28-year-old 4-4-2, No 221.A.14, which in 1935 was operated with a special steamlined train set between Paris and Lyons. In regular service speed was limited to 75mph (120kmph), but on a special test run from Paris to Dijon the engine was worked up to 97mph (156kmph) and covered the first 159 miles (256km) out of Paris in 136min.* / La Vie du Rail

Below right: *One of the streamlined push-pull double-deck units built for the Lübeck-Büchen Railway in the mid-1930s, the 2-4-2 tank engine by Henschel and the coaches by Wegmann. The privately-owned railway was absorbed by the Reichsbahn in the late 1930s and the engines then became Reichsbahn Class 60.* / Alfred B. Gottwaldt

Bottom: *This remarkable shroud applied to a 4-6-0 of the French State Railways in 1937 was known as the Huet streamlining system. It was intended to achieve great aerodynamic efficiency without encasing moving parts.*

Once the Germans' new diesel train-sets had made their spectacular debut, it seemed highly improbable that steam would take any further share in the speed development of that country. After all, there had been precious little visible attempt to extract more speed from steam even before the diesel units' development; published records showed nothing better than the 95.7mph (154kmph) obtained on special test from a Bavarian Class S2/6 4-4-4 way back in 1907 between Munich and Augsburg. When German locomotive industry approached the Reichsbahn at the end of 1931 for encouragement to develop a 150kmph (93mph) steam locomotive design, it wasn't rebuffed, but it wasn't greeted with much enthusiasm either. Few of the top brass had any faith in the higher speed potential of steam power.

But eventually grudging assent for construction of prototypes was forthcoming. If there were to be any merit in the development majority opinion, convinced with the diesel train-sets in mind that the high-speed inter-city passenger future lay in low-slung, limited-capacity lightweights, favoured something along the lines of two extraordinary double-deck, articulated twin-set push-pull trains each with a streamlined 2-4-2 tank engine that Henschel and Wegmann were building for the then privately-owned Lübeck-Büchen Railway. So it was that in 1935 Henschel turned out the impressive streamlined Class 61 4-6-4T No 61.001 and Wegmann a splendidly furnished four-car train-set, closely resembling one of the diesel units in its external styling, to go with it. A second of these huge tank engines was built in 1939 as a 4-6-6. The Henschel tank and train took up Berlin-Dresden service, but the records hold no really outstanding performance by them.

It was the prototypes built by Borsig which made the Reichsbahn's final mark in steam speed history. The genius largely responsible for their design was Dr Richard Paul Wagner of the Reichsbahn's central office responsible for all traction, and his achievement was the more laudable because he had little of the supporting technical resources of, for example, a Chief Mechanical Engineer of a British railway of the period, each of whom had at least one major

Above: *The parentage of the Lübeck-Büchen design is evident in these views of the Reichsbahn's Henschel-Wegmann train, photographed first at the Reichsbahn Centenary Exhibition at Nuremberg in 1935, and second headed by Class 61 4-6-4T No 61.001 on a 1937 Berlin-Hamburg trial run in the Sachsenwald.*
/ Deutsche Bundesbahn

Right: *In the summer of 1934 some proposed streamlining detail was tested on an existing Reichsbahn 4-6-2, No 03.154, to see if it improved efficiency and whether the complete casing of wheels and motion caused overheating. The guinea-pig is seen at Hamburg Altona.* / Lokomotivbild-Archiv Bellingrodt

Below: *The fully streamlined 4-6-4 Pacific locomotives No 05.002 and No 05.001 of 1935, showing in the lower picture the remarkable number of hinged flaps built into the casing for maintenance access.* / Deutsche Bundesbahn

locomotive works under his care and the full range of design and engineering staff to go with it. But Wagner had a close acquaintance with the British locomotive engineers Gresley and Stanier, who kept him fully briefed on their experience in meeting British demands for higher speed in the early 1930s and who were happy to put their acquired knowledge at Wagner's disposal.

In developing their design, Wagner and Borsig paid special attention to streamlining efficiency, conducting lengthy wind-tunnel experiments and testing some of their ideas on an existing Pacific, No 03.154, in the summer of 1934. Eventually the project took shape as two three-cylinder 4-6-4s, No 05.001 and 05.002, designed for 175kmph (109mph) capability with a 300tonne train and thus promising an economy in high-speed passenger service decidedly superior to that of the lightweight diesel trains. In a production series, Wagner claimed, the 4-6-4 and a 300 tonne train would cost no more to build than two of the diesel sets, but would offer 50% more passenger seats: steam could work to the same schedules, moreover, but on indigenous fuel, not imported oil — a consideration weighing more and more with the Third Reich at the time.

In streamlining, Borsig and Wagner, went further than Britain's Gresley. Not merely the upperworks of this pair of three-cylinder 4-6-4s but their wheels, cylinders and motion were encased down almost to rail level by sheeting windowed below the running plate with ventilation grilles. The running plate was high, for the driving wheels were a remarkable 7ft 6½in (2.30m) in diameter. The engines were outshopped in 1935, the Reichsbahn's Centennial year, but the Germans spent much of that year in methodical tests of the machines to eliminate any weaknesses before they were put on public high-speed display. At the same time they needed to fettle up the track and modify the signalling on the streamliners' planned course between Berlin and Hamburg. By 1936 the pair were in regular use on new high-speed morning and evening business expresses of four cars and a restaurant, booked over the 178.1 miles (286.6km) between the two cities in 145 minutes eastbound and 144 minutes westbound for end-to-end averages of 73.7mph (118.5kmph) and 74.2mph (119.4kmph) respectively.

In May of 1936 No 05.002 was taken out of public service for what were said to be special brake tests. More likely, though, another propaganda triumph for the greater glory of Hitler's Third Reich was the covert objective, since the Transport Minister, Dorpmüller, just happened to be among the four-car, 200 tonne test-train's occupants on the day that counted, 11 May 1936. On that Hamburg-Berlin trip, it was claimed, *Oberlokführer* Langhans had urged his 4-6-4 up to a top speed of 124.5mph (200.4kmph) on the almost imperceptible 1 in 333 downgrade to Zernitz, near Neustadt on the final stages of the run in to the then German capital city.

No detailed supporting data for that record have ever been published, though the claim was based on dynamometer car readings, but not far off the same peak was certainly attained *and* irrefutably recorded later that same month by the dean of British train timers, the late Cecil J. Allen. He was in Germany with a distinguished party from Britain's Institution of Locomotive Engineers. Eager to impress the guests, the Reichsbahn naturally staged a demonstration trip from Berlin to Hamburg and back behind No 05.002. This time the load was three cars of 137 tonnes — one of them again a dynamometer car, whose comprehensive instruments confirmed Allen's chronograph reading.

At the start out of Berlin the 4-6-4 was driven at about two-thirds throttle, with little more than half its rated boiler pressure of 285lb per sq in in the steam chest and on a long cut-off. That was enough to keep speed hovering just below 100mph (160kmph), however. Then on dead level track after

Above: *Streamlined 4-6-4 No 05.002 pauses during the 118mph (190kmph) demonstration laid on for the British Institution of Locomotive Engineers in May 1936. The previous year the Institution had awarded the 05 design its Gold Medal.* / The late Cecil J. Allen

Wittenberge the *lokführer* gave her just a touch of the spur, edging the throttle open enough to raise the steam-chest pressure to 225lb. At that speed climbed sweetly to 118mph (190kmph); 7.49 miles (12km) were timed at an average of 111.4mph (179kmph) and 19.4 miles (31km) at an average of 101.0mph (162.6kmph). More eminent members of the British party had been invited to ride the 4-6-4's footplate, among them London Midland & Scottish Chief Mechanical Engineer William Stanier, and they were mightily impressed by her smoothly solid riding at 100mph plus: as steady as in the coaches, they said.

On the return leg from Hamburg, incidentally, the Britons had a dramatic demonstration of braking power. They were cruising at 100mph when, wrote Allen later, 'a feed pipe between tender and engine came adrift and, dragging along the ballast, threw up a shower of stones against the underside of our coach. There followed the most abrupt stop that I have ever known in a train, for we came down from 100mph to a dead stand in precisely 60 seconds and in a distance of 0.85 mile (1.37km).' Then the 4-6-4 was given the gun again; 70.1 miles (112.8km) from Wittenberge to an unscheduled signal stop on the outskirts of Berlin were gobbled up at a start to stop average of 86.7mph (139.5kmph), more than a third of them at an average of 100mph. In the course of the day No 05.002 had treated the visitors to 250 miles (402km) of travel at an average speed in excess of 90mph (145kmph).

A third and very distinctive Class 05 was built in 1937. No 05.003 was arranged to burn pulverised coal dust and hence turned end for end, with cab in front and smokebox end coupled to its tender: some sources suggest that the fuel arrangements may have been adopted in part as a means to

design a cab-in-front coal-burning steam engine, which would then be capable of push-pull operation despite being paired with a tender. Little more was heard of No 05.003 and it was rebuilt as an orthodox non-streamlined 4-6-4 in 1944.

Several more streamlined steam types were turned out for the Reichsbahn in its final years. The origins of most could be traced to the birth period of the 05s, but although some sterling work was reported of the latter on Reichsbahn inter-city passenger services up to the outbreak of the Second World War they had their troubles, ranging from steaming problems to track wear on curves. The Krupp-built Class 06 4-8-4s of 1938 and the 03.10 and 01.10 Pacifics of 1939, therefore, were devised with considerably lower speed ceilings in mind.

As for the Class 05s, at war's end all three were discovered derelict in Eidelstadt yards, Hamburg, though still forlornly displaying plates in their cabs advising enginemen that they could be driven up to a maximum of 175kmph (108.8mph). Eventually they were reconditioned, in the course of which the early pair were divested of their streamlining, and put to work from Hamm depot. They were marked up for scrap in 1958, but No 05.001 was salvaged for display in the Nuremburg Transport Museum.

The potential, implicit in the telling demonstration runs of North America's pioneer diesel streamliners in the mid-1930s did not deflect US railroads from fresh high-speed locomotive development for a number of years. As late as the summer of 1938, for instance, the Committee on Further Development of the Reciprocating Steam Locomotive of the Association of American Railroads was organising track trials to determine the drawbar horsepower needed to keep a 1,000 tonne passenger train moving at a steady 100mph on level track. The tests were conducted with a 1,005 tonne rake of standard Pennsylvania coaches on the Pennsylvania, Chicago & North Western and Union Pacific systems. Star of the show in terms of peak speed was Union Pacific's massive 4-8-4 No 815, which, with its 300lb/sq in boiler pressure and 6ft 5in (1.96m) driving wheels, summoned up well over 4,000 drawbar hp to keep the huge train rolling at 102.4mph (164.8kmph) on its home ground. Far from discomfited, though, was one of the much more compact Pennsylvania Class K4 Pacifics which were the trialists in Pennsylvania territory. On level track they managed to accelerate the

Above left: *The Deutsche Reichsbahn's cab-in-front, pulverised coal-burning 4-6-4 No 05.003, built in 1937. / Cecil J. Allen collection*

Left: *One of the two Krupp-built Class 06 steamlined 4-8-4s for heavy express passenger work introduced in 1938, seen in a builder's pose and in action at Frankfurt/Main Hbf soon after entering service. / Alfred B. Gottwaldt*

Above: *A wartime shot of one of the two Deutsche Reichsbahn streamlined Pacific types of 1939, in this case the 01.10 for heavier duty, with ten-wheeled tender. No 01.1088 was photographed near Dresden in 1941. / Locomotivbild-Archiv Bellingrodt*

Right: *Kilroy was here: US Army engineers who repaired this Class 03.10 at the Henschel works in 1945 signed their work with a replica of the Atlantic Coast Line logo on the smokebox casing. / Henschel-Archiv*

same train to 92mph (148kmph) between Chicago and Fort Wayne.

The K4s, one of North America's most venerated and proficient steam passenger engine designs, were in the van of US railroads' determined assault on higher speed in the mid-1930s. If the Eastern US railroads attracted less attention at this time than some of the dramatic accelerations elsewhere in the country — for instance, the Frisco road's overnight cut of *five hours* from its 'Firefly' Kansas City-Oklahoma City timecard to keep up with Santa Fe and Rock Island's new streamliners — it was because systems like the New York Central and Pennsylvania were already leading the US speed table. But in a widespread 1935 speed-up the Pennsylvania, exploiting its largely level course between Fort Wayne and Chicago, set its K4 Pacifics to timings as crisp as 51 minutes for the 64.2 miles (103.3km) from Plymouth to Fort Wayne and 101 minutes for the 122.4 miles (196.9km) from Gary to Fort Wayne, the former exacting an average speed as high as 75.5mph (121.5kmph). That year, too, both Central and Pennsylvania trimmed their 'Twentieth Century Limited' and 'Broadway Limited' New York-Chicago times to 17 hours — a whole hour faster, incidentally, than Amtrak's 'Broadway Limited' managed in 1977!

The K4s were stellar performers well into the 1940s, for Pennsylvania, as will be demonstrated shortly, was among the major railroads that long resisted total dieselisation. From 1936 onwards some K4s Pacifics were subjected to the streamlining vogue of the day, supposedly in the cause of aerodynamic science. But what was scientifically valid and effective in fuel economy on engines like the British A4 Pacifics and German 05 4-6-4s, routinely driven in the

Above: *Union Pacific 4-8-4 No 829, sister engine of No 815, which was a star of AAR heavy-load speed tests in 1938, assists diesels over Sherman Hill on the 'City of San Francisco' in the late 1930s.* / Cecil J. Allen collection

Right: *Renowned US speed performer of the mid-1930s — the Pennsylvania Class K4s 4-6-2: this pair is heading the Chicago-New York 'Rainbow' out of Canton, Ohio.* / Cecil J. Allen Collection

Below right: *One of Chicago & North Western's Alco-built 4-6-4s of 1938 pauses at Cedar Rapids, Iowa, on the Los Angeles-Chicago 'Pacific Limited'. Locomotive livery is green with gold stripes.* / Cecil J. Allen collection

Far right: *A Baltimore & Ohio Pacific on the 'Cincinnatian' takes water at Athens, Ohio.* / Cecil J. Allen collection

Left: The Pacific-hauled New York-Philadelphia-
Buffalo 'Black Diamond' of the Lehigh Valley.
/ Cecil J. Allen collection

Below: Chesapeake & Ohio's New York-Cincinnati-
Louisville 'Fast Flying Virginian' makes speed between
Ashland and Russell, Kentucky, behind a streamlined
4-6-4 rebuilt from a 4-6-2. / Cecil J. Allen collection

Bottom: One of the five 'Jubilee' 4-4-4s acquired in
1936 by Canadian Pacific to work high-speed multi-
stop services between Montreal and Quebec, Toronto
and Detroit (the 'Royal York') and Calgary and
Edmonton (the 'Chinook'). / Cecil J. Allen collection

Right: Florid styling devised in 1937 for a Union
Pacific 4-6-2 seen at Cheyenne, Wyoming; colours
were basically brown and yellow with a broad red
stripe at waist-level. The casing was removed in 1942.
/ R. H. Kindig

Below right: Milwaukee pioneer: Class F6 4-6-4
No 6402 draws a grandstand at Milwaukee on 20 July
1934 after topping 100mph on the record run from
Chicago that paved the way for the 'Hiawatha'.
/ Cecil J. Allen collection

90-100mph speed range, was pure flummery where speed
restrictions of 80mph officially prevailed, as they did on most
US main lines in the 1930s. In those conditions streamlining
was quite unproductive economically. Whatever publicity
value it may have had was negated by its inconvenient
shrouding of vital parts, the casing's extra weight and even,
sometimes, its reverse aerodynamic effect if the engine was
buffeted by a strong side wind. Not surprisingly, many
railroads persuaded by their salesmen to jump on the
streamlining bandwagon didn't take long to unfrock the
engines they had dressed up, all too often in a pretty tawdry
gear. Much more significant was the refinement of steam
locomotive technology proper: in the case of the
Pennsylvania K4s, for instance, the application after 1937 to
several engines of poppet valves and redesigned steam
passages that realised the full steam-generating potential of
the tubby K4 boiler, enabling the engines to run close to an
illicit 100mph (160kmph) on the Fort Wayne-Chicago level
with trains like the 'Broadway Limited', 'Manhattan
Limited' and lightweight 'Detroit Arrow', and to sustain
averages in excess of 80mph (128.7kmph) for 20-25
continuous miles (30-40km).

The most exhilarating US inter-city rail race of the mid-
1930s was fought out between Chicago and the Twin Cities of
St Paul and Minneapolis, where three railroads were in
contention with routes of roughly equal length and speed
potential: the Chicago, Burlington & Quincy; the Chicago,
Milwaukee, St Paul & Pacific; and the Chicago & North
Western. The latter two had the commercial bonus of serving
intermediately the sizeable city of Milwaukee. Until 1934 all
three had been content to compete overnight for the
approximately 400 miles (645km) haul, but by then you
could motor from Chicago to the Twin Cities in a little over
eight hours and the drift of passengers into buses as well as
automobiles was beginning to hurt. On 20 July 1934 The
Milwaukee fuelled up its Class F6 4-6-4 No 6402, hooked it
on to the morning train out of Chicago, a five-car train of 352
tonnes, and proved that the 85 miles (136.8km) of the route's

Above: *The first 'Hiawatha' train-set and streamlined 4-4-2 No 2 parade at Milwaukee.*
/ Cecil J. Allen collection

Right: *The original 1935 'Hiawatha' at speed behind streamlined 4-4-2 No 2.* / Milwaukee Road

Far right: *The 1935 'Hiawatha' from the rear, showing the beaver-tail observation car of the period.*
/ Milwaukee Road

well-aligned section from Chicago to Milwaukee could be rolled off in a fraction over 67½ minutes. When Engineer William Dempsey opened up his 4-6-4 20 miles out of Chicago, they averaged 89.9mph (114.6kmph) for 68.9 miles (110.9km) off the reel — whereat the Milwaukee insisted that the riband for sustained high speed claimed by Britain's Great Western with its 'Cheltenham Flyer' *tour de force* of 1932 was now theirs — and, so it was claimed, held a top speed of 103.5mph (166.5kmph) throughout the 5 miles (8.1km) from Oakwood to Lake, Wis.

Within a month all three railroads announced that at a stroke they would slash their Chicago-St Paul daylight transit times from around 10 to 6½ hours. One of the trio, the Burlington, elected to go diesel straightaway. The Chicago & North Western opted to run its new 'Twin Cities 400' with existing Pacifics, but rebuilt, and traditional coaching stock. The Milwaukee, however, went for brand-new train-sets and a fresh breed of locomotive that evolved into one of the world's high-speed steam locomotive prodigies.

The reasons influencing the Milwaukee's decision to persist with steam are worth recall: they typified the considerations which railroad managements were having to weigh up now that diesel traction was showing such promise. First, said the Milwaukee, the new generation of streamlined diesel train-sets lacked the carbody space to create maximum travelling comfort, and the fixed train-set was inflexible, impossible to shorten or lengthen according to troughs and peaks of demand. With steam and individual cars there was no need to invest in new servicing plant. Given determination to employ full-size coaches, only steam, at that stage of diesel development, offered enough power to meet the schedules in mind, and particularly to put out sufficient horsepower at the top end of the speed bracket. A minor but important consideration in the US environment: the ironclad front-end of a steam engine promised better protection for engine crew — and passengers too — than the more lightly armoured cab front of a diesel should the train come on a rogue driver at one of the many open road-rail grade or level crossings. Finally, and by no means least, diesel traction cost four time as much as steam.

For 'Hiawatha', as Milwaukee christened its new service, the road built America's first new 4-4-2s since 1914. These 131 tonne, oil-fired machines were the country's first steam engines to be streamlined from birth and the first to be designed expressly for high speed, with roller bearings on every axle, 300lb/sq in boiler pressure and 7ft (2.13m) driving wheels. The colour scheme devised for the new engines and matched on the train was a delight: the traditional Milwaukee orange set off by horizontal maroon

Inside the early 'Hiawatha'. Above: A reclining-seat car of the 1935 trains; Left: *The observation car of the 1935 train;* Above right: *Diner of the 1937 train;* and Right: *'Tip-Top-Tap' bar of the 1937 train.*
/ Milwaukee Road

stripes, with huge stainless-steel wings draped around the front of the streamline cowling below the headlight.

On 8 May 1935 new Atlantic No 2, engineman Ed Donahue at the throttle, was sent out from Milwaukee to New Lisbon for a spin with a full six-car set of the new 'Hiawatha' stock. The trackside swarmed with bystanders — at least one school trooped out *en bloc* to line the local ballast — and the Milwaukee gave them full value. Their new Atlantics, they had announced, were designed to cruise at 100mph (160kmph) and attain 120mph (193.1kmph). No 2 came pretty close to the prospectus that early in its career.

A battery of clicking chronometers in the train said she held 112.5mph (181kmph) for 14 miles (22.5km) continuously. And the faster she went, the smoother she rode, crowed the enthusiastic Donahue. Back in the train, a few engineers kept an eye on a glass of water and proudly reported not a drop had splashed: the car riding was pluperfect.

Commercially, the steam-hauled 'Hiawatha' never looked back. The public service schedule it took up at the end of May 1935 was well within the speed ceiling established by the test run, but even so the pace and creature comforts (they featured what was probably the USA's first on-train cocktail bar in the restaurant-buffet car's Tip-Top-Tap Room) stimulated such demand that the 'Hiawatha' formation had to be steadily enlarged. The train had only been running for a year and a half before the Milwaukee built a handsome new train-set for it. Such early updating was unprecedented anyway, but by the 'Hiawatha's' third anniversary, when its passenger count was near 900,000 since birth, a third renewal order, for 55 new cars, was on the production lines. Simultaneously ALCO was building six

mighty new streamlined 4-6-4s to supersede the 'Hiawatha' Atlantics.

Arguably these Class F7 4-6-4s were the finest high-speed passenger engines America ever saw, superbly handsome as well as almost legendary in their performance. Like the Atlantics they had 7ft driving wheels, but powered by bigger cylinders fed from a bigger though still 300lb/sq in boiler. Unlike the oil-fuelled 4-4-2s, they were stoker-fired coal-burners, which predicated a big 12wheel tender. Engine alone weighed 188 tonnes and total weight including fully loaded tender ran out at 350 tonnes.

The so-called 'Hiawatha of 1939' entered public Chicago-Twin Cities service on 19 September 1938. By now the service each way had been doubled and there was a 'Morning Hi' and an 'Afternoon Hi'. Some curves had been realigned, too, so as to raise the degree of cant and make 100mph perfectly comfortable over more mileage. At the start the Milwaukee had applied a 90mph limit to normal 'Hi' operation, but had given enginemen the nod for 100mph in legitimate pursuit of lost time. Now there were no inhibitions about 100mph at any time.

There couldn't be. To keep up with diesel 'Zephyrs' on the rival Burlington route, the Milwaukee had by the start of 1940 trimmed the 'Hi' Chicago-St Paul timings to 6¼ hours for the 410 miles (659.7km). Taking into account intermediate stops and enforced slow running in the busy rail complexes of the route's big cities, the overall schedule could only be maintained by very tight timing over suitable open track — in fact, timing never before or after equalled in steam locomotive history. From Sparta to Portage, 78.3 miles (126km), the 'Morning Hi' eastbound was for a period allowed just 58 minutes start to stop, average 81mph (130.3kmph); on the Chicago-Milwaukee stretch westbound 'Hi' pass-to-pass allowances for the 57.6 miles (92.7km) between Signal Tower A12 and Lake were no more than 38 minutes, demanding an average for the distance of 90.9mph (146.3kmph). Such scheduling didn't just encourage regular 100mph running: it demanded it.

The magnificent F7s freely provided the speed, day in and day out, on the usual nine-car load of 388 tonnes (they were load-pullers too, mark you: one had once to tackle an emergency assignment of two night sleeper trains coupled as one and had the gargantuan 1,690 tonne load up to 70mph (112.6kmph) within 12 miles (19.3km) of a standing start on level track). The most sparkling run to see printed detail, recorded by a meticulous North American train-timer, was made one snowy January day of 1941, when No 100 on the eastbound 'Morning Hi' was making 100mph (160kmph) or more for 31 miles (49.9km) consecutively from near Sturtevant to a slowing for level crossing removal works near Rondout. Speed peaked twice at 110mph (177kmph).

The eastbound 'Morning Hi' schedule over the Milwaukee-Chicago racetrack of 85 miles (136.8km) was then 75 minutes. Despite the severe, unscheduled Rondout slowing and the usual cautious gait through the outskirts of Milwaukee and Chicago, not to mention the makings of a blizzard from Rondout on to Chicago, No 100 chalked up only 69½ minutes for the run that day.

The Milwaukee was convinced that even this was well short of the optimum performance of the F7s. Experiment, they said, had shown that once it has accelerated 12 cars to 105mph (169kmph), an F7 could maintain that speed comfortably on just 25% cut-off with only 150lb showing in the steam chest. On this trial, it was claimed, the 4-6-4 had needed little extra effort to climb to 125mph (201.1kmph) and hold 120mph (193.1kmph) on practically level track. In the light of this practical data the Milwaukee was minded to raise the line speed limit to 105mph (168.9kmph) and prune the Chicago-Milwaukee time to an even hour with a heavier train. But because its rivals were not equipped to follow suit and there was an unwritten pact between them to keep in schedule line, the plan had to be pigeonholed.

The Milwaukee's 'Hiawatha' engines were to the rest of the world the best-known symbols of American high-speed steam power in the late 1930s. But fresh vitality was summoned from an extraordinary range of steam engines to fuel the brushfire of acceleration that suddenly, in 1936, had US railroads operating over 29,000 passenger train-miles every day at schedules of a mile a minute or better. Never before or since, probably, has any industrialised country

Far left: *The magnificent Milwaukee Class F7 4-6-4; No 102 heading out of Chicago with the 'Afternoon Hiawatha' at the end of August, 1941.* / R. H. Kindig

Left: *Inside the 'Hiawatha' — the observation saloon.* / Cecil J. Allen collection

Below: *Another view of a Milwaukee Class F7 4-6-4, heading the 'Morning Hiawatha' at St Paul Union Station in 1945.* / Cecil J. Allen collection

Right: *A New York Central 4-6-4 hammers over the crossing with the Pennsylvania main lines at Crestline, Ohio, on the 'Cleveland Special'.* / Cecil J. Allen collection

Far right: *The streamlined version of the New York Central 4-6-4, ready to leave Chicago's La Salle Street station for New York.* / Cecil J. Allen collection

Bottom: *Despite its small-size drivers, a Norfolk & Western Class J 4-8-4 was timed at 110mph (177kmph).*

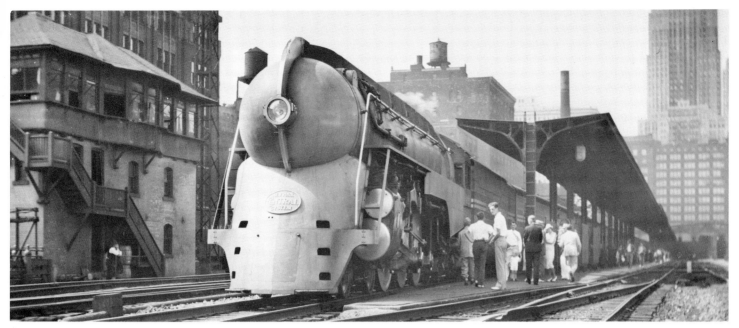

experienced such a rapid and widespread speed-up. Rallied to the cause of speed were veteran Atlantics and Pacifics of the Wabash and Chicago & Eastern Illinois, which managed to hold their own with Illinois Central's new diesels in the simultaneous acceleration of the four rival Chicago-St Louis route services to near mile-a-minute standards. Before the 'Hiawatha's' debut, the Pennsylvania had coaxed its venerable Class E6 Atlantics and K4 Pacifics to the world's first regular 75mph (120kmph) start-to-stop running on the 'Detroit Arrow'.

Two more US steam locomotive designs must be honoured with extended mention before this chapter recrosses the Atlantic to complete the European high-speed steam story. The first is the Norfolk & Western Class J 4-8-4. The fully attested 110mph (177kmph) by one of these engines on a 830 tonne train was an astonishing feat for an eight-coupled engine in any event, but the more so because the J's driving wheels were only 5ft 10in (1.78m) in diameter; on the particular engine being tested, moreover, tyre wear had reduced the measurement to 5ft 8½in (1.74m). The J's maximum piston speed must therefore have been a staggering 2,878ft (877m) per minute.

US rail history records only one instance of higher steam locomotive piston speed. The New York Central was at the time studying the balancing of its magnificent Class J3 4-6-4s and on pre-greased rails one of them was deliberately slipped up to the equivalent of 164mph (264kmph) — very probably the fastest rate at which any locomotive was ever steamed. At that peak the J3's piston speed was 3,370ft/min (1,026m/min) and its 6ft 7in (2.03m) drivers were rotating at a dazzling 11.6 revolutions per second. The nearest European approach to these US feats known to me is the attainment more than once of 90mph (145kmph) by one of British Rail's ultimate steam designs, the 5ft (1.52m) driving wheel Class 9 2-10-0 freight engines, when they were occasionally commandeered to work extra summer Saturday passenger trains over the Eastern Region main line between Grantham and London in the last years of BR steam working.

What has been termed the 'Custer's Last Stand' of high-speed US steam was Baldwin's endeavour to obtain the punch of eight-coupled drive without the transmission snags of orthodox wheel coupling. Baldwin's solution: duplex drive — divide the coupled wheels into two pairs, each with its

Above: *One of Pennsylvania's huge duplex-drive Class T1 4-4-4-4s, No 5527, here seen assigned to secondary work and coming off the Calumet River drawbridge at River Branch Junction, South Chicago.* / Cecil J. Allen collection

Above right: *The LMS 'Coronation Scot': Glasgow-bound, streamlined Stanier Pacific No 6223* Princess Alice *makes haste through Northchurch, having just cleared the London suburbs, in August 1938.* / E. R. Wethersett/Ian Allan Library

own set of cylinders. Articulation was ruled out because of likely stability problems at high speed and the probability that a hinged connection between the two power units would demand over-costly maintenance. So a long, rigid-framed engine was conceived: and on that count Baldwin's concept was at first rejected by several systems — Baltimore & Ohio, Florida East Coast and New Haven (B&O was eventually persuaded, but decided to produce its own not overly-successful variant with opposed cylinders and watertube firebox, Class N1 4-4-4-4 No 5600 *George H. Emerson*).

It was the Pennsylvania that finally embraced the Baldwin doctrine. Pennsylvania, like Norfolk & Western, was one of the great coal-carrying railroads and thus both politically and economically motivated to persist with steam power so long as its technology could sustain a challenge to the insurgent diesels. But at the end of the 1930s Pennsylvania had nothing newer than its basically World War I-designed Pacifics to power inter-city trains which were not merely faster but growing remorselessly heavier as air-conditioning became standard equipment. So in 1939, after exhaustive consultation with every major locomotive builder in the country, Pennsylvania laid down at its Altoona works its own concept of duplex-drive steam engine capable of exerting 6,500ihp and keeping a 1,000 tonne train rolling along straight and level track at a steady 100mph.

The outcome, Class S1 No 6100, was a breath-taking creation. A 6-4-4-6 with 7ft (2.14m) driving wheels, 300lb boiler pressure and 22in by 26in cylinders, the engine alone weighed 276 tonnes; throw in the 16-wheel tender and the scales were turned at a total of 481 tonnes. And the whole was flamboyantly streamlined by industrial designer Raymond Loewy. As for performance, No 6100's career has been crisply summed up thus by American writer David Morgan: 'She was extremely fast, extraordinary powerful — but slippery as glass and simply too darned big.' She was scrapped in 1949.

In July 1940, however, Pennsylvania decided to take the Baldwin duplex-drive design. Two poppet-valve 4-4-4-4s, again with distinctive Loewy sharknose styling, were ordered and delivered in the spring of 1942.

The newcomers, Class T1 Nos 6110 and 6111, were set to the 713 mile (1,147km) run between Chicago and

Harrisburg, which they had been designed to command with a single fuelling stop en route, since there were track troughs and the huge 16-wheel tender held 40 tonnes of coal. At once they showed Baldwin had comfortably met the specification. On her very first through trip No 6110 held a steady 100mph most of the way from Crestline to Chicago with a 14 car, 900 tonne train, while sister engine No 6111 was timed to average 102mph (164kmph) throughout the 69 miles (111km) of the route's Fort Wayne Division. Soon afterward, on Pennsylvania's stationary test plant rollers at Altoona, No 6110 chalked up power, steaming and calorific efficiency ratings that were a street and its sidewalks ahead of anything previously recorded. So, as late as 1945-6, Pennsylvania had 50 more T1s built.

At that eleventh hour, with the diesels' North American bridgehead expanded to near-occupation of many railroads, this was a startling investment decision. In the words of the US businessman's bible *Fortune*, it 'had the railroad industry by the ears'. For in the TI, proclaimed Baldwin, Pennsylvania had a machine that could 'outperform a 5,400hp diesel locomotive at all speeds above 26mph'.

Yet little more than a year after the last of the 50 production series T1s had taken the track Pennsylvania announced that it was immediately dieselising its Harrisburg-Chicago main line.

Why the abrupt volte-face? First and most obviously, the plain facts of the diesel's availability for work, capability and economy were by now so patent that even Pennsylvania, never a system to be led by the nose, could no longer ignore them — especially when, as happened in 1946, its accounts were sliding into the red. But in addition the T1s could not conceal their Achilles heel — or heels. Their unprecedented

steaming efficiency, power and speed were unarguable: one was alleged to have whipped a 16 car train of nearly 1,000 tonnes up to 130mph (209kmph), though the claim was never validated by acceptable evidence. Against its assets, though, had to be set the appalling costs in time and manpower of keeping the intricate poppet valve duplex-drive arrangements in good order. Moreover, notoriously prone to lose their feet in a frenzied slip, the T1s were unkind to the track. Pennsylvania motive power men desperately experimented with other valve gears, but it was too late. Diesels had long since tolled the bell even for such impressive steam performers as the T1s.

Steam technology was flowering in Western Europe too in the late 1930s, particularly in France under the hand of the Paris-Orleans company's brilliant locomotive engineer André Chapelon. Generally speaking, though the effort on the mainland of Europe was directed to economical movement of increasingly heavy loads at standard speed, regardless of grade to the greatest extent possible, rather than (for the period) extraordinary end-to-end speed on specially selected services. Line speed limits well below 100mph were rigorously applied.

A surprising exception was the Belgian State Railways. In 1933 this system at last completed its long-cherished project of a direct, finely graded and well-aligned route from Brussels through Ghent to Bruges and the port of Ostend. The general level of inter-city service on the new line was promptly accelerated to a creditable enough standard for Europe in the late 1930s.

Then, in 1939, the Belgians indulged themselves in a *feu de joie*. A small stud of bulbously streamlined, two-cylinder, 6ft 10½in (2.1m) driving wheel Atlantics was built to shuttle a service of three-coach high-speed flyers over the 70.9 miles (114km) between Brussels and Ostend Quay in the even hour, inclusive of a stop at Bruges. Between Ghent and Bruges the line speed limit was lifted to 90mph (145kmph) for these trains, so that they could be timed over the 57.8 miles (93km) from Brussels Midi to Bruges in 46 minutes start to stop, which predicated an average speed of 75.4mph (121.3kmph); and that for a brief spell snatched the world's fastest daily steam train riband from the Milwaukee's 'Hiawatha'. The *rapides* were taken off in

September 1939, but briefly reinstated in March 1940 when the Low Countries were deluding themselves that the Second World War was a non-event.

The only country in Europe to make new speed ceilings with steam power something of an objective in itself was Britain. Following its publicity success with the 1935 'Silver Jubilee', the London North Eastern Railway had two years later unveiled companion streamliners, the Kings Cross-Edinburgh 'Coronation' and Kings Cross-Leeds and Bradford 'West Riding Limited'. But its West Coast rival was stirring too. In 1936 the London Midland & Scottish Railway had felt the wicket by sending one if its comparatively new Pacifics, the unstreamlined No 6201 *Princess Elizabeth*, on a test run from London to Glasgow and back in which the 401½ miles (646km) were despatched in 5 hours 53½ minutes northbound and 5 hours 44 minutes southbound, a shattering reduction of the everyday schedules then in force between the two cities. In 1937 the LMS therefore launched its own high-speed, lightweight streamliner, the Euston-Glasgow 'Coronation Scot'.

In August 1936 the LNER had inched the British speed record a fraction higher in a rather desperate effort on the southbound 'Silver Jubilee'. The LNER was out for marked advance on *Silver Link's* 112.5mph of the previous year, but finesse was lacking on the footplate of sister engine *Silver Fox*. To get a run at the long descent from Stoke summit, she had been hammered so fiercely up the northern climb from Grantham that as she raced away downhill the big-end bearing metal of the middle of her three cylinders overheated to melting point. That allowed the big end itself so much play that it knocked out the cylinder end.

Everyone gritted their teeth as they heard the disintegrating metal strike showers of ballast against the floor of the leading coach, but they held on grimly until the graph of the dynamometer car specially inserted in the train registered — just — a new peak of 113mph (181.8kmph). At that the footplate crew were ordered to rein in fast. Live steam jetting from its gaping middle cylinder end, the streamlined Pacific limped the rest of the way to London sounding more like a mortally wounded bull than a silver fox. This, incidentally, was the only occasion in British history — and one of the few in all rail history — when management, not just a footloose engine-driver on his own initiative, deliberately set out for a speed record with a public service train carrying oblivious paying passengers.

The aura that now glowed publicly about the LNER and its 'Silver Jubilee' stung the LMS to attack the record on the pre-launch press demonstration trip of its 'Coronation Scot' on 29 June 1937. Unfortunately the LMS had nothing like the enticing LNER racetrack down from Stoke summit, their nearest approach being 6½ miles (10.5km) of steady downhill at the southern approach to Crewe. Streamlined Pacific No 6220 *Coronation*, one of a quintet of new four-cylinder 6ft 9in (2.06m) driving wheel engines created by William Stanier for the new service, was given the gun on the last few miles up to this stretch and they turned downhill with speed already on 93.5mph (150.4kmph). Her exhaust, in the words of one observer, 'humming with a continuous roar like that of an aeroplane engine', *Coronation* just made it to a new record of 114mph (183.4kmph) — or so it was claimed on the evidence of tape from the Pacific's automatic speed recorder; three expert stopwatch timers on the train had recorded no better than a dead-heat with *Silver Fox*.

At that critical moment Crewe and its maze of trackwork were already in sight. *Coronation's* regulator was shut fast, the brakes were slammed on and flames spurted from the Pacific's flanges as the brake blocks fought for a hold, but speed was down only to 57mph (92kmph) as she hit the first of the crossovers leading to her platform berth in the station. Fortunately, as one of *Coronation's* footplate party recounted it later, 'she rode like the great lady she is. There wasn't a thing we could do but hold on and let her take it. Take it she did. Past a sea of pallid faces on the platform we ground to a dead stand, safe and sound.'

The electrifying sensations of that deceleration can be imagined from the fact that the final 2.1 miles (3.4km) to the grinding halt at the platform occupied only 1 minute 53 seconds. Bruises were the only physical marks of the experience the relieved passengers in the train could discover as they picked themselves off compartment floors or disentangled unwonted embraces. Carnage, miraculously, was confined to cascading crockery and utensils in the restaurant-kitchen cars; the horrendous din from this quarter as the train keeled drunkenly through the crossovers had convinced many passengers within earshot that the coaches were disintegrating.

The following year the LNER put the record firmly out of LMS reach. The pre-announced pretext for the events of Sunday 3 July 1938 was braking trials, but an invincible speed record was clearly the prime objective. By then four of the Gresley Class A4 Pacifics had been fitted with one of the highly successful French devices to streamline internal steam flow, the Kylchap double blastpipe and chimney. Sensibly resisting friendly pressure from colleagues to turn out the A4 which a grateful LNER had named *Sir Nigel Gresley* in his honour, Gresley mobilised one of the double-chimney engines, No 4468 *Mallard*, to head the 244 tonne test train of dynamometer car and three articulated twin-units from a 'Coronation' train-set.

Starting southbound from Barkston, just north of Grantham, Driver Duddington gave *Mallard* full regulator up the northern slopes of Stoke. They entered the summit tunnel at 74.5mph (119.9kmph), then streamed away. Within 6 miles (9.7km) she was making 116mph (186.6kmph), and for 3 miles (4.8km) — now with steam shut off — she held 120mph (193.1kmph). The dynamometer

Right: *In 1939 a 'Coronation Scot' train was shipped to the USA for display. Pacific No 6220* Coronation *(in reality No 6229 in disguise) poses alongside the Baltimore & Ohio 'Royal Blue' streamliner on Relay Viaduct, near Baltimore.*
/ Cecil J. Allen collection

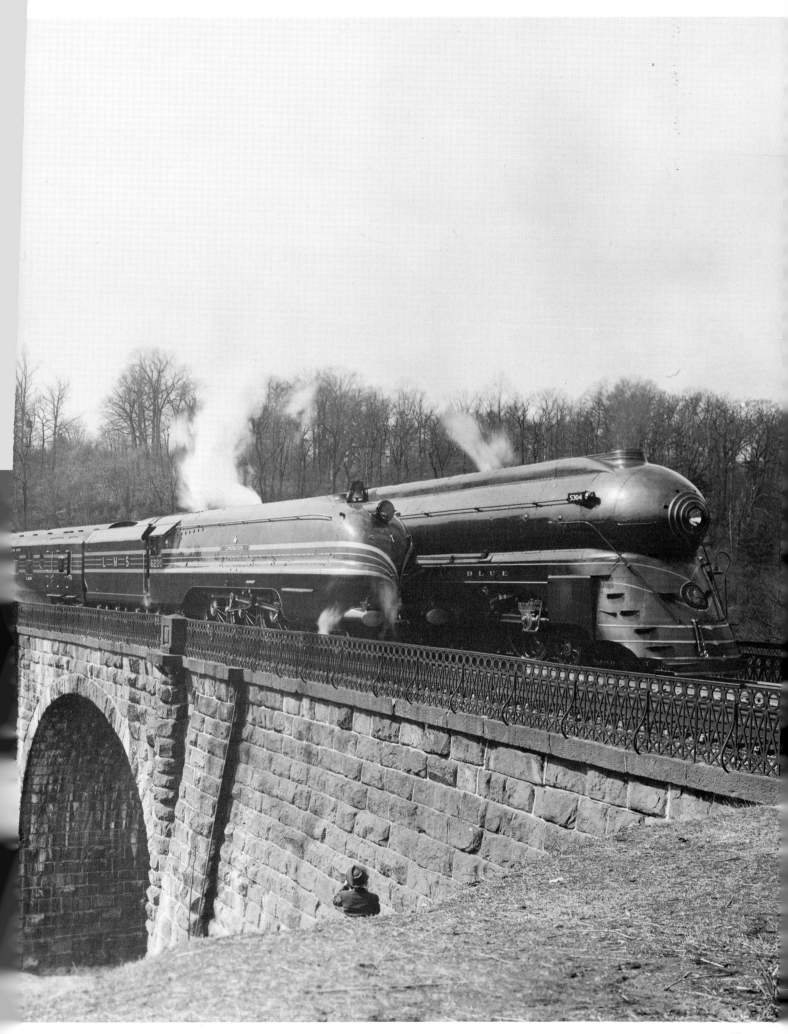

Right: *Photographers rarely caught steam at 100mph (160kmph), but there was an expert timer on the train to confirm former Great Western 'King' 4-6-0 No 6018* King Henry VI *was hitting 102.5mph (164kmph) when the shutter froze the 'Bristolian' descending Dauntsey bank en route from London to Bristol in July 1956. Highest known speed by this type was 108.5mph (173.3kmph).* / Kenneth Leech

Below: *Mixed-traffic member of the '100' club in the last years of British steam was the BR standard 'Britannia' class Pacific. This one is No 70025* Western Star, *hurrying for London with an express from South Wales in the 1950s.* / G. F. Heiron

Bottom right: *Another '100' club member near the close of its career: one of the three-cylinder Bulleid 'Battle of Britain' Pacifics of the former Southern Railway, No 34053* Sir Keith Park, *emerges from the New Forest near Brockenhurst with a Waterloo-Bournemouth express in July 1965.* / K. R. Pirt

car rolls registered an unarguable top speed of 126mph (202.7kmph), which is, short of the belated discovery of full supporting data for some of the superior claims mentioned in this chapter, the uncontestable world record for steam power.

After the Second World War most of the world's major railways were dieselising or electrifying as fast as resources would allow. British Rail was the conspicuous laggard. Though its inter-city timetables were for weary years pegged well below pre-war speed standards by the war's legacy of skimped track, traction and rolling stock maintenance and by a scarcity of good steam coal, and though 90mph (145kmph) was the maximum officially permitted on any British main line until the diesel/electric era, steam engines would still be pushed up to three-figure miles-an-hour speeds on occasion. Sometimes it was quite illicit, sometimes the civil engineers had relaxed the rules for a special. It was with a railway enthusiasts' special, for instance, that the ex-LNER streamlined A4 Pacific *Sir Nigel Gresley*, by now also equipped with Kylchap double chimney, attained the highest speed reliably recorded in the post-war twilight of British steam. The venue was, as always, Stoke bank, down which the now 22-year-old Pacific had its eight-coach 300 tonne train rolling at a peak of 112mph (180kmph).

In these last years the list of 100mph British steam engines lengthened. The Great Western 6ft 8½in (2.04m) 'Castle' 4-6-0s and 6ft 6in (1.98m) driver 'King' 4-6-0s, after rejuvenation with boiler modifications that included double chimneys and blastpipes, were authentically timed at just over the three-figure mark on more than one occasion. Another 4-6-0 design irrefutably timed at just over 100mph was the 6ft 9in (2.06m) ex-LMS 'Royal Scot', on the sweeping 1 in 200 descent of the London St Pancras - East Midlands main line from Ampthill down to Bedford.

Engines that were nominally mixed traffic units, with driving wheels only 6ft 2in (1.88m) in diameter, also joined the '100' club. Among them was one of British Rail's post-war standard designs, the two-cylinder 'Britannia' Pacific, which like the 'Royal Scots' passed its entrance test on the Midland main line from Ampthill to Bedford. Denied easy membership by a rigid 85mph (137kmph) limit throughout their territory were, for several years, Oliver Bulleid's remarkable three-cylinder 'Merchant Navy', 'West Country' and 'Battle of Britain' Pacifics on British Rail's Southern Region. Weaknesses they certainly betrayed, but their boilers with Lemaitre multiple-jet exhausts were not among the frailties; given free rein from the start of their careers, the first of which began in wartime, their free-running propensities would have placed them very quickly amongst the elite of Britain's high-speed steam power. It was at the very end of their all-too brief lives, when the 1967 electrification of the Southern main line from London's Waterloo to Southampton and Bournemouth was about to rob them of their last jobs, that management turned a veiled if not a blind eye to drivers determined to see steam out on a high note. Even though by then the Pacifics were in some cases shamefully run down, a considerable number of 100mph maxima were recorded, up to a peak of 105mph (169kmph), both on the long descent at 1 in 252 past Winchester and also between Basingstoke to Woking, in the latter case on a profile flattening from 1 in 249 to practically level track.

3. Diesels and Electrics Show their Paces

There were dreamers of 125mph (200kmph) electric locomotives even before the last century had turned. Stimulated by reports from America of a quest for speed on the New York-Philadelphia route, two engineers of the French PLM Railway set out determinedly to devise such a machine for the Chicago Exhibition of 1893. But the limitations of the electric traction art at that time defeated them.

They were not to defeat the Germans much longer. The German engineer Werner von Siemens had in the summer of 1879 achieved the world's first railed electric locomotive. Granted, it was only a 3hp midget running on narrow-gauge track, drawing current from a centre third rail, which perambulated trainloads of 30 passengers on open 'knifeboard' cars at 4mph (6.4kmph) round some 900ft (275m) of track in the Berlin Exhibition grounds. But it spurred some remarkably rapid development. Little more than two decades later German technology had proved electric traction was indeed capable of 125mph on rails.

The practical outcome of the early German development was the spread of dc electric tramways, beginning at Lichterfelde in 1881. At the same time, however, there was eager pursuit of three-phase ac traction and a consortium for the study of high-speed electric railways (*Studiengesellschaft für Elektrische Schnellbahnen*) was formed. By the end of the 19th Century it had its first prototype to test.

An appealing test track was the easily graded 14.5 miles (23.3km) of military railway between Marienfelde and Zossen, near Berlin. It was furnished with catenary supplying 15,000 volts ac, generated at the AEG power station at Oberschönweide, and here, in 1901, an experimental eight-wheeled centre-cab locomotive built by Siemens & Halske was run up to a world record of 101mph

(162.5kmph). Later that same year two new vehicles were ready for testing.

Both were 50-passenger railcars, mounted on two six-wheel bogies, each with a power output of 1,000hp. The mechanical parts of both vehicles had been built by Van der Zypen und Charlier, but one had Siemens & Halske and the other AEG electrical equipment. The two cars were distinguishable by their quaint current collection arrangements. The line's three-phase current supply was arranged as three vertically spaced and parallel conductor wires strung up to masts at the trackside, so that the wires were to one side of the rail vehicle. The AEG had two sets of three pantographs, one set at each end of the car, the members of each set stepping up in size to align their sideways-facing contact pans to the supply wires. The Siemens & Halske car, on the other hand, had each set of three pantographs mounted one above the other on the same roof-mounted standard, looking like some contemporary sci-fi vision of an esoteric radar device.

As soon as they had the two cars up above 75mph (120kmph) on the Marienfelde-Zossen line they were in trouble. Faces blenched as the ungainly vehicles pitched and swayed on the lightly-laid track and the sky erupted in vicious arcing as pans lost contact with the supply wires. At 160kmph one car momentarily bounced a bogie clean off the rails, thumped it back and spread the track alarmingly. That was enough. The tests were suspended until the whole route had been comprehensively relaid with heavier rail and better foundations and the railcars had had their bogie wheelbases lengthened.

By 1903 the rebuilding was complete and on 6 October that year the Siemens & Halske car was hustled the length of the railway in just eight minutes, reaching a peak of 126mph (202.7kmph). It did much the same on 23 October, except that it edged the record up to 128.5mph (206.8kmph). A few days later the AEG car snatched the laurels with a peak of 130.5mph (210kmph). Shortly afterwards a more significant achievement was recorded when the Siemens & Halske electric locomotive worked a train up to 130kmph (81mph).

The running of the railcars on the rebuilt track was, they said afterwards, so smooth that top speeds of 230kmph (143mph) were attainable had not 'caution outweighed a thirst for knowledge', to quote one technician. However docile the ride, it can't have been a nerveless experience, with the unwieldy clerestory-roofed cars, quite innocent of

streamlining, churning up the ballast to beat a frenzied tattoo on the underside of the floor and spraying a maelstrom of flying soil and pebbles in their wake.

These exploits sparked off a number of plans to electrify the Berlin-Hamburg main line for high-speed railcars, but the expense was too much of a deterrent. Oddly, despite the Siemens & Halske locomotive's performance on the test track, no one seems to have advocated the obvious alternative of developing high speed locomotive-hauled services, even though as early as 1911 members of the Reichstag were treated to a 135kmph (84mph) trip behind an electric locomotive from Dessau to Bitterfeld.

With these early electric exploits the Germans held the all-comers' record for rail speed for 30 years. Then, in 1931, they pushed it a bit higher with a still more unorthodox vehicle.

Quite soon after the Wright Brothers' first flight an inventive German had visualised the speed potential of a prop-driven train. In 1917 the idea was put crudely to the test by mounting an aero engine on an orthodox railway van. The hybrid was run on the Berlin-Hamburg main line and is said to have shown a rare turn of speed, but there was no follow-through until 1931.

Eight years earlier there had been formed in Germany the *Gesellschaft für Verkehrstechnik* (GVT), or Association for the Advancement of the Science of Transport. For its first line of research it picked the monorail concept, with the idea of driving the suspended gondolas by airscrews; this it put to joint study with the country's leading railway rolling stock manufacturers. But in 1929 it switched to thoughts of powering an orthodox railcar the same way. In conjunction with the country's Aeronautical Research Association (DVL) in Berlin, the 1917 vehicle was dusted off, refitted with two BMW engines of 230hp apiece and reputedly taken up to a speed of 109mph (17.5kmph).

A year later the partnership yielded a more refined version, Dr. F. Kruckenburg's so-called *Schienenzeppelin*, or 'Zeppelin of the Rails'. This pencil-slim, aluminium-bodied

and aerodynamically streamlined railcar was aluminium-bodied, weighed a mere 17¼ tonnes and was mounted on just two axles at a lengthy wheelbase of 65ft 7in (20m). Its propulsion was a rear-mounted four-bladed airscrew, driven by a 12-cylinder Otto petrol engine delivering 600hp at 1,200rpm. The forward passenger saloon seated 40, but not in memorable comfort to judge from the slender configuration of the body — one has to surmise, because the *Schienenzeppelin* never carried paying customers. It did, though, establish a new world rail speed record.

After a preliminary 23 September 1930 jaunt between Hannover and Celle when the car showed it could bolt from a standing start to 100kmph (62.14mph) in 66 seconds and 985m (3,230ft), and 113mph (182kmph) was reputedly attained, the *Schienenzeppelin* was let out on the German Reichsbahn's recognised racetrack, the Hamburg-Berlin main line, shortly before dawn on midsummer's day, 21 June 1931. Pressmen had chartered a plane to follow the *Schienenzeppelin's* progress, but they had to keep the taps well open to hold the railcar in their sights, for she droned the 159¾ miles (256km) from Bergedorf to Spandau West merrily away in 98 minutes at an average of 95.7mph (154kmph), and held an average as high as 142.9mph (230kmph) for 6.25 miles (10km) on end between Karstädt and Dergenthin.

History records little further track testing of the *Schienenzeppelin* in its original guise. For one thing, the slipstream as it hummed through stations was a menace to anyone or anything movable on the platform. Intrinsically, though, the concept had little to offer bread-and-butter railroading. The nature of the animal precluded anything but single-unit operation; and to have kept the tracks adequately clear of conventional trains for such a low-capacity passenger vehicle would have been ludicrously uneconomic. Kruckenburg's name was to recur in rail speed history before the outbreak of the Second World War, as we shall record shortly, but his *Schienenzeppelin*, after a period of trial as an orthodox axle-powered diesel-hydraulic railcar with a Maybach engine and the airscrew dismantled, faded from rail history in 1936.

Some three decades later, incidentally, an equally aimless stunt with aero engines was perpetrated in the USA by New York Central. In the mid-1960s, naturally, the power plant was jet engines — two General Electric J-47s, military surplus, which NYC mounted on the roof of a standard Budd

Below left: The AEG three-phase electric railcar which achieved 130.5mph (210kmph) in the Berlin-Marienfelde-Zossen military railway tests of 1903. / Deutsche Bundesbahn

Below: Dr Kruckenburg's airscrew-driven Schienenzeppelin *of 1930, reputed to have averaged 142.9mph (230kmph) over 6.25 miles (10km).* / Alfred B. Gottwaldt

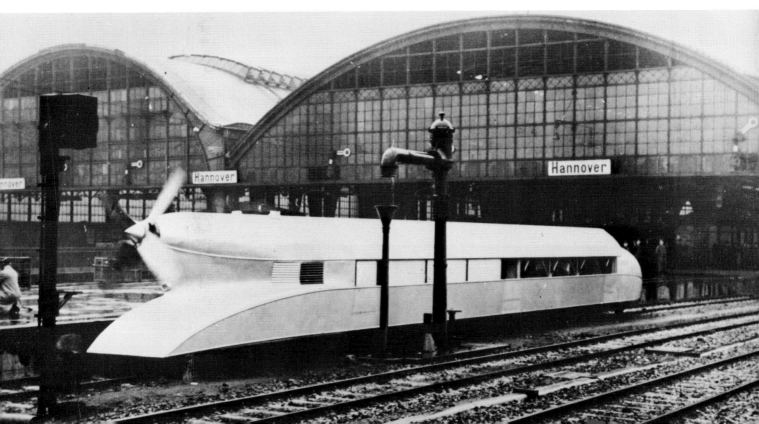

Above: *New York Central's experimentally jet-propelled Budd RDC railcar on its way to a maximum of 183.85mph (295.8kmph) in the tests staged on 23-4 July 1966.* / Tom Miller

Above right: *The three-car, Budd-built 'Pioneer Zephyr' on its record-breaking 26 May 1934 dash from Denver to the Century of Progress exhibition in Chicago.* / Burlington Northern

RDC-3 diesel railcar built for branch-line baggage-passenger service in 1953. They gave the RDC new wheels, added shock absorbers to damp down vertical oscillation, grafted a streamlined prow on to the end beneath the jets, then at the end of July 1966 sent it careering down a piece of standard straight and level track between Butler, Ind., and Stryker, Ohio. The car's normal diesel-hydraulic transmission had been disconnected and it was being driven solely by the jets.

Two minutes of full power from the screaming jets were enough to get the car up to 120mph (193kmph) from a standing start. Another four minutes and it had hit a maximum of 183.85mph (295.8kmph). At that it was braked, having secured America a rail speed record still unbeaten by anything but electric traction. And the sensations? One of the testing staff was reported as affirming that the car rode better at its peak speed than it did at 90mph (145kmph), but the din from the jets was on a scale 'from horrendous to just tolerable'. 'Most comfortable' though, was, NYC President Al Perlman's stoic comment to pressmen.

But so what? The real objective of the affair was probably no more than that of some publicity thunder from the rival Pennsylvania, which was struggling up to the starting line with its Federally-sponsored New York-Washington electric Metroliners, of which more in a subsequent chapter. Only a matter of months later Perlman was publicly threatening total withdrawal from inter-city passenger service because of the NYC's rapidly dwindling passenger patronage.

Returning to the proper chronological sequence of this chapter, the internal combustion engine's potential in rail traction had been appreciated very early in this century. The first significant applications were of petrol engines to low-powered petrol-electric railcars — ie, vehicles whose electric traction motors were supplied with current from a petrol engine-driven generator — but soon after the First World War Dr Rudolf Diesel's compression ignition engine was sufficiently developed for diesel rail traction to make a diffident debut in the shape of modestly-powered yard locomotives. At that stage, though, the diesel engine itself was too heavy and ungainly to impress anyone as a potential high-speed train mover.

It was the early 1930s' perfection of the compact, high rpm diesel engine which altered the course of rail traction history. Dedicated research work by the US company Electromotive, which had been absorbed by General Motors in 1930, evolved the historic 201A engine that promptly quadrupled the contemporary diesel engine power/weight ratio, thanks chiefly to adoption of two-stroke instead of four-stroke design and welded construction with new alloy steels.

By now Henry Ford's Model T automobile has just become the prized possession of countless American households and the railroads were being drained of passengers. One such was the Chicago, Burlington & Quincy, which had seen its passenger receipts quartered in a decade. The Burlington had already been intrigued by news that the Budd company of Philadelphia, a pioneer in several facets of automobile bodywork, was adapting what it had learned in that field to construction of a revolutionary lightweight stainless steel alloy rail coach body. This seemed a likely tool for greatly accelerated rail passenger service to recapture lost business and Burlington had ordered a train-set of the new vehicles. Now the enterprising Burlington had the train equipped with Electromotive's new diesel engines.

Streamlining was in vogue and Burlington's Budd-built 'Pioneer Zephyr' saw almost its first calculated application to an American train. The three-car articulated unit was not exactly a mass transportation unit, but the Burlington had only specified accommodation for 70 passengers (the service in mind was a daily out-and-home run between Kansas City and Lincoln, 250 miles (402.3km) apart). The first vehicle of the 196ft (59.8m)-long, 88.5 tonne unit was entirely occupied by the 600hp diesel-generator set, Railway Post Office and mail storage accommodation; there was more baggage and mail space in the second car, leaving room for just 20 passenger seats and a buffet-grill; and the third car had 40 more seats plus a 12-seat solarium observation lounge at the rear end.

Within two days of emergence from the Budd works in early April 1934 the 'Zephyr' had glided up to 104mph (167.3kmph) on a 25mile test run in the vicinity of Philadelphia. Then, in the course of a five-week promotion of

the new Budd-Electromotive technology around the cities of the Eastern US it zipped over the Pennsylvania racetrack between Fort Wayne, Ind, and Englewood, on Chicago's outskirts, at an average of 80.2mph (129kmph) for the whole 140 miles (225.3km). It was 26 May 1934, however, when railway history unmistakeably turned the page.

That day the Century of Progress exhibition in Chicago was to be reopened and to publicise both the event and the new high-speed train concept Burlington agreed to stage an attempt on the transcontinental rail speed record. At the time the best regular schedule over the 1,015 miles (1,633km) from Denver to Chicago was 26¾ hours, inclusive of 40 intermediate stops, but in 1897 a special had been hurried between the two cities in seven minutes under 19 hours. Burlington set its 'Zephyr' a target of 15 hours.

There was an eleventh-hour trauma when, on the afternoon before lift-off, one of the traction motor armature bearings of the 'Zephy' was found to be cracked — and she was due out as early as 04.00 next day. Frantic phoning at last unearthed a replacement in Union Pacific's workshops at Omaha and an emissary was hustled off by air to fetch it, with orders to charter a plane home so as to be back in Denver as near midnight as possible. Already more than a little unnerved by mature appreciation of the unprecedented endurance feat he had set his relatively untried 'Zephyr', the Burlington president nevertheless decided to stake his last handful of chips and go ahead with a nationwide broadcast outlining what was to be attempted next day. Meanwhile a local newspaper had rung that fraught afternoon asking if it could send a local breed of donkey along in the 'Zephyr's' baggage car as a neighbourhood publicity gimmick. The request was put to the Burlington president. 'Why not?', he replied helplessly, 'One more jackass on this trip won't make any difference.'

But the component arrived safely, was installed and at 05.05, later than billed, they were away, cutting through a tape activating a timing machine specially set up on the platform of Denver's Union Station. Extraordinary steps had been taken to keep the 1,015 mile path of the 'Zephyr' clear. In the preceding days track and track structures had been meticulously examined; and as the 'Zephyr' winged out into the early morning nearly 1,700 railroad men were on special duty at open level or grade crossings. Excited by the radio publicity, too, grandstands were congregating from one end

of the route to the other; around half-a-million people are said to have lined the track to watch the streamliner's astonishing progress.

They took it quietly at first, but crossing from Colorado into Nebraska the 'Zephyr' was notched up to average 90mph (144.8kmph) for 129.5 miles (208.4km) on end, run 19.1 miles (30.7km) at 106.2mph (170.9kmph), 6.4 miles (10.3km) at 109mph (175.4kmph) and hit a peak of 112.5mph (181kmph). By Lincoln, Neb, 482.6 miles (776.5km) from the Denver start the clock showed an elapsed time of only 6 hours 7 minutes, so that they had been averaging 78.9mph (127kmph) the whole way. And there was no sign of frailty in any 'Zephyr' component, though one mischance could have rung down the curtain on the show but for the sort of knee-jerk reaction that subsequently earns a bravery medal. Severed by a slamming door, a faulty instrument cable set up a short circuit that burned out an engine starter cable and had the technicians scenting fire. The engine was promptly shut down while the technicians scrabbled madly for means to repair the split cable. The idling 'Zephyr' had come down almost to walking pace before one technician decided enough was enough, seized the wire ends in his hands, made contact between them in a searing flash that burned him quite severely, but restarted the engine.

When they cut the complementary timing tape at Halstead Street, Chicago, the 'Zephyr' had reeled off 1,015.4 miles in two seconds under 13 hours 5 minutes. The whole dawn-to-dusk hop had been wrapped up at an average speed of 77.6mph (124.9kmph) — a record for long-distance non-stop running which, in terms of mileage, has still to be surpassed. And they had done it on 418 gallons (1,900 litres) of diesel oil; at 1934 prices, would you believe, that represented a fuel cost for the journey of $16! To top of its triumph that day the 'Zephyr' was run around Chicago's lakefront tracks to purr into spotlit place in a 'Wings of a Century' pageant at the 'Century of Progress' exhibition, moving thousands of the show's wildly cheering audience to stream out of their seats and crowd round this herald of a new age of rail travel.

Burlington's 'Pioneer Zephyr' was not, the sole diesel streamliner on show at the 1934 'Century of Progress' show in Chicago. The Burlington had been just beaten to the post of displaying America's very first diesel streamliner by the

Above: *The pioneers: Union Pacific's first diesel streamliner the three-car M-10000, later 'City of Salina', meets Burlington's 'Pioneer Zephyr' in Kansas City Union station.* / Burlington Northern

Right: *Rear-end view of Union Pacific's M-10000.*

Below right: *A new travel era opens on 11 November 1934; a grandstand gathers as Burlington's 'Pioneer Zephyr' opens daily round-trip service between Lincoln, Omaha and Kansas City.*

Far right, top: *No 10001 was Union Pacific's second diesel streamliner, star of a record-breaking transcontinental trip in October 1934.* / Cecil J. Allen collection

Far right, bottom: *Burlington's 'Pioneer Zephyr' on Denver & Rio Grande Western tracks in the spectacular Royal Gorge of the Arkansas River, beneath the 1,053ft-high (321m) Hanging Bridge.* / Burlington Northern

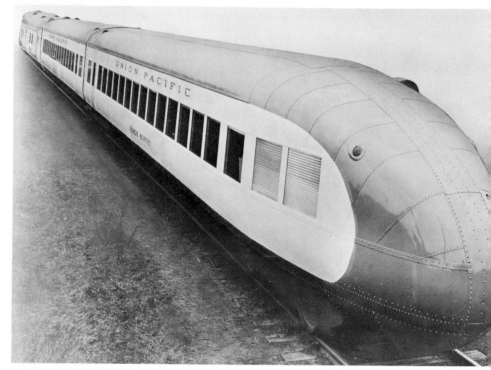

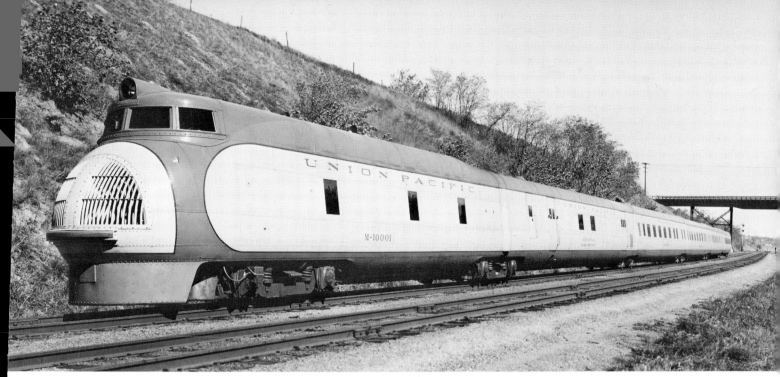

unveiling in February 1934 of a train-set built by Pullman
Standard for Union Pacific, another road to appreciate very
early the potential of diesel traction. Unlike the 'Zephyr',
UP's oddly fish-headed and fin-tailed three-car articulated
unit, the M-10000, was built of aluminium alloy and
powered by an Electromotive 12-cylinder V-type distillate
engine — that is, one fuelled with diesel oil but still using
spark-plug ignition — as opposed to the 'Zephyr's'
eight-cylinder in-line diesel engine proper. The boldly
yellow-styled M-10000 had seating for 116 and was designed
to cruise at 90mph (145kmph).

Prior to its static showing at Chicago M-10000 had toured
the country coast-to-coast and engrossed upwards of a
million visitors — the first of them President Franklin D.
Roosevelt — in the 68 city stops that punctuated its
12,625 mile (20,314km) itinerary. None of the sharp
contrasts of climate or variations in track, it was said, had
remotely discomforted the streamliner; moreover, at one
stage it was claimed to have run smoothly up to a top speed
of 111mph (178.6kmph). Another two million visitors
clambered over M-10000 during its spell at the Chicago
exhibition.

Putting the M-10000 to post-exhibition revenue-earning
service as the 'City of Salina' between Kansa City and
Salina, where it immediately attracted and held a near 100%
loading of passengers day in and day out, Union Pacific
eagerly ordered a twin. This time a six-car unit was
specified, with a 16-cylinder 1,200hp engine and including
Pullman sleepers, which were not only the first articulated
Pullmans seen in the US but which sported unique
collapsible lavatories in each berth. On 22 October 1934 this
second UP streamliner, M-10001, was sent out on the year's
second record-shattering transcontinental run, this time
from coast to coast.

At that date the coast-to-coast rail speed record still stood
at 71 hours 27 minutes, set by a steam special laid on from
Oakland, Calif, to New York for E. H. Harriman as long ago
as 1906. As for public service trains in the autumn of 1934,
the best schedule operative over the 3,259 miles (5,244km)
from Los Angeles to New York was 84 hours, inclusive of
stops. M-10001 set out at 22.00, hummed easily up the severe
grades through the Rockies, and by the time it pulled into
Chicago, 2,299 miles (3,699km) from the California start, it
had already notched up a gain of 20 hours on the best
contemporary public service timing. It had averaged 59mph

Above left: *One of Burlington's 12-car 'Denver Zephyr' sets of 1936, with 3,000hp twin-unit power. / Cecil J. Allen collection*

Left: *Union Pacific's 'City of San Francisco' pulls in the business at Oakland Pier in 1940; the second section, on the right, is formed of one of the original streamlined train-sets. / Cecil J. Allen collection*

Above: *Union Pacific's 'City of Denver' was the USA's fastest regularly scheduled train in the late 1930s. With a 3,600hp cab-and-two-booster unit of Electromotive's 1936 build up front, the train cruises into Denver in September, 1940. / R. H. Kindig*

(95kmph) start to stop over terrain when the long climbs had previously pegged averages at 35-40mph. Over the plains between Cheyenne, Wyo, and Omaha, Neb, 508 miles (817km) had been reeled off at an average speed of 84mph (135kmph) and it was said that 120mph (193kmph) had been touched, but the only basis for this last claim seems to be one passenger's excited cry that he'd just seen two miles go by in a minute by his fob watch. Be that as it may, despite a 40 minutes' pause in Chicago and discreet forbearance to put 'Twentieth Century Limited' timings to shame over the New York Central tracks onward to the East Coast, M-10001 glided to a stand in New York City in 56 hours 55 minutes overall from Los Angeles, a thumping 14½ hours ahead of the long-standing 1906 coast-to-coast record time.

Trailing clouds of glory from this feat and graced with the title 'Streamliner City of Portland', the six-car set was launched on regular public service between Chicago and Portland from 6 June 1935, working to a 39¾ hour schedule for the 2,272 miles (3,656km) that straightway lopped 18 hours off the previous steam timecard for the route. Scorning the slump that was impelling other railroads disconsolately to curtail their passenger services in the mid-1930s, the euphoric UP now laid orders with Pullman Standard for two eleven-car streamliners, with twin power units — a 900 or 1,200hp booster articulated to the 1,200hp cab unit by a span bolster — to encompass the added load. These, the original 'City of Los Angeles' and 'City of San

Francisco', were inaugurated in the early summer of 1936. That year, confounding the trend on most other railroads, UP's passenger takings climbed by more than a third. Frequently, said UP in its annual report, business had to be turned away, so the road would now be stepping up to 17-car formations — which, following the debut later in 1936 of the 12-car 'City of Denver' on a 16 hour end-to-end schedule for the 1,048 miles between Chicago and Denver, inclusive of eight intermediate stops, duly materialised in 1937-8.

Meanwhile the other US diesel pioneer, the Burlington, hadn't been sitting on its hands. The first Zephyr had so entranced the public that, to quote American railroad writer David Morgan in his book *Diesels West*, 'the Burlington couldn't order them nor could Budd build them fast enough... All of a sudden, train riding had become The New Experience for the country. One sat in a soft individual reclining seat amidst modern, sound-proofed air-conditioned surroundings, and was effortlessly swept up to astounding speeds of 70, 80, 90 — even 100 miles per hour. Riding the "Zephyr" was more than merely transportation in the 1930s; it was sophistication, The Thing To Do.'

In the spring of 1935 came the first 'Twin Cities Zephyrs', still three-car units but with reduced mail space to lift the seating space to 88, which went into immediate contention with Milwaukee's new steam 'Hiawatha' and Chicago & North Western's brave '400', with its vamped-up conventional steam Pacifics, on the thriving Chicago-Minneapolis and St Paul route. After only ten weeks of single out-and-home workings by each unit the load factor was averaging 97.7%, so at the start of June 1935 the Burlington rostered each unit to make two return trips daily totalling 882 miles (1,419km) per set. Of course the diesel 'Zephyrs' were now and then crippled by the usual ills to which all diesel hardware is prone, but that year their availability ran out at 97% — an astonishingly high figure for units as yet so briefly serviced-hardened. And the accountants reckoned their revenue was exceeding direct operating costs by 160%!

By early 1936 the Burlington too had decided diesel traction was handsomely clear of its probation period. It could now be applied confidently to really long-distance service. Orders were handed to Budd for two 12-car 'Denver Zephyrs' (also for two new seven car 'Twin Zephyr' sets). In the 'Denver Zephyr' units the diesel streamliner for the first time took on the full interior trappings of the American rail transcontinental, with a cocktail as well as an observation lounge (that featured a soda fountain and a radiogram), a wide range of sleeping accommodation (which included special 6ft 8in berths for tall passengers, and something new on any train, power sockets for the then new-fangled electric razor) and a dormitory for train staff. And there was still more power up front: the 'Denver Zephyr's' cab unit mounted a pair of two-stroke 900hp V-12 engines, its booster a single 1,200hp V-16.

Ever since 1934 the Burlington had been miffed by repeated sniping that the original 'Zephyr's' record run from Denver to Chicago had been done the easy way, because the west-to-east profile was effectively downhill all the way from a starting point some 5,000ft above sea level at Denver to around sea level at Chicago. On 23 October 1936 the Burlington set out to squelch the sceptics by pointing one of its new 'Denver Zephyr' 3,000hp twin power units and six trailer cars from east to west. This time the route was slightly different and thus a trifle shorter, at 1,017 miles (1,636km).

It was a cold, grey morning spattering snow as they left Chicago's Union Station and for a long time the gods seemed to have thumbs down on the whole exercise. Some way out they discovered that, because of a maintenance man's negligence, they had been getting no power to the booster unit's traction motors. Not long after there was a thunderclap flashover in the lead unit. That repaired, an overspeed governor on one of the cab unit's engines tripped and shut it down temporarily to idling speed. After that, the breaking of an air line and the sudden jamming of the air horns must have seemed mere pinpricks.

Once the casualty ward had been cleared, though, there was no holding the 'Zephyr'. Over one 26.6 mile (42.8km) stretch of Illinois level average speed was held at 105.8mph (170.2kmph) and in Colorado they claimed the streamliner hit 116mph (186.6kmph). They touched down in Denver in 12 hours 12½ minutes from Chicago, which meant, despite the irritations along the way, a start-to-stop average speed of 83.3mph (134kmph). That still stands as a world record for sustained rail speed over a run of 1,000 miles or more.

The 'Denver Zephyrs' scored as instantaneous a commercial success as their shorter-run sisters. Until extra train-sets were available, of course, there were not enough units to operate the long-distance services daily, particularly transcontinentals like the UP 'Cities'. At the start the 'Cities' ran only five or six days a month and their departures were picturesquely described in the public timetables as 'sailings'.

The acceleration of American inter-city services spearheaded by the diesel streamliners and the last refinements of steam power like the Milwaukee 'Hiawatha' engines accumulated mileage with extraordinary rapidity in the second half of the 1930s. It got a fresh fillip in 1938 when Electromotive perfected its famous 567 range of diesel engines and launched the world's first range of successful production-line diesel-electric locomotives in the E6, fitted with a pair of the new 567 series 1,000hp V-12 engines. From 29,301 miles daily in 1936, the runs covered at scheduled start-to-stop speeds of a mile a minute or more had jumped to 48,247 miles by the summer of 1938. Union Pacific led the

Right: The Santa Fe 'Super Chief' rolls into Chicago in the 1940s behind an ALCO DL-109 4,000hp cab-and-booster unit. / Cecil J. Allen collection

Above: *Fronted by an Electromotive E5B 4,000hp cab-and-booster unit, the Burlington Route's 'Denver Zephyr' pulls out of Denver in August 1940 on its high-speed run over Union Pacific tracks to Omaha.* / R. H. Kindig

Left: *Rugged country confronts US transcontinentals: this is the former Great Northern's 'Empire Builder' in the Rockies, with Mount St Nicholas in the background.* / Cecil J. Allen collection

field with an 81.4mph (131kmph) sprint over the 62.4 miles (100.4km) from Grand Island to Columbus and another at 80.3mph (129.2kmph) over the 95 miles (152.9km) from North Platte to Kearney by its 'City of Denver'. But diesel locomotive-hauled trains were close on its heels: Santa Fe's exclusive all-Pullman 'Super Chief' and supporting all-coach 'El Capitan', timed over the 202.4 miles (325.7km) from La Junta to Dodge City at a start-to-stop average of 78.3mph (126kmph).

Inexorably, wartime notwithstanding, the acceleration continued until by the early 1950s the mileage scheduled for US trains at more than a mile a minute start to stop was over 150,000. By then, of course, over 80% of it was behind diesel power, a mere 3-4% with steam up front and the rest under live wires. There were to be no marked advances on the top average speeds already described in this book, not least because of the Interstate Commerce Commission's intervention with an edict that speed must be kept within 80mph (128.7kmph) on any line not equipped with both automatic cab-signalling and automatic train-stopping devices; few roads were prepared to lay out the money on that just to benefit a handful of passenger trains over lengthy routes predominantly occupied by massive freight tonnage. That ICC ruling ended, for instance, the remarkable schedule

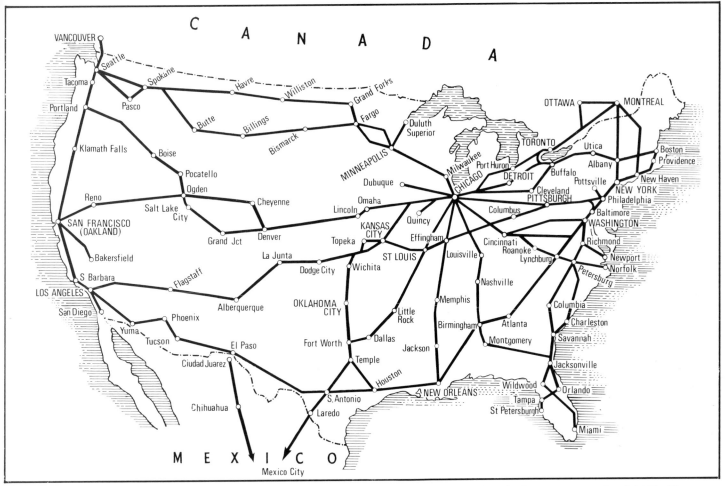

applied for several years to the 'Denver Zephyr' between Denver and Omaha, on Union Pacific metals, which stipulated coverage of 560miles (901km) at an average of 73.9mph (118.9kmph) *inclusive of seven intermediate stops* — probably the world's most demanding timing for a considerable period of the 1940s. Throughout the 1940s and early 1950s, until post-war air and road competition began to bite fiercely and bleed the US passenger train practically to death, the emphasis of development was on raising average speeds to a common standard, gilding the trains with ever more fanciful amenities and increasing frequency in the heavily populated corridors.

By comparison with today's impoverished one Amtrak train daily between Chicago and Milwaukee, in 1950 seven heavy streamliners were plying daily each way between Chicago and the twin Cities of Minneapolis and St Paul. Of these, the now diesel-powered Burlington 'Zephyrs' had intermediate start-to-stop timings as fast as 38 minutes for the 54.6 miles (87.9km) from East Dubuque to Prairie du Chien, average 82.6mph (138.7kmph) and 41 minutes for the 57.7 miles (92.8km) from La Crosse to Prairie du Chien, average 84.4mph (135.8kmph). The rival and now also diesel-powered 'Hiawathas' had timings almost as fast. On both routes 100mph (160kmph) was essential routine to maintain schedule with these trains.

On paper the end-to-end times of the Pacific Coast streamliners looked far less sparkling, apart from the intermediate flatland sprints of the kind which I have already acknowledged to the UP 'City of Denver' between Grand Island and North Platte, west of Omaha. Considered against the background of the formidable terrain these 15-17 car trains and their 6,000hp diesel multiple-unit combinations had to surmount between the prairies and the West Coast, their schedules — and, equally, some of the record runs described earlier in this chapter — take on a different complexion. The UP's San Francisco and Portland

'Cities', in particular, had to conquer the 8,013ft Sherman Hill summit west of Cheyenne, Wyo. Santa Fe's 'Super Chief' and 'El Capitan' confronted four summits each over 7,000ft (2,135m) up in succession, the highest, at 7,622ft (2,325m) in Raton Pass Tunnel, approached from the east on a fierce 1 in 28½ slope. The later 'California Zephyr', that most buff-beloved of all the golden age streamliners, which was jointly operated by the Burlington, Denver & Rio Grande Western and Western Pacific, had no less than 9,191ft to climb up to Moffat Tunnel, west of Denver.

Now steps must be retraced in time and space to recount the major European developments in diesel and electric speed up to the eve of the Second World War. Cynosure of interest on that side of the Atlantic was the other and parallel pioneer of diesel rail traction, Germany.

Another reason for German disinterest in Kruckenburg's *Schienenzeppelin*, despite its startling demonstration run in 1931, was Dr Rudolf Diesel's perfection of his art. Even as the Kruckenburg car was winging from Hamburg to Berlin, the Reichsbahn had a file of conclusive data to show that its long-cherished ambition of an unassailable world speed crown was within the grasp of a diesel-powered twin-car set. So that same year the Görlitz works of Wagen und Maschinenbau AG, or WUMAG, was handed the order to build a diesel-electric prototype, its two cars articulated, and horsed with a pair of 12 cylinder high rpm 410hp Maybach engines.

The prototype was finished in 1932 and put to exhaustive proving trials. Then, on 15 May 1933, it was committed to public service over the Berlin-Hamburg racetrack as the *'Fliegende Hamburger'*, or 'Flying Hamburger', and premiered a new epoch in European inter-city rail travel.

Comfort was not the outstanding characteristic of the 78 tonne articulated unit, of which the streamlined contour derived from extensive research at the Zeppelin works in Friedrichshafen. Into the two open saloons they crowded 102

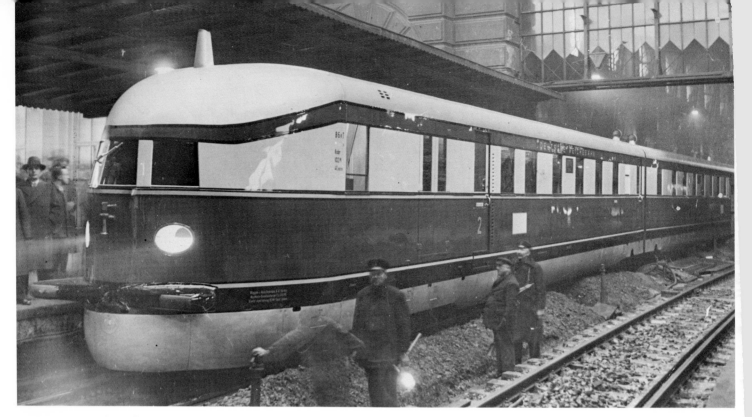

seats, arranged in bays three-and-one athwart a central gangway, and catering service was limited to a four-seater Mitropa bar serving only drinks and snacks. In sharp contrast, at least two British railways were at this time verring towards a two-a-side compartment layout in the first class accommodation of crack services like the 'Royal Scot' and 'Flying Scotsman'. No wonder the London North Eastern Railway brass counted the German diesel unit's spartan facilities a serious debit in drawing up the balance sheet that persuaded them to commission Gresley's steam-powered 'Silver Jubilee' streamliner, as described in Chapter Two.

In speed the 'Fliegende Hamburger' immediately opened up a new European chapter. Its schedule of 138 minutes for the 178.1 miles (270km) between Berlin and Hamburg demanded a start-to-stop average speed of 77.4mph (124.6kmph). Not only was that, in 1933, the quickest scheduled start-to-stop timing in the world: to observe it and take account of certain fixed speed limits en route the new diesel train had to run regularly at 160kmph (99.4mph) over substantial stretches of the route — the first time such a pace had been accepted as day-to-day routine.

The German Reichsbahn was not indulging this new range of speed without additional safety precautions. The trains themselves had both quick acting Knorr air brakes and electro-magnetic track brakes, capable of decelerating the unit from 160kmph to a dead stand in 2,790ft (851m). The Berlin-Hamburg route had been fitted throughout with the Indusi automatic train control system, an inductive apparatus that has each running signal protected by track sleeper mounted electro-magnets; if the adjacent signal is adverse, the ground device transmits a distinctive frequency which, reacting on a train-mounted receiver, either brakes the train to an immediate stand, or issues an audible warning and, if the driver fails to acknowledge, applies brakes automatically after a few seconds' interval, or sounds a warning bell in the cab to advise the driver he is exceeding the speed limit in that area. The 'Fliegende Hamburger's' immediate commercial success and demonstrable economy in running costs compared with steam soon had the Reichsbahn scheming an inter-city network of similar units, but not without preliminary groundwork: a route had to be fettled up to a 'Special Class' category of track maintenance

and be equipped throughout with the Indusi apparatus before the Reichsbahn would open it to the new diesel trains.

Orders for 17 more units were placed in 1935. Thirteen of them were diesel-electric twin-units basically similar to the prototype, which the Reichsbahn classified SVT877 (and which now reposes in the Nuremburg Transport Museum), but the production series Class SVT137 or 'Hamburg' sets embodied refinements of exterior styling and internal layout; in particular, seating was thinned out to a more relaxing 76 places in a two-and-one layout and the outher ends were fitted with Scharfenburg automatic couplers, so that the sets could be run in multiple. Set weight was increased to 91 tonnes.

Four of the 1935 order, the Class SVT137 'Leipzig' series, were three-car units that took advantage of the newly-perfected Maybach 600hp diesel engine. Two of these sets, moreover, had a new feature that was later to be the signal difference between German and American diesel rail traction practice: Voith hydraulic as opposed to electric transmission. The three-car sets, seating 139 each, had engine compartments at each end, unlike the two-car units. In the diesel-electric version, the two inner articulation bogies were both motored (it was only the centre bogie of the two-car set that was powered), but in the diesel-hydraulic sets it was the two outer bogies that were motored. According to German sources, one of the diesel-electric 'Leipzig' units was tested up to a peak speed of 127.4mph (205kmph) on the Berlin-Hamburg route between Ludwigslust and Wittenberge shortly after delivery in February 1936, but I have never come across full supporting data: the three-car sets were, however, designed with a slightly higher service speed capability of 170kmph (106mph). A major change applicable to all the three-car sets, as compared with the two-car units, was that they were two-class and that their 139 seats were laid out entirely in compartments; there was no seating in the buffet, from which passengers were served in their compartments. Weight per set was 117 tonnes.

The diesel railcars stimulated as sensationally rapid an advance in German rail speed overall as the diesel streamliners had in the USA. In the mid-1930s the Reichsbahn gradually interlaced all the country's major population centres with each other and with the capital, Berlin, in a network of services with the same cardinal

Top left: *The 'Fliegende Hamburger' makes its debut at the Lehrter station, Berlin, for a trial run to Hamburg.*

Above: *One of the production series of Reichsbahn 'Hamburg' type diesel twin-units.* / Alfred B. Gottwaldt

Left: *A three-car 'Leipzig' near Berlin on the 'Fliegende Schlesier' service from the capital to Frankfurt/Oder in 1936.* / Alfred B. Gottwaldt

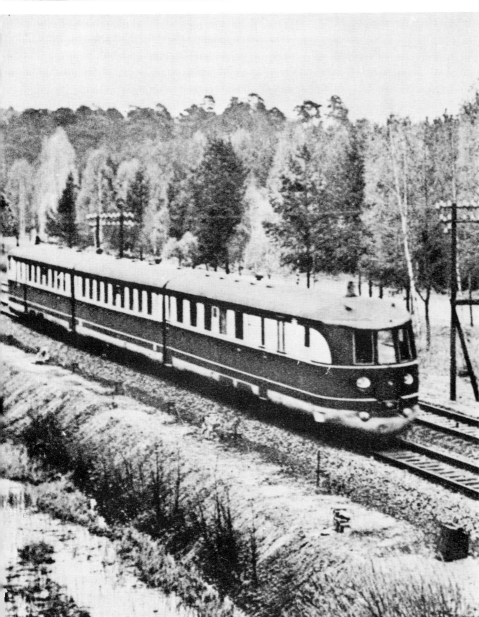

Above: *The MAN-built 'Berlin' diesel train-set of the Reichsbahn was the last in this pre-war format to be built with two-class accommodation. These pictures show a second-class compartment and the diner.* / Alfred B. Gottwaldt

Right: *Final standard three-car inter-city diesel multiple-unit of the Reichsbahn was the 'Köln' type, one of which is seen after the Second World War at Hamburg Hbf in Deutsche Bundesbahn service as Class VT 06.* / Deutsche Bundesbahn

commercial objective that informed much of Western European inter-city development after the Second World War: establishment of primarily business services that would get executives to destination by midday in time for a reasonable day's work and have them comfortably home to bed the same evening. Most of the services were promoted under a common *'Fliegende'* brandname — *'Fliegende Kölner', 'Fliegende Münchener'* — and so on.

By the summer of 1935 the Reichsbahn had not merely swept the European rail speed board comprehensively, but had grabbed the world lead in daily scheduled start-to-stop runs with not one but 13 services. Topping the table were the world's first timings in excess of 80mph (128.7kmph) — four of them: Berlin (Zoo) to Hannover, 157.8 miles (254.1km) by the evening train FDtl6 in 115min, average 82.3mph (132.6kmph); Leipzig to Berlin (Anhalt), 102.2 miles (164.4km), by both the morning train from Frankfurt and the morning flyer from Stuttgart in 76 minutes, average 80.7mph (129.8kmph); and Sagan to Güben, 37.5 miles

(60.3km) in 28 minutes, average 80.4mph (129.4kmph). As outstanding as these tightly-timed sprints were the long distances covered by some of the railcars in a single high-speed day. The *'Fliegende Kölner'*, for instance, had a daily itinerary of 719 miles (1157km), all run at an average of 71.2mph (114.6kmph); the Berlin-Munich train's daily stint was 851miles (1,369km), for which the overall average of 64.5mph (13.8kmph) may look superficially unremarkable, but was outstanding for the times considering the reduced speed enforced over the sinuous and sharply graded stretch of its route through the hills between Leipzig and Nuremburg. Attention to timekeeping of the railcars were punctilious; operating staff had strict instructions from Reichsbahn headquarters not to delay them for late-running connections.

In their final series of high-speed railcar units the Reichsbahn abandoned articulation of coach bodies so as to increase coach length and augment seating space. A new specification had been issued in 1936 and both MAN and Linke-Hoffman-Werke prepared designs. The MAN prototype, which appeared in 1938 and was known as the 'Berlin' type, was distinctive in style from any other unit in the fleet. It had a single power car, shorter in length than the other three vehicles in the set, which was unusually powered by a single low-speed, 700rpm MAN engine developing 1,400hp and driving through electrical transmission to traction motors on inner bogie of the power car and the inner bogie of the end passenger car; the latter had no driving cab so the set was not flexibly reversible. Fully laden weight of the MAN essay was 207 tonnes, which made its power/weight ratio markedly inferior to that of the other railcar sets.

Not surprisingly, perhaps, the Reichsbahn standardised the so-called 'Köln' series version from Linke-Hoffman-Werke, of which 14 were ordered and deliveries began in 1938. In these three-car non-articulated units the centre car was a trailer and both outer vehicles power cars, each mounting a Maybach 12 cylinder high-speed turbocharged 600hp engine with electric transmission. As a matter of policy the Reichsbahn had now made its diesel flyers exclusively one-class, which in the 'Köln' series was of compartment layout seating a total of 102 in one power car and the centre trailer combined. The other power car was a full-scale 30-seater kitchen restaurant.

One recently published world railway history has it that the Reichsbahn's diesel flyers were all withdrawn in the 1937-8 winter and never restored. This is a canard. A number of services were certainly suspended for a period at that time, partly because axle fatigue flaws had shown up and the whole fleet needed inspection, partly because the Third Reich was exerting great strains on the whole national economy, particularly in its drive for self-sufficiency and hence reduced consumption of imported oil. The great majority of the railcar services were reinstated within a matter of weeks, however, and not finally killed off until the outbreak of war. Many of the units survived the Second World War and served either the West German or East German systems for a number of years: both 'Hamburg' and 'Köln' series units were active on the East German Deutsche Reichsbahn until 1959.

One last German pre-war high-speed diesel railcar exploit must be recorded. Here the redoubtable Dr Kruckenberg re-enters the stage. In 1937 the Cologne firm of Westwaggon was persuaded to build an aluminium-bodied and articulated three-car streamliner, with an overhanding nose that looked like a cartoonist's grotesque distortion of the post-war German Trans-Europ-Express diesel multiple-unit. After considerable problems in securing two 600hp Maybach engines and Voith hydraulic transmissions to power the prodigy, Kruckenberg got his so-called 'Flying Silver Fish'

on the track towards the close of 1937. Next year it was reported to have reached 121mph (195kmph) on test between Berlin and Cologne. Then, on 26 June 1939, it was set at the favourite Berlin-Hamburg course and reputedly held 200kmph (125mph) for a considerable distance, touching a maximum of 215kmph (133.6mph). Wherever the speedometer needle really fetched up, the exertion wrought such havoc with the outfit's power plant and running gear that it had not recuperated sufficiently for further operation until late in June 1938. It was consigned to limbo with the war's outbreak.

Just before the onset of the Second World War, with electrification from Munich to Berlin programmed (because of the war catenary got no further north of Munich than Dessau), the Germans at last set about high-speed electric locomotive development. Progenitor of the new range was the Reichsbahn's Class E18 (later Deutsche Bundesbahn Class 118), a 4,075hp 1-Do-1 with a maximum speed of 93.2mph (150kmph) which AEG put on the drawing board in 1933; 55 were built, the last two after the war's end. Tests showed that the E18, which won a grand prize at the Paris World Fair of 1937, could summon up a short-term output as high as 8,000hp for pace in excess of 100mph (160kmph), which made it by a clear margin the world's most powerful electric locomotive of the age. And that prompted a step up to a specifically high-speed design for express service over the Munich-Nuremburg-Leipzig-Berlin route when the latter's electrification was ready.

The first Class E19 (later DB Class 119) was delivered by AEG at the close of 1938. Again a 1-Do-1 it was visually almost a twin of the E18, but with a continuous power rating lifted to 5,360hp it was designed for a maximum speed of no less than 140mph (225kmph) and its specification called for ability to accelerate an eight-car, 360-tonne train from rest to 112mph (180kmph) within 4½ minutes on straight and level track. The E19's maximum short-term output was well over 8,000hp and on test one of the first pair was said to have bettered its specification to the extent of hustling 400 tonnes up to 125mph (200kmph) within 4min 48sec of a standing start. The first two E19s were never run at their designed maximum speed and in fact their permitted ceiling was eventually lowered to 112mph (180kmph), but German records hold that the final pair, built by Henschel and classified E19.1, were definitely run up to the intended maximum of 140mph (225kmph) during their acceptance trials. The war rang down the curtain on further expansion of the class, but the original quartet survived to be taken into Deutsche Bundesbahn use between Munich and the East German border at Probstzella after the war. Throughout their post-war service, however, the E19s were restricted to 87mph (140kmph). The last, No 119.12, was retired for preservation in 1977.

No one else in Western Europe held much of a candle to the Germans in pre-1939 development of high-speed diesel traction. By the late 1930s the French were actually operating more internal combustion-engined railcars of all types, local stopping as well as inter-city express, than the Germans. But in France 120kmph (74.5mph) was imposed on the whole rail system by law (whether under the duress of statute or not, the same ceiling was steadfastly observed throughout most of mainland Europe at the time). As French inter-city railcars or railcar sets multiplied, first petrol and then diesel, their regular line speed ceiling was eased out to 140kmph (87mph), but that was not generous enough to lift any French service into the same start-to-stop schedule league as the Germans. Some speeds above 160kmph were attained on test trips, but again nothing to rival the German feats.

The same inhibitions — plus, as I have already remarked, short-sighted disinterest in going for the horizons opened up

Above: *The Kruckenberg aluminium-bodied diesel train-set of 1937, the so-called 'Flying Silver Fish', which was said to have reached 133.6mph (215kmph).*

Left: *Deutsche Reichsbahn's crowning high-speed electric locomotive development, the Class E19 1-Do-1; this one is seen in post-war Deutsche Bundesbahn employment as No 119. 011-5. / Deutsche Bundesbahn*

Below left: *One of the twin Maybach-engined 820hp diesel-electric train-sets which the Northern Railway of France introduced between Paris, Lille and Tourcoing in 1934, seen at Paris Gare du Nord. On test one was worked up to 98.3mph (158kmph).*

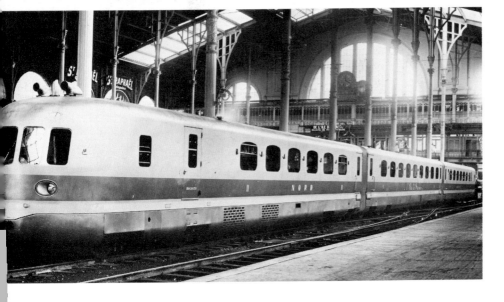

as early as 1903 by the Marienfelde-Zossen experiments —
limited the pace of electric traction before the Second World
War. But there were occasional *feux de joie*. One such was
reported in 1938 from Switzerland, of all unlikely places,
with its generally sinuous and often sharply graded main
lines. On the Simplon route through the Rhone Valley
between Geneva and Brigue there are some temptingly
straight and level tracts, and it was here that one of the
Swiss Federal Railways' two three-car articulated 'Red
Arrow' electric multiple-units, built in 1937-8 for day round
trip excursion work, was tested up to a peak of 180kmph
(111.9mph). For years a jaunt on one of the 'Red Arrows',
whether one of the 1935-8 single-units or the later triplets,
could be fairly guaranteed to turn up higher speeds than the
Swiss main line norm; the triplets, in fact, were geared for a
top service speed of 150kmph (93.2mph).

That triplet's attainment of 180kmph stood as the Swiss
national record until the summer of 1977, when the Swiss
Federal borrowed a German Federal Class E103 electric
locomotive for a test programme in the tunnel of its new
Heitersberg cut-off line and ran the visitor up to 132mph
(212.4kmph). Object of the exercise was to examine the high-
speed performance of a new design of catenary against the
possible construction of a new Gottherd base tunnel under
the Alps.

The most significant pre-war pointers to the electrified
way ahead came from France and Italy. During 1938 French
National Railways staged a high-speed test programme over
the Paris-Bordeaux main line, which is admirably aligned
for pace at its northern end. The test locomotive was
No E704, one of a quartet of 4,950hp 2-Do-2s (ie, with idle
front and rear bogies enclosing four independently motored
driving wheels) which had been commissioned in 1934 to
evaluate machines of considerably higher output than the
standard traction units of the time. Foreshadowing what was
to come in the 1960s, when this route was to become a
shopwindow of French high-speed rail technology, No E704
crowned the tests by hustling a 176 tonne rake of four
coaches up to 185kmph (115mph) and averaging 170kmph

Top: *The PLM and State Railways of France were also
extending the use of railcars for inter-city service in the
mid-1930s. Best-known type was the 76ft (23.2m)-
long Bugatti railcar adopted by the State Railway in
1933 and driven by four 200hp petrol engines through
mechanical transmission, two axles on each of the
unusual four-wheel bogies being powered. During a
pre-service trial of the prototype near Le Mans in May
1933 a top speed of 106.3mph (171kmph) was said
to have been touched. This power car-and-trailer
version was put on to Paris-Lyons first class-only
service in 1934 by the PLM and timed at start-to-stop
average speeds as high at 72.8mph (117kmph)
between Laroche and Dijon.* / La Vie du Rail

Above: *The two-car version of the Swiss Federal 'Red
Arrow' electric railcar. This one, Type RAe 4/8
No 1021, was built in 1939 and is named* Churchill
*following its use by Sir Winston Churchill in 1946. It
was photographed near La Chaux-de-Fonds.*
/ Sébastian Jacobi

Left: *The German Federal Class 103 electric
locomotive and its German testing train on the Swiss
Federal's new Heitersberg cut-off line in 1977, when a
new Swiss rail speed record was set up.*
/ Swiss Federal Railway

(105.7mph) over 20km (12.4 miles) between Blois and St Pierre-des-Corps.

'First on land, on sea and in the air', was the Italian objective trumpeted by Mussolini's propaganda machine with tedious persistence in the 1930s. So far as the railways went, popular history credits Il Duce chiefly with making the trains run on time. Be that as it may, hard fact is that by the late 1930s no other European country's inter-city passenger service had been so transformed, speedwise, as Italy's. The 523 mile (841.5km) trip from Naples to Milan, for instance, which as recently as 1914 had sprawled over a wearisome 17 hours — and often more, because of chronically unpunctual working — was by the summer of 1939 down to eight hours by electric *rapido*. Compared with 1914 every trunk route timetable showed not merely cuts in average journey times ranging from 20 to 45% (the crack trains were generally 100% faster) but massive increases in service frequency, up to as much as 114% between Rome and Naples.

The new flagships of this revolutionised Italian train service were a series of articulated three-car inter-city electric multiple-units in Classes ETR201 and ETR221 that were introduced to the Italian State 3,000V dc system from 1936 onwards. These 110 tonne, 1,100kW train-sets were built with 160kmph (100mph) maximum speed capability in regular service, but were tested at considerably greater pace. On the recently completed Rome-Naples *direttissima* line via the coast, for instance, No ETR201 itself was taken up to a maximum of 125mph (201.3kmph) on 27 June 1938 in the course of eating up the 130.5 miles (210km) in 83 minutes start to stop at an average of 94.3mph (152kmph).

That exploit though, was eclipsed by the extraordinary feat of ETR201 on 20 July 1939. The second of Italy's new rail *direttissima* lines, superseding some of the system's most tortuous or adversely graded routes with a more favourable alignment, had lately been opened through the mountains from Florence to Bologna via the impressive new 11½ mile (18.5km) Apennine Tunnel. Chiefly for the greater glory of the regime rather than calculated railway purpose, one

guesses, a special run was laid on over the new route that July day for the Minister of Communications and some hundred other invitees.

Now although the *direttissima* was a vast improvement on the old line in terms of curvature it is still beset by a fair share of sharpish bends. I still vividly recall a trip over this route in the Italian State Railway's latter-day 'Settebello', the extravagantly luxurious emu that has the driving cab in a sort of mezzanine so that the streamlined nose of each end-car can be given over to a passengers' observation lounge. I defy any motorist to sit in the front armchairs of the 'Settebello's' forward lounge on the Forence-Bologna leg of its Rome-Milan itinerary and avoid sub-consciously stabbing his foot hard on a non-existent brake pedal as each bend looms up. Especially where the curves break up descents, the driver seems to leave it to an impossibly last moment to slow the streaking train.

Ever since that trip, what was achieved on 20 July 1939 has astounded me. The traction current voltage had been specially boosted from 3kV to 4kV dc but so far as I know the track was not specially fettled up or any extraordinary precautions taken, yet they ran the whole 195.8 miles (315km) from Florence to Milan in 115¼ minutes at a start to stop average of 102mph (164kmph). Passage of those curves must have been trepidating. Even on the *direttissima* the climb up to the tunnel through the Apennines is 1 in 106, and there is nearly 11 miles (17.7km) of it, but the train strode up the hill at a steady 80-90mph (130-145kmph), then surged up to 109mph (175.4kmph) on the level deep under the mountains. Climax of the day was coverage of the entire 124 miles (199.5km) from Lavino, north of Bologna, to Rovoredo, south of Milan, at a pass-to-pass average of 109.2mph (175.8kmph), with a top speed of 126mph (203kmph). It was the fastest long-distance journey on rails anywhere in the world until the post-war inauguration of a new rail speed era by the Japanese New Tokaido Line.

Below: An Italian State Railways Type ETR200 electric multiple-unit of the type which made the remarkable 102mph (164kmph) average run from Florence to Milan in July 1939. / Italian State Railways

4. The French Point the Post-War Way

Before the Second World War, you will have correctly inferred from their brief appearance in the preceding chapter, French Railways were not front runners in rail speed. The line speed limit of 120kmph (74.5mph) statutorily imposed on steam trains was still enforced by the discipline of self-recording speed indicators on the locomotives long after 90mph (145kmph) had become commonplace on some neighbouring British trunk routes and 100mph (160kmph) was daily routine with US and German diesel trains — even with steam on the Milwaukee's 'Hiawatha' in the US and the London North Eastern streamliners in Britain. At the outbreak of the Second World War the fastest scheduled start-to-stop runs in French timetables represented averages of only 67.2mph (108.2kmph) with steam, 70.1mph (112.9kmph) with electric and 73.0mph (117.6kmph) with diesel traction.

But the groundwork for the splendid flowering of French train speed to come had been laid in the aftermath of the First World War. War damage to France's richest coalfields, then labour unrest, throttled the supply of coal and sent its price soaring. So in 1920 the Government spurred the Orleans, Midi and Paris-Lyons-Mediteranée (PLM) Railways to channel the water resources of their mountainous areas into hydro-electric power stations that would fuel homes and factories as well as power the railways. The initial plan was too ambitious and by the onset of the Second World War the only main lines fully converted, on the 1.5kV dc system, were those from Paris to Le Mans and from Paris through Bordeaux to the Spanish frontier at Hendaye.

Railwaymen kept their plans dusted throughout the German occupation, though, and French Railways were at the starting gate with a detailed programme of further electrification almost simultaneously with the ceasefire. As early as 1946 the plan's centrepiece, conversion of the ex-PLM main line from Paris to Lyons, was under way. Within six years — and six years of irksome post-war discomforts at that — some 380 miles (611km) of main and diversionary routes between the two cities were electrified at 1.5kV dc. In the 1952-3 winter French Railways rewrote the Paris-Lyons timetable to take account of the new traction's potential and thereby Europe acquired its first post-war inter-city rail service in the 70-75mph (110-120kmph) start-to-stop schedule range.

Right: *From 1931 onwards a number of French railways used railcars with rubber-tyred wheels that had been developed by the Michelin company in pursuit of quieter, shock-free riding. One of the earliest post-war French Railways developments, in 1948, was the introduction of three streamlined locomotive-hauled train-sets employing lightweight coaches running on Michelin-designed chassis with novel bogies of ten wheels, all rubber-tyred. Hauled by streamlined 4-6-0s nicknamed the 'Whales' by virtue of their appearance, the equipment operated between Paris and Strasbourg and a Michelin train on this service is seen at Nancy.* / Y. Broncard

Right and below: *Buffet and restaurant car of a 1948 Michelin train-set.*

Far right: *Spearheading the revival of French Railways speed in the immediate post-World War II years on the Paris-Dijon main line were the 1.5kV dc 2-D-2s built before the war or constructed post-war to the same basic design. 2D2.9103 is one of the 1950-1 series with an output of 4,950hp and is heading the 'Mistral' of the 1950s, with two Pullmans behind the leading van, out of Paris Gare de Lyons for the Riviera. / Lucien Viguier*

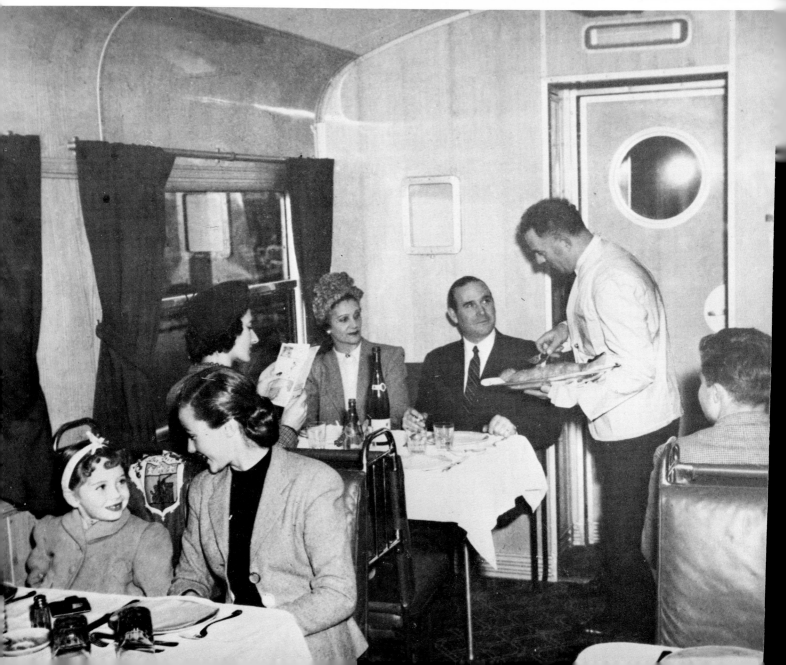

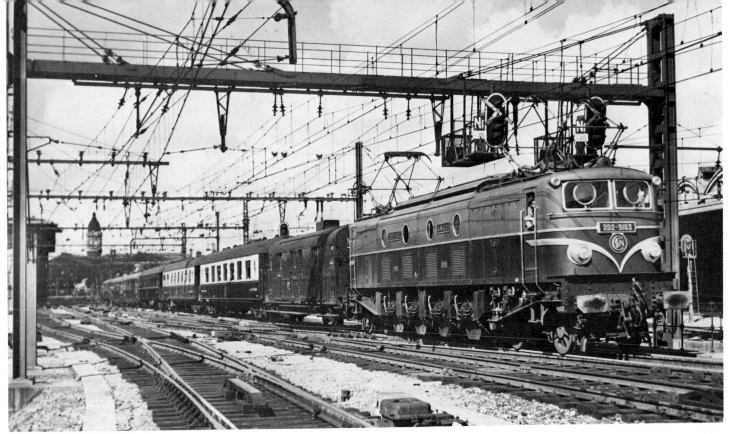

Coal was again a scarce commodity and the savings from this electrification were so significant that the French Government was eager for a rapid spread of catenary. But the railways' economists balked. Too few lines carried enough traffic to justify the huge installation costs of dc electrification. The electrical engineers, meanwhile, were beginning to glimpse the solution. The bones of it had come into French hands with the end of the war, but a great deal of flesh was to be grafted on by French genius.

When Germany was partitioned into occupation zones at the close of the Second World War, French territory embraced the short Höllental line in the Black Forest. In the 1930s the Germans had experimentally converted this to make direct use for rail traction of high-voltage alternating current at the national industrial frequency. The temporary overlords quickly grasped the implications: simpler lineside supply apparatus and far less ponderous catenary would be possible, and the railway would no longer need to build its own power generating stations, all of which added up to a big cut in the first cost of electrification. No need to delve here into the further research and development needed before, with the important aid of development in semi-conductor rectifiers, the modern ac traction unit was perfected: but that had been achieved by the mid-1950s.

The economies of the new system were not so dazzling that it paid to rip out all existing dc catenary and start again. Existing dc electrification, therefore, was logically extended — for instance, from Lyons southwards to Marseilles. Moreover, the engineers were soon to devise multi-current locomotives that could operate with equal facility under the wires of up to four different current systems, Central Europe's 15kV 16⅔Hz ac and the Low Countries' and Italy's 3kV dc as well as France's 25kV 50Hz ac and 1.5kV dc. But from 1957 onwards there was an explosive burst of ac electrification that knitted together a system right across Northern France, including the main lines from Paris to Amiens and Lille, to the Belgian border at Aulnoye en route to Brussels, and to Metz, Strasbourg and Basle. Moreover, the perfection of multi-voltage traction technology allowed ac extension of dc networks, from Marseilles on to Nice and the Italian border at Ventimiglia, for example.

High-speed inter-city passenger service was always a main plank in the SNCF's post-war reconstruction plan. Besides electrification, the other key tool for the objective's achievement was a thoroughgoing redraft of the timetable, so as to make the most of the prodigious reserve of power the French built into each successive breed of locomotive as a matter of policy. With this high power on tap for rapid acceleration from rest to full running speed, then to sustain maximum permissible track speed almost unvaryingly uphill or down, and by segregating the principal express trains in timetable groups, or 'flights' of equal schedule' speed, the French built up on each main line a basic operating pattern that was commercially valid for a period of years. That done, the engineers could apply themselves uninterruptedly to an orderly programmed exploration of new technological frontiers.

As early as 1952 the French showed how the theories worked in practice. On a July evening one of the 5,550hp 2-Do-2s of 1950-1 vintage that traced their lineage back to the 1934 locomotive which earned mention in the previous chapter confronted arrears of 14 minutes on schedule when it pulled out of Paris with a 642 tonne evening *rapide*. Despite some enforced slowings en route they covered the 196.3 miles (315.8km) to Dijon in 138 minutes at a start-to-stop average of 85mph (136.8kmph), but without ever exceeding the prevailing line speed limit of 145kmph (90mph).

In 1954 French Railways' technicians set up a far-sighted high-speed research and development exercise. Principal objectives were to determine the practical performance limits of orthodox electric locomotives, to study the high-speed behaviour of rolling stock, and to determine the resilience of the track, the efficiency of the current supply apparatus and the capability of the electrical equipment — fixed and mobile — to withstand the maximum loads exerted by the highest speed operation. A string of record-breaking performances ensued.

Track tests got off the mark in February 1954 on a 23 mile (37km) stretch of track that was almost dead straight and practically level south of Dijon, between that city and Beaune. Guinea-pig was one of French Railways' first dc electrics with all wheels motored, the 106 tonne, 4,740hp

No CC7121. These machines had already revolutionised day-to-day working on the newly-electrified Paris-Lyons line, sailing up the route's only significant slope, the climb into the Burgundy hills that culminates in 1 in 125 to Blaisy-Bas, with 700 tonne *rapides* at 80mph (128.7kmph). No CC7121, then just a few months old, was taken straight out of traffic and given no special preparation.

The tests lasted from 17 to 21 February 1954. While the three-coach, 109 tonne train of standard stainless steel coaches was on the move, the Dijon-Beaune section was closed to other trains and station platforms cleared of all but railwaymen. At that early stage of exploring high speed's side-effects, the French took the added precaution of tying down wagons in adjoining sidings in case they be set rolling by the test train's slipstream.

On the first two days comparatively modest marks of 112mph (180kmph) and 121mph (194.7kmph) were set without extending the locomotive. The third day saw France's first 100mph (160kmph) start-to-stop sprint in the record books when the 22.9 miles (36.8km) from Dijon to Beaune were gobbled up in 13¾ minutes and 143mph (230kmph) was touched. Sparkling acceleration distinguished the next run, for although curves restrained speed for the first 1¼ miles (2km) out of Dijon, No CC7121 reached 100mph (160kmph) within 3¼ miles (5.2km) and by 8½ miles (13.7km) from the start had edged the maximum a little higher, to 145mph (233.3kmph). Then on the final outing of 21 February No CC7121 needed only 3 miles (4.8km) from the start, inclusive of the speed-restricted exit from Dijon, to accelerate the train to 115mph (185kmph). Eight miles (12.9km) out it registered the peak speed of these trials and a new world record, 151mph (243kmph) as the climax of an average of 145½mph (234.1kmph) over the preceding five miles (8km). At that point the current supply fluctuated slightly and speed dipped to 138mph (222km) over the next kilometre, but within another two kilometres they had just about regained the peak speed of the run before they deliberately eased her down.At her highest speed the locomotive was putting out 4,100hp, well below her rated maximum. Instrumented recordings of the lateral movement and thrust of both locomotive and coaches attested that these were well within safety limits, corroborating the impression even of uncommitted journalists on board that

Above: *The 'Mistral' with its stainless steel, air-conditioned coaching stock of the early 1960s, headed by one of the 4,700hp CC7100 class of 1952-4 which was to produce a still unbeaten world rail speed record-breaker.* / French Railways

the test train had been riding as smoothly as a Paris-Lyons *rapide* at the line's normal maximum pace.

The 1954 trials turned out to be just a curtain-raiser to the main event. French engineers now determined to leap clean out of the generally accepted limits of rail speed. The February trials had proved that modern locomotives could reach at least 150mph without overtaxing their power or absorbing more current than their electrical equipment could tolerate. It was comparatively simple to regear the drive from traction motors to wheels for still greater speeds. The only essential was a different venue: the Dijon-Beaune section was not long enough for the target in mind.

The most likely alternative was the ex-Midi Railway route from Bordeaux to the Spanish frontier at Hendaye. For mile after mile across the flat Landes the route is practically level; and in a 52¾ mile (85km) stretch from Lamothe, south of Bordeaux, to Landes there is a solitary curve, and that a very gentle one, through Labouheyre station. It was the ideal racetrack and would have been selected for the February 1954 trials except for one drawback.

The Midi had been electrified in 1927 and its catenary structure, suspended from quaint portal-shaped supports, was comparatively lightweight. In normal service the maximum permitted speed beneath it was 75mph (120kmph), despite the otherwise speed-inviting characteristics of the route. Would it stand up to quite unprecedented stresses envisaged?

In June 1954 French Railways sent No CC7122, a sister of the February trial protagonist, to the Midi for reconnaissance. For the purpose No CC7122 was slightly modified with a new-model tubular pantograph, designed to reduce air resistance and also pressure on the catenary. The omens looked good. On 22 June No CC7122 took out a three-coach train and was held at 125mph (200kmph) or more for 12 miles (19.3km) up to a peak of 140.5mph (226kmph). Next day a 10 coach, 430 tonne train was assembled to examine catenary and pantograph performance under heavier load conditions. The train was a *mélange*

Left: *The world's steam rail speed record holder, LNER Class A4 4-6-2 No 4468* Mallard, *now preserved in its original condition in Britain's National Railway Museum at York.* / D. A. Halsall

Below: *One of the Belgian steamlined 4-4-2s which briefly worked the world's fastest daily train in 1939.* / G. Freeman Allen

Left: *This is the Russian ER200 electric train-set, designed for a maximum of 125mph (200kmph). It was forecast to take up the 'Aurora' service between Moscow and Leningrad in 1978 and to cut the previous end-to-end time of 4hr 59min for the 404 miles (650km) to 4hr or even slightly less, for an average of at least 100mph. As this book went to press, however, there was considerable doubt that the track works necessary to permit this speed would be completed by 1978.* / John Dunn

Top: *A series of 4,920hp and 6,000 monomotor-bogie, multi-voltage locomotives with double gearing built by French Railways between 1964 and 1970 were equipped for very high speed on their higher gearing, though the top speed has not yet been regularly employed in public service. Nos CC40101-4 have a maximum speed of 149mph (240kmph), Nos CC40105-10 a maximum of 137mph (220kmph). No CC40103 was photographed under French 25kV ac catenary on the Northern Region main line, heading an Amsterdam-Paris express near Survilliers.* / Y. Broncard

Above: *A Japanese Shinkansen train-set against the Tokyo skyline.* / John Dunn

Top: *A German Federal Class 103 8,000hp electric at the head of a 'Trans-Europ Express' near Heigenbrücken, Spessart.* / German Federal Railway

Above: *A UAC Turbo-train in the new Canadian VIA RAIL livery.* / Canadian National

Right: *France's 8,000hp, 125mph (200kmph) electric power of the 1970s — No CC6568 at the head of the Paris-Nice 'Mistral' near Brunoy.* / Yves Broncard

Above: An HST diesel train-set on British Rail's 125mph (200kmph) Paddington–Wales service hurries through Sonning Cutting, near Reading. / British Rail

Below: A driving trailer of British Rail's pre-production APT-P, scheduled to enter high-speed service between London and Glasgow in 1979. / British Rail

Right: *French Railways high-speed, turbine-powered test unit TGV001, prototype of the TGV Sud-Est train-sets.* / French Railways

Below: *The four-car 'Pendoline' automatic tilt-body electric train-set designed and built by Fiat, which has been operating on the Rome-Rimini service.* / Fiat Ferrovia Savigliano

Above: No CC7107 accelerates up to its still unbeaten 205.6mph (331kmph) world speed record of 28 March 1955. / French Railways

presumably improvised in the neighbourhood, since it included some vintage-looking coaches. Perhaps that was the reason speed on the second sortie was not pushed much beyond 160kmph (100mph), though that pace or better was held for 15 miles (24km).

These opening tests had satisfied the engineers that the catenary could stand up to the purely mechanical stresses of moving pantograph contact at well over 100mph (160kmph) and for a considerable time. But the power transmitted had been some way off the strength needed to reach the speeds in mind. At 115mph (185kmph) with the 430 tonne train the current demand had been within 2,000 amps; it might reach 4,000 amps at the extreme speeds contemplated, and with that a single locomotive's traction motors could not cope if they were normally geared. For the next series of tests in early December 1954, therefore, the engineers coupled a pair of Co-Cos, Nos CC7107 and 7113, but arranged them so that their combined current feed was taken through a single pantograph on the leading locomotive. To ensure adequate current strength throughout the test section, its five sub-stations were supplemented by the output of a mobile generating plant.

On 30 November the two Co-Cos were coupled to a 17-coach train of 715 tonnes. That day and the next they had three outings, attaining successively 102½, 115 and 121mph (165, 185 and 195kmph) with this heavy load. For the final essay on 2 December, two coaches were subtracted, slimming the formation to 620 tonnes and with this the pair of Co-Cos maintained an average of 118½mph (191kmph) for 10½ miles (16.9km), peaking at 131.3mph (211.3kmph). Throughout this high-speed stretch the single pantograph in use was taking current at 4,000 amps, so the engineers now had more of the data they needed.

Some of it was disconcerting. The engineers were particularly dismayed by the severe arcing between locomotive wheels and rails when current was flowing at maximum amperage. It was the current's normal return path, but ordinarily, of course, at a strength that gave no trouble. Fierce arcing in this area might dangerously deform either

the locomotive wheels or the rail profile. Another problem was the serious wear of the current collector strips at the tip of the pantograph. That was bad enough to rule out reliance on a single pantograph at the speeds in mind; but on the other hand simultaneous use of both pantographs on a locomotive was equally a non-starter, as their random oscillations at 150mph (240kmph) and more would be bound to snap the conductor wire.

The engineers now set themselves to intensive wind-tunnel study of new pantograph designs to meet the very exacting specification thrown up by the tests so far. The chosen model had to be capable of rapid and efficient raising and lowering against extreme wind pressures, since the plan was now to lower one pantograph of the test locomotive halfway through the speed trial, simultaneously raising the other to take over its function with split-second precision. The pantograph must also retain maximum stability once it was raised, despite the tremendous air resistance, to minimise the strain on the conductor wire. Eventually a new model, equipped with contractors of greater durability, was perfected, capable of elevation in six seconds and lowering in one.

To mitigate arcing the three-coach test train was wired up so that the return current would be dissipated through the wheels of the train as well as the locomotive. The three coaches, together weighing 100 tonnes, were specially prepared in other ways. Further wind-tunnel research had shown up the extent of drag reduction possible at really high speed if the sides and roofs of the vehicles were effectively air-smoothed. So all protruding fitments like door handles, ventilators and external steps were removed and rubber fairings were stitched between the ends of each vehicle, including those of the locomotive and the leading coach; additionally, a streamlined tail nearly 8ft (2.4m) long was grafted on to the rear of the end coach. Every axle was fitted with roller bearings, a two-shoe braking gear was substituted for the usual single-shoe and the train was equipped throughout the monobloc wheels, to eliminate the risk of a conventionally-assembled wheel disintegrating either at the high rpm in prospect or under brutish braking stress.

Nos BB9004 and CC7107, the two locomotives picked for the ultimate trials, were also given monobloc wheels, as well as acquiring the new design of pantograph and having their

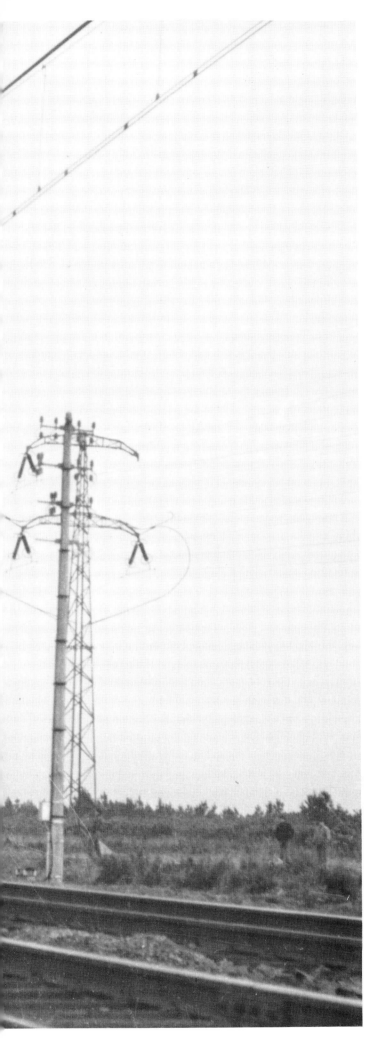

gearing modified; on the four-axle locomotive this last was varied from 2.517 to 0.849 to 1, on the six-axle from 2.606 to 1.145 to 1. As a safety precaution protective resistances were inserted in series ahead of the ventilators and compressors and such inessential apparatus as the lighting and heating circuits were temporarily disconnected. Traction motors and every rotating part of each locomotive were submitted to ruthless workshop bench tests up to an equivalent 280mph (450kmph) before the road trials were started.

Out on the track the solitary bend at Labouheyre, superelevated for a comfortable 75mph (120kmph) in normal service, had its cant increased and its entrance and exit curves realigned to ease the radius to 4,370yds (4,000m), which was deemed fit for 137mph (220kmph). The curve was actually a long way — some 8½ miles (13.7km) — beyond the anticipated peak-speed location at Ychoux, but the engineers were anxious to avoid sharp braking in the top speed range.

Elaborate photographic equipment was set up at the lineside to record speeds meticulously. At each kilometre post of the selected high-speed stretch they laid treadles which, when actuated by the locomotive's leading axle, would electronically fire off a camera and flashlight enclosed in a lightproof lineside box and focused on a brace of chronometers reading down to two-hundredths of a second. Finally, a second mobile power station was drafted to the area and linked to the catenary alongside the existing sub-station at Lamothe, where the train would be making its maximum accelerative effort.

On 17 March every static and mobile item of the equipment was given a field test by a standard locomotive, No CC7113, which glided down the racetrack at 100mph-plus (160kmph) and leaned safely to the Labouheyre curve at 114mph (183kmph). Nevertheless this curtain-raiser showed the engineers they had some touching-up to do: it revealed a few track irregularities that were insignificant at normal pace but potentially troublesome at the highly abnormal speed to be attempted, and a few nagging worries about current collection. Eight days later the specially prepared No CC7107 was let out at a modest 112mph (180kmph), which seemed to satisfy the stewards of the course. The 'big one' was on.

On the morning of 26 March the Bo-Bo was let out of the slips. Minutes later No BB9004 had chalked up a new world rail speed record of 171½mph (276kmph) with so little concern to the engineers that they decided they were ready to go for the 300 — in kmph, that is — which had been their objective from the start.

The morning of 28 March looked good. Forecasters predicted a temperature not exceeding 15deg C (60deg F), which was important because an unseasonably high temperature had frustrated an earlier high-speed test: expanding in the heat, the conductor wire had undesirably lost tension. So, at 13.25 that afternoon, No CC7107 was signalled off the starting line at Facture.

All too soon nerves were jagged. The pantograph changeover was scheduled at the 70mph (112.5kmph) mark, but the test staff had not foreseen that the critical point would be reached near a sectioning point in the conductor wire. At that crucial spot the rising rear pantograph kissed the wire. Immediately there was violent arcing from which the pantograph collector strips emerged decidedly the worse for wear, and that upset the current feed, so that from 100mph (160kmph) onwards the locomotive did not accelerate as smoothly and rapidly as expected.

Left: *A remarkable photograph that caught No BB9004 at its 205.6mph (331kmph) peak on 29 March 1955. The forward pantograph has just been raised and its collector strips are already red-hot from the clearly visible arcing.* / French Railways

Above: *French Railways began to gear their electric locomotives for 100mph (160kmph) maximum with their 5,160hp, 82tonne Class BB9200 B-Bs for the 1.5kV dc system introduced in 1957. One is in charge of the 'Mistral' in this 1969 photo, taken after the train's re-equipment with new air-conditioned stock.* / Y. Broncard

The first coach of the train had been fitted up with periscopes so that the testing staff could keep eyes glued to the all-important behaviour of the pantograph. It was a painful job now: vicious arcing marked the passage of every catenary support and it was almost blinding the periscope watchers. But in the ever briefer interludes between the arcing, as speed surged up to 150mph (240kmph), they could see enough to set them nervously debating whether to call off the attempt. Anxious calls went out over the direct-wire telephone to the locomotive cab and the radio-telephone link with the test directors at the trackside headquarters.

Then suddenly the current flow became less erratic. Gradually, with speed climbing to around 185mph (300kmph), it stabilised. The news was passed excitedly to the command post and back came the order: take the risk — so long as performance remains normal, carry on so long as the pantograph will stand it.

The pantograph stood it — but only by threads of metal. At 190mph (305kmph) or thereabouts the periscope watchers were appalled to see the collector strips burn red hot and then deform so grotesquely that they threatened to foul parts of the catenary. Barely had the locomotive crew been warned to prepare for instant lowering of the pantograph — they were now hurtling at 199mph (320kmph) — than one disintegrating strip did brush a catenary fitting and get partly shorn off. That actually eased the risks momentarily.

But it wasn't long before the remnants of the collector strips began to melt: soon it was the pantograph frame itself that was rubbing the conductor wire.

That was the danger point. The periscope watchers jabbed a button, a red light flared on the locomotive's driving desk and at this prearranged signal the driver instantaneously lowered the wrecked pantograph. At that moment speed was 205.7mph (331kmph). For nearly seven miles (some 11km) the train had been careering at over 185mph (300kmph) and for nearly four miles (all but 6.5km) at over 199mph (320kmph), whipping up ballast to carriage-window height with the force of its slipstream. Despite its realignment, the Labouheyre curve imparted some fairly sick-making lurches to the train during the careful deceleration, but otherwise the riding at least had added nothing to the day's alarms.

The science of safe braking from this unheard-of speed had been studied beforehand just as anxiously as every other facet of the operation. Exhaustive research had probed the levels of braking possible without damage to the brakeshoes, wheels and other components of the running gear, and without risk to the train. One conclusion was that braking of locomotive and coaches should be independently controlled: the locomotive's brakes were the more powerful and at this speed it was vital that the train should hang back on the locomotive, not vice versa, during deceleration.

Two carefully planned braking routines were compiled, normal and emergency (which was not used). The normal programme prescribed that, initially, the brakes be applied only to the coaches over the first eight miles or so (13km) after Ychoux, predicted location of maximum speed, until speed was down to about 120mph (195kmph), which was expected to be the level at the Labouheyre curve. During this initial deceleration the carriage windows would be lowered to increase wind resistance until the locomotive's brakes were brought into play at Labouheyre. This last provision, incidentally, spawned a fiction that the test train had been allowed to coast down from the peak speed, curbed only by the opening of the windows.

Despite its erratic acceleration rate after the pantograph change, No CC7107 attained the top speed some 2½ miles (4km) ahead of the expected location. In the ensuing weeks, after precisely the same speed had been claimed for No BB9004, and some British and American commentators were openly sceptical that two runs at such hurricane pace could have been so nicely judged, one journal alleged a secret confidence from one of the trial's partipants that the six-axle locomotive had been reined in at 197mph (317kmph). French Railways officially rebutted the report. Even if it were true, a discrepancy of 8-9mph in this speed range is no speck, let alone a blot, on a stupendous technical achievement. Anyway, no one has ever contested that on 29 March 1955 No BB9004 certainly achieved 205.6mph (331kmph), this time a whole 4½ miles (7.2km) ahead of the predicted location.

For this second trip new precautions had been taken to ease the strains on the pantograph. Copper collector strips had been replaced by ones of harder-wearing steel and the conductor wire had been thoroughly greased to reduce the friction-generated heat. This time the pantograph exchange was to be deferred until speed was around 110mph (175kmph), to shorten the time during which the rear pantograph would be subjected to the really severe high-speed stresses. That set up a new hazard, of course: at the higher speed the driver would need to deploy still greater dexterity, to make sure both pantographs were not in simultaneous contact with the conductor wire, or conversely that no more than a fraction of a second elapsed with neither pantograph in contact, which would interrupt acceleration. Finally, the second run was timed to start much earlier in the day, at 7.35, to avoid any risk of rising ambient temperatures slackening the catenary's tension.

This time the early stages of the run had no one nailbiting. The change of pantographs was deftly executed at the planned higher speed and at first all that bothered the train party was billowing smoke from burning grease on the conductor wire. But then, steel strips or no, pantograph troubles recurred.

As on the first trip, a deformed and disintegrating strip was partly hacked off when it caught a catenary support. Peering through a periscope increasingly fouled by a spatter of burning grease and liquescent red-hot metal, the train staff's anxiety mounted by the second as they were dazzled by fiercer and fiercer arcing. At around 180mph (290kmph) the driver was warned by telephone to get ready for disengagement of the pantograph — and almost at once the collector strips melted completely away.

But in the cab of No BB9004 they had decided on a desperate gamble. Once more — but this time with speed mounting towards 200mph (320kmph) — they changed pantographs. And once more it was done with supreme dexterity. Despite its earlier stint in maximum acceleration from rest there was enough resilience left in the forward pantograph to withstand the final stages of the climb to 205.7mph (331kmph), but then its collector strips too were glowing red. The peak reached, it was hauled down and the controlled deceleration began.

Those 1955 records have yet to be surpassed and it may be years yet before they go under. At the date they were set, they showed the great scope practically existing for higher speed by conventional steel wheel on steel rail. But I have described the painstaking groundwork and the traumas of the test runs themselves in detail to underline the vast difference between a one-off exploit and everyday operation. Before regular working in a higher speed bracket can be entertained, every last trifle of equipment must be proven immune month in, month out, to all the foreseen risks against which special precautions were taken before those French runs and to those which were not avoided. Track and vehicles must be well-nigh invulnerable to the extreme stresses of daily movement at that speed. Not least, of course, a whole new range of signalling and safety arrangements will probably be essential throughout the route to be accelerated. And, as I have stressed in an earlier chapter, for any substantial acceleration to be economically sensible, the speed range of every train using the route concerned will need to be accelerated in proportion.

For several years after the 1955 record runs French Railways concentrated on acceleration by sustained speed rather than sensational maxima. Not until 1965, in fact, was the ceiling raised from 150kmph (93mph) to 100mph (160kmph) on favourable stretches of the Paris-Lyons main line following the development of new braking systems on rapide stock. Long before then, however, French Railways had in 1957 bestowed on Europe its first regular post-war start-to-stop 80mph (128.7kmph) schedule by running the 'Mistral' from Paris to Dijon, 195.3 miles (314.2km), in 146 minutes; and in 1959 the French had wrested the 'world's fastest' title from the fading American inter-city service by covering the 41.1 miles (66km) between Arras and Longueau in 29 minutes, average 84.9mph (137kmph), with one of the rapides introduced between Paris and Lille following 25kV ac electrification of the former Nord main line. These star performances, though, were merely the frills tipping a fan of inter-city services radiating from Paris to every major French population centre that was unequalled for average speed in Europe.

By the early 1960s French Railways were calculatedly preparing to step up top speeds, and from 1961 to 1964 they conducted several series of lengthy tests to evaluate the costs that would be incurred in such areas as additional signalling and safety devices, tracklaying with heavier rail, easing of curves and strengthening in bridges. The theme of this research programme was consistent high speed with substanital trainloads rather than exceptional maxima.

One notable sequence of tests lasted from December 1963 to June 1964. Again the locale was the Landes, south of Bordeaux, on a 15 mile (24km) stretch of the up line between Solférino and Caudos, straight and level apart from the sweeping curve through Labouheyre. As on previous exercises, the adjoining line was kept clear when the test trains were on the move; the public was cleared from station platforms; at the 31 level crossings circuit-breakers were installed to cut off current in an emergency; and electrified fencing was erected to deter straying cattle. The main protagonist was one of the then latest 1.5kV dc Bo-Bo types, No BB9291, specially modified in such details as gearing (to allow maxima up to 250kmph, or 155mph), insulation to increase the one-hour traction motor rating to 5,940hp, flange lubricators and rheostatic braking. In all No 9291 made 99 high-speed runs with a five-coach train, two-thirds of them at least at 200kmph (125mph) and 11 of them at up to 250kmph (155mph). Riding was reported faultless, even on vehicles that had run as much as 100,000 miles (161,000km) since overhaul.

French Railways began their first 125mph (200kmph) operation in daily service in 1967. The selected stretch of track, the 31.1 miles (50.1km) of the Paris-Limoges-Toulouse main line between Les Aubrais and Vierzon, on the Orleans cut-off, was actually equipped with signalling and safety devices sophisticated enough to permit 250kmph (155mph), and four standard BB9200 class 1.5kV dc electric locomotives were modified to operate at that pace. But although a considerable number of units in the French locomotive fleet now have that capability, they seem unlikely to exercise it publicly in the foreseeable future. Like their colleagues in other major railway managements, the

French have recoiled from the high cost of superimposing special-purpose signalling on the existing system to benefit a comparative handful of trains, and from the economic consequences of trying to operate traffic of very widely contrasted maximum speeds over one route. Instead, as we shall discuss later in the book, French sights are now on the construction of brand-new passenger-only railways where present and prospective traffic flows will justify the investment in a really glittering transformation of end-to-end speeds.

The automatic cab signalling and control apparatus installed between Les Aubrais and Vierzon employs both sleeper-mounted *balises*, or transponders, and coded currents superimposed on the track circuitry of the conventional automatic block signalling system through the running rails (this last method was pioneered in Europe by Netherlands Railways, who applied it to their Amsterdam-Amersfoort line in 1965 and have since spread it throughout a large part of their main-line network). In the French system, the *balises* impart inductively the aspects of signals immediately ahead to a receiver on the underside of the locomotive; the role of the coded track circuits is to cancel the information when a signal's aspect changes. In conjunction, therefore, the two sets of devices feed the locomotive's receiver with continuous advance information on the state of signals to come. Some of the *balises* have a fixed single-frequency circuit, but others are multi-circuit and can be switched in conformity with up to five signal aspects; the simple, single fixed-circuit *balise* is used to transmit invariable data, such as warning of a permanent speed restriction, indication of a change of gradient or the starting-point of safe braking distance to a stop signal ahead.

The high-speed locomotives are fitted with mini-computers that decode the impulses picked up by their receivers and translate them into a continuous signal-aspect display at the driver's control desk. The *balises* are arranged to mark a five-stage deceleration distance to a stop signal, and when a train approaches an adverse aspect the apparatus not only works out instantaneously and displays to the driver an ideal deceleration curve but checks his braking response and adds a touch of pressure if he is not bringing speed down at the correct rate. One should add that control is only taken out of the driver's hands if he exceeds prescribed speed limits. The main point of the special signalling system is to eliminate the engineman's exclusive reliance on sporadic information from lineside signals, give him continuous and much more advanced knowledge of the state of the road ahead, and to aid his judgement.

Over the Les Aubrais-Vierzon stretch the special signalling was arranged to provide for treble-block working of high-speed trains. That meant that a driver got the first warning on his cab signalling display of an adverse stop signal ahead when he was some 4½ miles (7.5km) away from it and had two whole block sections in which to decelerate just to 100mph (160kmph). When 125mph (200kmph) operation was subsequently extended to much of the Paris-Bordeaux main line and the French had concluded this was the likely maximum operational speed for years to come on existing routes, a greatly simplified double-block system was installed on that route. Here the 125mph train gets its special advice of an adverse stop signal ahead from a flashing green aspect — the *préannonce* — at the signals in advance of the normal amber aspect, backed up by impulses from a sleeper-mounted *balise*.

Level crossings are a bigger problem on the European mainland than in Britain. French Railways confronted no fewer than 350 in their planning of 200kmph operation on the Paris-Bordeaux main line, for example. At every one it was impossible to suppress or too costly to replace with a bridge the safety arrangements had to be expensively modified. The

protecting treadles that operated 'train approaching' warnings to road traffic had to be supplemented by a twin-treadle device that measured the speed of an oncoming train and activated the road signals earlier if the pace was above the 140kmph norm. At important crossings the keepers were equipped with emergency controls enabling them not only to throw all adjacent signals to danger but to illuminate a line of brilliant red warning signals specially installed along the track in the immediate vicinity of the crossing.

The first regular 125mph (250kmph) train over the Les Aubrais-Vierzon stretch was the 'Capitôle', introduced at the end of May 1967 on a six-hour evening schedule over the 443 miles (713km) between Paris Austerlitz and Toulouse in each direction. At the start it was worked exclusively by six specially-modified Class BB9200 locomotives and two distinctive air-conditioned train-sets, basically of the then standard UIC (International Union of Railways) pattern but with several refinements, such as electro-magnetic track brakes as well as normal electro-pneumatic braking. Electromagnetic track brakes, incidentally, are spring skids suspended just above the rails from the equalising beams of coach bogies. Their retarding effect is derived not from friction, but from magnetic strength when they are energised by windings connected to the vehicle's electrical system. A braking force of some 30 tonnes can be exerted when all four electro-magnetic brakes on a coach are applied simultaneously; consequently they are cut out to leave control entirely to the vehicle's conventional braking in final deceleration to a stand from about 30mph (50kmph). Both locomotives and train-sets were finished in an individual red livery with a broad gold band at waist level.

With evening working each way, the service initially made decidedly extravagant use of two complete train-sets, each with its own restaurant car crew serving only dinner as a day's work. But from September 1968 the operation was doubled to a 'Capitôle du Matin' and 'Capitôle du Soir' in each direction, giving each train-set a much healthier roster of an 886 mile (1,426km) round trip daily — and, moreover, one at consistent high speed.

But though the 'Capitôles', with the aid of 125mph between Les Aubrais and Vierzon, were timed as tightly as an allowance of 2 hour 54 minutes for the 248.5 miles (400km) from Paris Austerlitz to the first stop at Limoges for an average of 85.7mph (138kmph), the spread of 100mph (160kmph) authorisations to considerable lengths of other French main lines — Paris-Lille, Paris-Aulnoye (on the way to Brussels), Paris-Le Havre and Paris-Bordeaux — was already allowing the power of French electric traction to attain still faster end-to-end speeds elsewhere. By the end of 1967 the record Arras-Longeau time of the Nord Region's Paris-Lille service had been screwed up to a start-to-stop average of 88.1mph (141.8kmph) and two trains were covering the 135.1 miles (217.4km) from Paris to Douai at a booked start-to-stop average of 86.2mph (138.7kmph).

By 1970 French Railways had a dossier of evidence that higher speed pays dividends. The 'Capitôles', despite first-class exclusivity and supplementary fares, had more than doubled peak-hour travel on the Paris-Toulouse route and attracted fresh passenger revenue 70% in excess of the extra direct costs debitable to provision for 125mph (200kmph) operation. Their publicity side-effect was substantial, too. Concurrently passenger carryings as a whole on the route from Paris to the South-West increased nearly 9% and the rate of growth on parallel domestic air routes was trimmed by two-thirds.

Nor had running costs been startlingly inflated. Technological improvements had so mitigated the stresses imposed by the latest traction and coaching stock that the track maintenance standards set for 100mph (160kmph) proved to be stringent enough for the higher speed. True,

Left: *The restaurant car of the 125mph (200kmph) 'Capitôle' was fitted with moving-band wall speedometer, seen at the top right of this picture.* / Cie Int des Wagons-Lits

Below: *Proof that high speed pays off: the four trains on the right of this view of Paris Austerlitz on Friday 28 May 1971 are all labelled 'Capitôle du Soir', for demand required the train to be run in four parts that day, all headed by 8,000hp CC6500s. The three parts in the centre platforms are formed of 'Grand Confort' stock, the one on the extreme right of original 'Capitôle' equipment. Another CC6500 heads the 'Aquitaine' and to the left of that is the overnight train to Madrid, the 'Puerta del Sol'.* / Y. Broncard

coach wheelsets had to be dismantled and checked ultrasonically for flaws three times as frequently as those run no faster than 100mph (160kmph), but even so upkeep costs of the 'Capitôle' locomotives and train-sets were running out only 10-15% higher than the French Railways' inter-city norm; and that extra debit would be almost covered by the revenue from two extra fare-paying passengers attracted to each trip.

So, in the later 1960s, French Railways prepared for 125mph (200kmph) running over a much greater distance than the characteristics of the Paris-Toulouse line allowed. The focus was now on the Paris-Bordeaux line, probably the best aligned in all Western Europe for sustained high speed. Its original builders kept it so free of curvature and junctions that nearly two-thirds of the 359.8 miles (579km) from Paris to Bordeaux in the flat farmlands of Central France were practical 125mph (200kmph) territory, before the route strikes harder going across the foothills and beautifully wooded valleys sweeping westards to the Atlantic from the Massif Central. In May 1971 the French were ready on this line to amaze Europe yet again with the fastest really long-distance train the continent had yet seen, the 'Aquitaine'.

The 'Aquitaine' brought a new look to French high speed. Up front was the latest expression of French high-power traction policy, one of the new range of double-sixwheeled-bogie electric locomotives built to an extraordinarily taxing performance specification. The machines were required to hold 100mph (160kmph) up a 1 in 200 gradient with an 800-850 tonne train, not drop below 93mph (150kmph) with same tonnage in tow on a 1 in 125 slope, and be able to sustain 125mph (200kmph) on the level with 550-600 tonnes. Three versions of these 8,000hp machines now command the cream of France's fastest and heaviest inter-city *rapides*: the 1.5kV dc CC6500 class, the 25kV ac CC8500 class and the dual-voltage ac/dc CC21000 class.

The 'Aquitaine's' coaches had both a new livery — grey contrasted with horizontal bands of red and slender lines of orange — and a new profile. The vehicle bodysides had a marked outward taper from high domed roof to well below the waistline, almost to floor level in fact, and in length the coaches were a foot or two shorter than the French and general European standard in inter-city coach construction by the 1970s. The reason for the change in profile was that the design was drafted for easy adaptability to 'pendular suspension', or automatic body-tilting through curves to permit the negotiation of bends at speeds higher than the latter's superelevation would permit for conventionally suspended coaches without subjecting passengers to unpleasant *g* effects.

Left: *Close-up of a 'Grand Confort' coach.* / French Railways

Centre left: *Interiors of 'Grand Confort' compartment and saloon.* / French Railways

Bottom left: *Compare the 'Grand Confort' saloon interior above with this saloon of 'Mistral' TEE stock and the difference in side-wall taper to allow for body-tilting in the 'Grand Confort' vehicle is noticeable.* / French Railways

Right and below: *These two photographs of Swiss Federal 'Inter-City' trains of the system's recent MkIII stock illustrate more graphically than most the effect of automatic body-tilting on a vehicle's posture as it negotiates a curve. Because of the incessant sharp curvature of most of its key main lines the Swiss Federal is one of the few systems that seems likely to employ the device extensively.* Swiss Federal Railways, Werkaufnahme SIG Neuhausen

At the time several European Railways were busy on automatic body-tilting research, but the French device was the first to reach the practical test stage. In the French version, the automatic action is motivated by variations in oil pressure in a hydraulic circuit linked to rams fixed transversely on each side of the bogie. Its effect is instantaneously to adjust the centre line of a vehicle to its true vertical axis, and to do it with such nicely graded reaction from the instant of entry into a curve that the passenger should comfortably retain upright composure in a coach vestibule even when the train is sweeping at 125mph round a bend that checks orthodox trains at 90mph.

By the end of the 1970s, however, the only European railways still planning to deploy automatic body-tilting as standard equipment in vehicles running over existing railway were the Swiss Federal and British Rail, in its Advanced Passenger Trains.

Every other system toying with the concept, the French included, had recoiled at the expense of the device balanced against its benefits. The French estimated that it added 15% to the capital cost of a new car. It is only over a considerable distance or over routes really beset by speed-inhibiting curvature (a characteristic of scarcely any French inter-city route of commercial stature) that the tilt-body coach's gain of speed achieves a marked improvement in end-to-end journey times, the consideration that counts with the great mass of travellers. Moreover, as has been hinted more than once in this book, railway planners have become more and more conscious of the economic disbenefits of widening the speedband of traffic over a given route. In other words, to equip a few crack trains with stock that gives them a substantial speed advantage of the rest of the line's services and pulls them still further ahead of the general run of freight trains may reduce track capacity; the benefit needs to be applied to at least the great majority of all passenger trains.

There is a final consideration which, all else apart, has dissuaded the French from increasing the daily services at very high speed over the electrified lines cleared for 125mph (200kmph): the existing traction current supply system was not designed to cope with the enormous demands made of it by two 8,000hp CC6500 and CC8500 locomotives pulling out the stops on 600-700 tonne trains in the same feeder section simultaneously. More widespread indulgence in 125mph (200kmph) operation on the existing network will force the French to costly renewal of fixed electricity installations. This, one may add, is a problem that clouds the very high speed future of Britain's Advanced Passenger Train in its electrically-powered form.

To revert from that digression to the premiere of the Paris-Bordeaux 'Aquitaine', its new-look coaches were dubbed 'Grand Confort' partly on account of the ride enhancement promised by their pendular suspension. Even though the body-tilting was not standardised, the serene, blissfully silent ride of the fully air-conditioned cars on orthodox suspension systems, and their relaxing spacious armchair comfort in themselves fully justified the title.

In another of the long French catalogue of sustained speed trials since 1950, the then almost new No CC6509 had set up in March 1970 a target schedule for a new Paris-Bordeaux *rapide* following the line's readiness for 125mph (200kmph) operation. With a 10 coach train grossing some 500 tonnes it had tossed off the 359.8 miles (579km) in 3 hours 33 minutes at a start to stop average of 101.4mph (163kmph) without exceeding 133.6mph (215kmph). The inaugural schedule of the 'Aquitaine' nevertheless was set at a prudent four hours.

Today the 'Aquitaine' has a sister train, the 'Etendard', and the outward-bound 'Aquitaine' and return 'Etendard' have come down to a non-stop timing of 3 hours 50 minutes. Their resultant averages of 93.8mph (151kmph) have no equal by locomotive-hauled train over such a distance anywhere in the world. In the reverse directions each train makes intermediate calls and here the 'Etendard' has one sprint at a start-to-stop average of 101.7mph (163.7kmph), over the 82.8 miles (101km) between St Pierre des Corps and Poitiers.

Apart from the 125mph (200kmph) routes discussed in some detail and some stretches passed for 106mph (170kmph), the ceiling over most of the high-speed sections of French Railways trunk routes stays at 100mph (160kmph). Within that ceiling, however, the standard of express train speed over every trunk route radiating from Paris is impressively high, thanks to the rapid acceleration and power to sustain unvarying speed built into modern electric traction. The heavy 'Mistral' from the Riviera to Paris, for instance, makes nine intermediate stops in its 675 mile (1,086km) haul from Nice to the capital, yet competes the journey in a minute over nine hours for an end-to-end average of 74.8mph (120.4kmph). On the Paris-Strasbourg line, one of the least amenable of France's key routes to high speed because of its topography, comparatively little route mileage is passed even for 100mph (160kmph) and in the final stretch from Reding to Strasbourg the limit hovers between 75 and 87mph (120-140kmph), yet the evening *rapide* from Paris makes Strasbourg, 313.2 miles (504km) distant, in two minutes over four hours, inclusive of two intermediate stops, for an end-to-end average of 77.6mph (124.9kmph). Nor are speed and comfortable new stock any longer the preserve of morning and evening, first class-only, extra-fare businessmen's trains and 'Trans-Europ Express'. In the late 1970s the new air-conditioned, delightfully-styled 'Corail' coaching stock, first and second class, was gradually re-equipping every major inter-city service, TEEs and the 'Grand Confort' stock trains apart. Broadly speaking, every exclusive *rapide* was preceded or followed by a no-supplement express of practically the same speed standard. And bit by bit those long and traditional mid-morning and afternoon gaps in the inter-city timetables were being filled. A particularly interesting development planned for 1979 was the creation of 100mph push-pull train-sets of 'Corail' coaches, with streamlined driving trailers, for operation on the Paris-Rouen-Le Havre and Paris-Tours-Poitiers routes. The BB

locomotives to power these formations (which include the six former 'Capitôle' machines) have been repainted to match in the 'Corail' colour scheme of two-tone grey and orange.

It now seems doubtful that French Railways will greatly expand 125mph (200kmph) running on their existing network. But by the early 1980s they will nevertheless have the fastest railway in the world — a largely new railway to abstract the entire long-distance inter-city passenger traffic of their busiest trunk route, the main line from Paris to Dijon and Lyons. Already there is talk of adding to this a second new high-speed passenger railway from Paris to the Atlantic coast. Perhaps, then, the French are about to pioneer a second post-war high-speed rail era, this time with new lines, just as they did the first post-war European rail speed resurgence on existing infrastructure in the 1950s. The technology which they are applying to the new-generation railway is described in Chapter Ten.

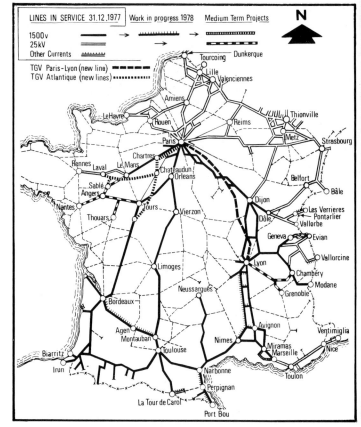

Left: *The Paris-Bordeaux 'Aquitaine' at speed near Ste Genevieve des Bois, between Paris and Orleans, headed by a CC6500.* / Y. Broncard

Above: *The 5,500hp 25kV ac BB16000s built in 1958-63 have 100mph (160kmph) capability. One heads this Strasbourg-Paris* rapide *of 'Corail' stock in the Meuse hills.* / Y. Broncard

Right: *Latest 100mph (160kmph) type is the 1.5kV dc BB7200 (and its related 25kV ac BB15000 and dual-voltage BB22200 designs). This example has charge of a heavy Paris-Ventimiglia* rapide *of largely 'Corail' stock near Villeneuve-sur-Yonne.* / Y. Broncard

5. Japan's Bullet Trains— The Shinkansen

On 1 October 1964, a few days before the Olympic Games opened in Tokyo, Japan ceremonially inaugurated a new vision of inter-city railroading. A brand-new, 320 mile (515km) railway dedicated exclusively to passenger trains, able to move over 6,000 passengers an hour at standard inter-city average speeds of 100mph (160kmph) almost like a long-haul Metro. It was a mass transit development without parallel anywhere in the world.

This, the New Tokaido Line, the first of Japan's Shinkansen, or 'new high-speed railways', was born of Japan's phenomenal economic boom following the Second World War. The country's geophysical character compresses its constantly swelling population into narrow belts, chiefly along the islands' coastlines. Little more than 15% of the country's land surface is flat enough to encourage industrial and population development and as a result 40% of the people are crammed into 1% of Japan's total area. That elongated antheap is the Tokaido belt of Honshu island, from Tokyo to Osaka, where nearly three-quarters of the country's industry is concentrated.

The original Tokaido railway was Japan's first long-distance line, laid to the 3ft 6in (1.067m) gauge that is standard throughout the traditional Japanese National Railway system. The post-war industrial resurgence was soon taxing it to the limit. Though it represented only about 3% of JNR's total route mileage, it was being loaded with nearly a quarter of the system's total passenger and freight volume, which had to be operated over a route of around 100 intermediate stations, no fewer than 1,060 level crossings, by no means easy grades and curvature, and with all the capacity limitations of narrow gauge. With road and motor transport development yet to take wing, and rail fares politically pegged at absurdly uneconomic levels as a social measure, the railway was clearly facing strangulation. Electrification and resignalling, completed in 1956, only deferred the crisis.

Japanese National Railways had sensed possible trends during the latter stages of the war and reconnoitred the outline of a new 3ft 6in railway in the Tokaido belt. The bold Shinkansen concept of an entirely new railway divorced from the existing JNR system, however, stemmed from the report of a study group set up by the Japanese Government in 1957.

Right: *A New Tokaido Line train against the characteristic industrial background of the Tokaido coastal belt. The railway is on the kind of elevated structure to which JNR has increasingly to resort, and to an increasingly massive design compared with that for the New Tokaido Line, to mollify the environmentalists by reducing noise and vibration . For instance, practically all the new Joetsu Shinkansen which is not in tunnel will be elevated 7-10 metres above ground, partly to reduce noise nuisance, partly because of the many roads and waterways that have to be bridged in this densely occupied country. Incidentally, since it has to pierce the spinal Mikumi mountains, the Joetsu line will feature 23 tunnels aggregating 65.9 (106) of its total 171 route miles (275 route-km); among them the Dai-Shimize tunnel alone is 13.8 miles (22.2km) long.* / Japanese Information Centre

It rejected any solution based on expansion of narrow-gauge capacity because of the route's heavy weight of passenger traffic: enlargement of the existing railway's traffic capacity could not eliminate its inherent speed limitations. The recommendation was smartly accepted by the Government and JNR immediately set up a massive research and development apparatus to define and perfect a technology for which it had no prototypes.

Four important principles were established from the start. First, new and old lines should each operate within the narrowest possible speed bands, to maximise use of their respective operating capacities. That predicated concentration on the old line of intermediate passenger business and practically all freight traffic, and dedication of the new railway largely to inter-city passenger traffic between a strictly limited number of conurbation railheads, plus some fast night-time container Freightliners. Soon, however, the Freightliner idea was dropped; halving the 11 hour Tokyo-Osaka transit time that was practicable over the old route would have no commercial advantage to offset the container trains' embarrassment of nocturnal track maintenance on the new railway.

Next, it was agreed the new railway must be of wider gauge than 3ft 6in to allow a substantial lift of the speed ceiling with comfort and safety. Despite the resultant incompatibility with the rest of the system, the standard 4ft 8½in gauge was eventually selected. Third, in the light of French developments in high-voltage electrification at the industrial frequency, it was decided to adopt the 25kV ac system, but at 60Hz, instead of the 1.5kV dc previously standard on the JNR. Finally, a multiple-unit format was adopted both to spread traction gear weight and reduce maximum axle-loadings, thereby allowing economy in civil engineering, and also to quicken terminal turnrounds.

For the next six years nine design teams applied themselves unremittingly to evolving the detail technology of the new railway — its track design, traction, dynamics and braking, overhead current collection system, signalling and traffic control. Not only was JNR's highly-developed Railway Technical Research Institute, with its 36 departments and 900 staff, at full stretch, but also the full research resources of Japan's industry, for in that country an enthusiastic partnership of state and the private sector in any project promising to further national trade and prestige is second nature. Over 170 different research and development exercises were mounted in those formative years. Just how exhaustive they were can be deduced from the fact that, for train braking, such untried exotica as rocket and air drag systems were painstakingly evaluated as well as more orthodox methods.

The first earth was turned to build the New Tokaido Line in April 1959 before the research work was complete. Incredibly, considering the massive civil engineering work involved, the new railway was complete and operational within five years.

Quite apart from the complexities of carving a path into and out of cities for the pre-stressed concrete viaducts that elevate the line out of road level-crossing difficulty, the engineers confronted some formidable tunnelling and bridging in open country. Three tunnels ranging in length from 5,500yds (5,030m) to 8,580yds (7,840m) had to be bored — Otoyahama, Nangoyama and Tanna — and numerous viaducts thrown over streams and rivers coursing down to the sea; longest was the 1,320yds (6,035m) 20-span Fukigawa viaduct near Shizuoka.

Intermediate stations on the new line were restricted to ten, all but three at Yokohama, Hajima and Shin-Osaka ('Shin' simply means 'new') alongside the platforms of the old 3ft 6in-gauge line to facilitate passenger interchange; for the same reason the new tracks' two island platforms at

Tokyo were made an annexe to the existing main station rather than endowed with a new station. This economy in stations reduced the pointwork throughout the line to just 230 turnouts, 80 of them with movable crossing noses to permit passage on the straight track at maximum speed without undue wear and tear of the crossing components. Needless to say, track was welded throughout. Gradients were allowed to run as steep at 1 in 65 in places, given the mighty traction power to be built into the train-sets. Minimum curve radius for the intended maximum speed of 130mph (210kmph) was fixed at 2,735yds (2,500m), a slightly more generous figure than the minimum research had established for passenger comfort and safety.

Among the most advanced and impressive aspects of a railway project that was striking enough as an entity were its signalling and telecommunications. This was the world's first trunk railway to dispense entirely with lineside signals. The intermittent train control of a lineside system and its strain on drivers' senses was totally unacceptable for the high speed and density of train service in mind. Continuous cab signalling was essential; and with that was associated a high degree of automatic control so that the whole line's operation could be commanded from a single nerve centre at Tokyo.

The Tokyo control centre has the whole line, the setting of its pointwork and the position of its trains on continuous view on a huge illuminated panel. Each train is reporting its position by transmitting an electronic code representing its timetable number that is picked up by successive track-mounted induction coils and relayed to the Tokyo panel, along which the train's illuminated number progresses accordingly. In the reverse communications direction, the train's cab signalling display is activated by commands picked up by trainborne induction coils from coded frequencies transmitted through the track-circuiting.

Above left: *New Tokaido Line trains pass at the approach to Tokyo Central station. These are the original design of train-set, designed for the originally envisaged maximum operating speed of 161.5mph (260kmph). Because of the strenuous campaigning against Shinkansen noise it now seems improbable that the present maximum of 130.5mph (210kmph) will ever be lifted; even though the new Shinkansen infrastructures are being designed for the higher limit, the prototype train-sets for the Tohoku and Joetsu lines are being built with less powerful motors than the first series.* / Japanese Information Centre

Above: *Bird's-eye view of Tokyo Central station, terminus of the New Tokaido Line, which because of a political tangle will now be physically segregated from the Tohoku and Joetsu Shinkansen; these will terminate some 2½ miles (4km) away at Omiya. Tokyo Central's four-platform Shinkansen section is now severely overtaxed with a daily traffic of 275 trains.* / Japanese Information Centre

Acceleration of a train is automatically governed. When the driver opens his controller, assuming the road is clear the train will climb at a steady rate of 0.56mph/sec (0.90kmph/sec) to the ceiling of 130mph (210kmph) without any essential action by the driver, though he normally takes personal control. The continuous cab signalling is linked with the traction controls so that braking is automatically controlled too. The second a restrictive signal aspect shows up, in response to a command from the track circuitry an appropriately reduced speed is automatically registered by the train's data-processing apparatus. An axle-driven generator measures the actual train speed and power is cut off and the brakes applied until the rate is down to the right level — or until the coded commands indicate that the obstruction ahead has cleared, whereupon the train will automatically accelerate back to top speed. The signalling

sections and train headways are arranged so that, whether a temporary or permanent speed restraint is the cause, the deceleration process is five-stage from full speed to a dead stand — 100, 68, 44 and 18mph (160, 110, 70 and 30kmph) to stop, the final braking to a stand being under the motorman's control.

At the intermediate stations trains set up their own routes. This was only a matter of fitting up each train to signal to lineside receivers an electronic code that identified it as stopping or non-stopping at a station ahead. None of the stations have idiosyncratic layouts, just the standard loop off each running line, so there was only one possible routing for each type of train to be activated according to which of the two descriptive codes it was beaming. That usefully reduced the routine workload of the Tokyo controllers.

Many other special devices were built into the New Tokaido Line control equipment. For instance, an ultra-high-frequency radio-telephone system embraces track-to-train, train-to-track and train-to-train channels as well as a link with the national telephone system from passenger booths on the trains. And it functions even in the tunnels, thanks to booster plant, tunnel-mounted cables and amplifiers. Regularly spaced lineside switching posts enable track staff to switch off all traction current in an emergency, or to short-circuit the automatic train control in such a way as to reduce the speed of an approaching train immediately to 30mph. And since Japan is earthquake prone, every sub-station is fitted with a seismographic control that automatically cuts off traction current if a shock above a set figure on the Richter scale is registered.

Every axle of a Shinkansen train-set is motored, giving the ultimately standard 16-car formation (initially trains were operated in 12-car format) of the first Shinkansen units a remarkable installed power of 15,875hp for a total train weight of 880 tonnes. Coaches are arranged in pairs to form a complete traction unit, with or without driving cab; all the equipment is mounted underfloor and distributed so as to equalise axle loadings as nearly as possible. The high power/weight ratio was won by maximum tonnage-reducing use of light-weight alloys and plastics within the fully air-conditioned car-bodies, which in the early units were of high-tensile steel, eliminating the conventional heavy underframe by a fabrication method that welded the bodyshell on to ladderlike welded framework of sidebeams and cross-members. Bogies are rubber-cushioned and air-sprung, and braking is dynamic down to 30mph (50kmph), when air-operated disc brakes are brought into play. As for the trains' streamlining, it didn't take long for the projectile styling of the driving cars to inspire the 'Bullet Train' alias by which most of the world now knows them.

Initially the Shinkansen trains were two-class, but in the late 1960s Japan abolished first-class and today the 'Bullet Trains' are not in the seating comfort class of, say, Britain's 'Inter-City 125' HST diesel units, let alone mainland Europe's exclusively first-class TEEs. Three-and-two seating athwart a central aisle packs 110 into each 82ft-long 'Bullet Train' saloon car.

As for catering, each train-set of the first series incorporated two cars that were half-buffet, with the bar in the centre of the floor area, standing room on one side of it and stools for sit-down light meal service at the other counter. If the bar was crowded, then you had the option of trolley service of packed meals and hot or cold drinks at your seat from the train's waitresses. The catering cars, incidentally, sport both a wall-mounted speedometer and a display that indicates, thermometer-like, the train's progress against a strip map of its route.

One more feature of the 'Bullet Trains' demands notice. In its evaluation of six prototype cars delivered before the New Tokaido Line's opening, JNR was worried by the sharp increases of air pressure inside the vehicles that were set up when they passed each other at top speed in tunnel. Sensitive ears found it extremely uncomfortable. The design team came up with the answer: compressed-air devices, automatically activated at the approach to a tunnel, which

force entrance and vestibule doors hard against their frames to seal the train as near hermetically as possible. At the same time the track circuiting automatically closes shutters over the tunnel's ventilating shafts until the train is back in the open.

The New Tokaido Line was the pride of Japan and an instantaneous — in fact, phenomenal — commercial success in its first few years of operation. A year of relaxed schedules was sensibly programmed for the new roadbed to settle and teething troubles to be overcome. But in November 1965 the minimum Tokyo-Osaka time for the limited-stop 'Hikari' trains, calling en route only at Nagoya and Kyoto, was trimmed to 3 hours 10 minutes, representing an end-to-end average of 101.1mph (162.8kmph) for the 320 mile journey.

Within a few years the New Tokaido Line timetable was offering over 80 high-speed trains each way daily. Every hour of the working day (the service was shut down in the small hours for track maintenance) and three times an hour in the morning and evening peaks a two-stop 'Hikari' set out from Tokyo and Osaka. Besides these 30 or so 'Hikaris' in each direction there were the 50-odd 'Kodamas' each way, most travelling the whole route and serving all ten intermediate stations, but some making fewer stops and others adding peak-hour short-haul trips to the service.

The fastest point-to-point bookings demanded a start-to-stop average of 106.5mph (171.5kmph) between Nagoya and Kyoto, 83.4 miles (134.3km), from a number of the 'Hikaris'. Fractionally slower were the 'Hikari' non-stop timings of only 120-123 minutes for the 212.4miles (342km) between Tokyo and Nagoya, the tightest of which represented a start-to-stop average of 106.2mph (171kmph). By the end of the 1960s the New Tokaido Line timetable yielded the staggering total of 444 daily point-to-point runs scheduled at average speeds in excess of 90mph (145kmph). Incidentally, any passenger delayed by more than an hour was guaranteed the refund of the substantial 'Hikari' supplementary fare — it roughly doubled the price of a second-class ticket — charged to ride the 'Bullet Trains'.

Just as electrifying as the trains themselves was the popular response to the new service. From around 60,000 a

day at the start, the New Tokaido Line's carryings surged up through 200,000 in 1967 to an unbelievable record on 5 May 1969, when holiday crowds aggregating a fantastic 520,000 were moved in a single day on this one route. Came the big international 'Expo 70' show at Osaka in 1970 and the New Tokaido Line's passenger count was averaging 254,000 a day for six months as packed 'Hikaris' and 'Kodamas' swarmed out of Tokyo at five- and ten-minute headways in the peak travel hours.

The classic simplicity of the railway operationally and its high quota of automation made it a model of cost-effective investment. By 1969 JNR deduced that their NRL staff were on average four times as productive and were earning per man nine times the revenue of their colleagues on the 3ft 6in-gauge network. Whereas the narrow-gauge system was sliding deeper year by year into a mammoth accumulated deficit, the NTL's consistently high passenger load factors were generating revenue that cleared direct operating costs by over 40%. As a result, in 1970, the new railway in isolation could show a healthy surplus of more than £175 millions even after coverage of depreciation allowances and interest charges on the construction bill.

The moment the New Tokaido Line had shown its mettle JNR planners were at work on its first extension, and the first 103 mile (165km) stretch of the New Sanyo Shinkansen, from Osaka to Okayama, was opened to traffic in March 1972. Here again major civil engineering works were entailed — nearly 60 miles (97km) of bridgework and 35 miles (56km) of tunnel, including the 10.2 mile (16.4km) Rokko Tunnel at Kobe, which took 4½ years to bore through solid granite.

Even before the first 'Bullet Trains' hummed into Okayama, the Japanese Government had proclaimed widespread Shinkansen extension to be an essential ingredient of the country's economic growth and the only way to encourage population dispersal from the teeming industrial complexes of the coastal belts. In May 1970 it promulgated a Law for the Construction of Nationwide High-Speed Railways which ordered further extension of the New Sanyo Line to Hakata, on Honshu island, and three entirely new Shinkansen: the Tohoku from Tokyo

Above: *On the platform at Tokyo Central's Shinkansen station. Although the first series of Shinkansen train-sets were equipped for automatic train operation, in practice driver control has been retained throughout the system. Moreover, the automatic provision is being omitted from the Series 962 prototype train-sets for the new Joetsu and Tohoku Shinkansen.* / Japanese National Tourist Organisation

Left and right: *Second-class saloon and dining car of the first series Shinkansen train-sets. The train-sets built for the New Tokaido Line were considered life-expired by the start of 1978, and all were to be replaced by units of similar design before the end of 1979.* / Japanese National Tourist Organisation

northwards to Morioka; the Joetsu from Tokyo north-westwards to Niigata, on the Sea of Japan coast; and the Narita from Tokyo to its new airport at Narita, then expected to pursue an untroubled course to full commercial operation in 1977. Three years later the prospectus was euphorically lengthened to include projection of the Tohoku line to the northern tip of Honshu island at Aomori and then to Sapporo, in the northernmost of Japan's three main islands, Hokkaido, by a Hokkaido Shinkansen burrowing under the Tsuguru Strait in a new Seikan Tunnel 33.5 miles (53.9km) long, no less; extension of the New Sanyo Line beyond Hakata to Nagasaki and Kagoshima by the Kyushu Shinkansen; and another Tokyo-Osaka Shinkansen, the Hokuriku, advocated partly because traffic strangulation of the original New Tokaido Line was a credible threat, and partly to open up another area of the country economically, as the Hokuriku would trace an inverted-'U'-shape route between Tokyo and Osaka so as to touch the western Sea of Japan coastline at Toyama. That added up to another 1,480 route-miles (2381km) of Shinkansen. But a further 12 Shinkansen routes were also endorsed in principle, so that the ultimate network envisaged would total about 4,350 route-miles (7,000km).

The New Sanyo Line extension to Hakata was opened to throughout service from Tokyo in March 1975. Yet again the engineering task was awesome — more so, probably, than in

Above: This Shinkansen scene vividly emphasises the sharp gradient changes which today's high-powered electric traction can take in its stride. Following a steady increase of rail breakages and wear of the original catenary under the very intensive train service, the whole of the rail of the original system is being replaced and the catenary rebuilt to a heavier pattern. Because of the problems of relaying pointwork and re-wiring junctions within the nightly six-hour shutdown for maintenance, in recent years the train service on the original line has had to be suspended all morning some eight times every twelve months to allow the civil engineers a continuous 12 hour possession.

Centre right: The concrete fencing which JNR have had to erect alongside Shinkansen in populated areas as a sound baffle is clearly visible here. The train is the comprehensively equipped inspection unit which JNR uses on the Shinkansen. Fitted out to detect and measure imperfections of both track and current supply, it is run weekly over a route at the same speed as passenger-carrying services to produce data for computerised compilation of maintenance work schedules.

Bottom right: A New Tokaido Line train against a backcloth of Mount Fujiyama. Snow at ground level has been a problem on the New Tokaido and New Sanyo lines and will be a much more serious concern over parts of the new Shinkansen now under construction. In the mountainous central area of the Joetsu line, for instance, winter falls to a depth of over 8ft are common. Here the short sections of line between tunnels will be protected by snowsheds and elsewhere the new line will have to be lavishly provided with snow-melting water-sprinklers.
/ Japanese Information Centre

any previous Shinkansen project. Not only was there the 11.6 mile (18.6km) tunnel, second longest in the world after Switzerland's Simplon, to be sunk under the Kammon Strait between Honshu and Kyushu islands, but on land the railway was cutting through mountainous regions of very different character from the heavily-populated Tokaido coastal belt. In the 247 miles (398km) from Okayama to Hakata 111 tunnels aggregating 138 miles (222km) had to be bored.

New Tokaido Line experience dictated a number of changes in design parameters for the New Sanyo Line. Above all they concerned the track. Despite the care lavished on weight economy and load distribution in the train-sets, track wear had become a mounting worry on the New Tokaido Line, becoming more expensive in cash and in time than JNR had estimated; the track engineers were all too often stretched to cram their work into the night-time lull in service. For the New Sanyo Line, therefore, a more solid track foundation was ordered with heavier rail (which was also applied to the New Tokaido Line whenever and wherever relaying was due).

Over two-thirds of the New Sanyo Line were laid with concrete slab track; it would have been adopted throughout but for susceptibilities to subsidence, which might have fractured the formation. In the JNR version the rails are attached directly to fastenings cast into 5m-long concrete slabs, which are then fixed by a mix of cement and bitumen into a cast-*in-situ* concrete roadbed. Several major railways have made scattered, short-stretch installations of concrete slab track, but most are still evaluating its economics; none as yet has laid it so extensively as the Japanese on their Shinkansen. There is no doubt that its semi-permanent solidity cuts maintenance under intensive traffic to an extent that should offset its high initial cost within a year or two. But not only does it cost at least twice as much to make and instal as orthodox sleeper-and-ballast track: the laying operation shuts the track under renewal for much longer and as yet the specialised laying machines are scarce.

The original maximum speed target for the New Tokaido Line was 162mph (260kmph), but in the event the operational ceiling was lowered to 130mph (210kmph). That is still the limit through the Shinkansen so far completed, though the New Sanyo Line and its train-sets were specifically designed for regular operation at the higher speeds. Amongst other things, this predicated an easing out of the minimum curve radius from the New Tokaido Line's 2,500m to the New Sanyo's 4,000m (4,280yds).

A new and still more powerful multiple-unit, the Series 961, was created to expand the coach fleet to over a thousand twin-sets for the full Tokyo-Osaka-Hakata service. Main change internally was that, with 6-7 hour journeys now involved in end-to-end travel of the line, the two separate buffets of the earlier 16 car formations were replaced by adjoining dining and buffet cars. Externally the new sets were distinguishable by a more bulbous fairing of the nose round to its translucent snout camouflaging the emergency drawgear. The 961's greater power punch was startling. A constructional switch to light alloys combined with more mettlesome traction gear endowed the 961s with a stupendous continuous output rating of 23,600hp for a tare 16 car weight of 930 tonnes. One of these units was tested up to 178mph (286kmph) in February 1972.

The first series of train-sets had often been in trouble from snow penetrating and damaging their underfloor equipment; harm could be particularly severe when lying snow whipped up by a top-speeding train took ballast fragments with it. JNR at first tried to combat this by installing lineside water sprinklers to encourage hard-freezing of fallen snow, but in the 961 train-sets the engineers took preventive action by thoroughly enclosing the vulnerable equipment and arranging its essential cooling through high-level intakes fitted with snow-melting devices.

Apart from building enough Series 961 units to cover the extended service to Hakata, JNR had to continue production to renew the entire Shinkansen fleet during the 1970s, for another mark of the intensive train service was that after only a decade of sustained high-speed pounding the original units were exhausted. During the 1974 summer, in fact, the New Tokaido Line suffered a traumatic four months' concatenation of track, rolling stock and signalling failures that made a fiction of its timetable for over six weeks. Thoroughly alarmed, JNR quickly decided to relay the whole route throughout with heavier rail at a cost of nearly £300 millions and to plan renewal of the entire catenary by 1984.

With the New Sanyo Line fully open, passenger business soared again and within two months, on 5 May 1975, the Shinkansen lines topped the million-passengers-in-a-day mark for the first time. Today, from the start of the Shinkansen's public service day at 06.00 to its shutdown for nocturnal maintenance as midnight approaches, over 100 trains each way are scheduled over all or part of the combined New Tokaido and New Sanyo Lines — on public holidays significantly more. In most hours of the regularly-patterned service there are six trains over the busiest Tokyo-Osaka stretch, but in the peak hours this is augmented to four 'Hikari' and four 'Kodama'. From dawn to early evening two trains in every hour speed the whole 664 miles (1069km) from Tokyo to Hakata, the faster of the pair calling at six of the 11 intermediate stations and on the best timings of the day completing the whole run in 6 hours 56 minutes for an end-to-end average of 95.8mph (154kmph) — a remarkable achievement given extensive limitation to 100mph (160kmph) in mining areas of the New Sanyo line where subsidence is a risk; this preoccupation has so far frustrated the aim of running the line's entire length at an average of just over 100mph on a 6 hours 40 minutes timing inclusive of stops. The fastest start-to-stop timing anywhere on the route now is the 59 minutes allowed one 'Hikari' to cover the 108.5 miles from Nagoya to Shizuoka, which exacts an average speed of 110.3mph (177.5kmph) that has no world equal at the time of writing. (Surprisingly, as recounted in Chapter Six, it is not electrics but the diesel traction of Britain's High Speed Train multiple-units which has been running the 'Bullet Trains' closest in the speed tables of the later 1970s.)

Despite the triumphs of Shinkansen technology, which has set other countries from South Korea to Iran counting the cost of having the Japanese build Shinkansens in their own backyards (besides generally strengthening the Japanese railway industry's already powerful grip on world markets), and despite the new railways' enviable profitability and productivity, the Shinkansen network builders were not working overtime in the late 1970s. One contretemps after another had cooled Japanese ardour for the concept.

First there was the energy crisis set off by the Arab-Israeli war of 1973, which had no severer impact than on Japan, a country dependent on imported fuel to generate 86% of its energy and drawing as much as 99.7% of its oil from overseas. The outcome was raging inflation and a sharp setback in Japan's economic growth. Even before the oil price explosion JNR had been facing serious cost escalation in Shinkansen construction. Back in the 1960s it had built the New Tokaido Line at an average of just over £1¾ millions a mile, but as early as 1972 that figure had doubled for the initial stage of the New Sanyo Line. By 1977 the average was reckoned to be over £5½ million a mile. But overriding national economic considerations apart, the 3ft 6in-gauge bulk of JNR was sliding helplessly into the financial mire, downtrodden by a combination of overmanning, a market share of both passengers and freight that was being sharply eroded by competition, maintenance of totally uneconomic rural services at political insistence and absurdly uneconomic fare scales, again the result of political fiat. Was this the time to throw a mint of good money after a heap of bad?

Nor was the case for Shinkansen as a means to encourage population and industrial mobility quite so strong as in the early 1960s. Road transport was much more highly developed, as JNR's balance sheet testified all too starkly. And wide-bodied jets, with the benefit of considerably improved city centre-to-airport access, had greatly strengthened air travel's competitiveness in time, convenience and cost. That was put to unhappy practical proof early in 1977, after the Government had at last grasped the uneconomic rail fare nettle and ordered a 50% price rise at a stroke, whereupon Shinkansen carryings slumped by a drastic 15% almost overnight and the airlines took most of the pickings.

Least expected, perhaps, was the disenchantment with Shinkansen that soured public opinion. It was sparked off by growing complaints of noise from people living near the new railways. In designing the New Tokaido Line JNR engineers had taken some care to limit noise and vibration to levels no worse than those experienced in the proximity of the 3ft 6in-gauge system, but they had not foreseen the effects of the intensive service which rising traffic demands quickly generated. By now Japan, which had previously tolerated the foulest industrial pollution, probably, of any industrial country, was on a highly emotive ecological kick. Self-seeking politicos pounced on the alleged environmental disturbance of the Shinkansen as a symbolic issue, public opinion was roused and controversy erupted over much of the projected new Shinkansen routes. Late in 1972 the Government's Environment Agency stepped in with a diktat on maximum permissible decibel level in the vicinity of Shinkansen routes, which forced JNR to spend nearly £200 million on noise-abatement measures throughout the original New Tokaido Line alone.

Worst sources of noise and vibration on the New Tokaido line were its countless bridges and viaducts. Specially difficult to treat were the steel truss bridges, where the track was not ballasted but laid on steel beams encased in concrete; to all these the JNR had to apply a combination of underside baffle plates and side barriers lined with absorbent material. On the concrete viaducts rubber matting had to be inserted between the track ballast and the floor. Wherever the route ran close enough to dwellings to threaten a noise problem, it had to be enclosed by sound barrier walls of concrete about 2m high; if the dwellings were so close to the railway that this protection did not meet the mandatory noise levels, then there was sound-insulation work to be done on the dwellings as well. One other noise problem, incidentally, had shown its head by now; that was the very palpable 'sonic boom' heard at a tunnel mouth when a train plunging underground at the opposite end at top speed pressurised the air to an extent that generated low-frequency vibration. JNR at least mitigated the nuisance by erecting steel hoods at tunnel mouths to contain the noise.

In the cold light of the inflationary and recessionary late 1970s expert Japanese opinion became more and more convinced that the outlandish routes projected in the vast Shinkansen network outline of 1973 would never cover even

their direct operating costs. Some JNR executives had bluntly said as much at the time. In fact, they had urged compression of the draft to a more economically realistic scale, worried that such wildly grandiose dreaming would have public opinions questioning the validity of the plan's more sensible components.

By the spring of 1978 the full 1973 plan had almost certainly become a dead letter, though the Ministry of Transport and elements of the political majority were still fighting for it. The Government department responsible for regional development was strongly recommending that the 1990 network objective should be trimmed to around 1,300 route-miles and that the ultimate target be set no higher than about 2,800 route-miles.

In that first quarter of 1978, the time of writing, the only extensions certain of fulfilment were two of the three on which construction had begun, the Tohoku and Joetsu. The short Narita line to Tokyo's new, second airport got little further than the empty shell of an airport station. One reason for lack of progress was that the airport itself became one of the most battle-scarred victims of Japan's eco-fanatics. But more critically, in the contemporary climate of environmental anxiety JNR ran up against almost intractable problems in trying to carve another Shinkansen route through metropolitan Tokyo. Residents of the Chiba suburb mounted a particularly virulent campaign against Shinkansen noise. The new airport struggled through to its completion in 1978, by which time it was crystal clear that the Narita Shinkansen project was at best shelved, and that the Government intended to serve the airport by a projection of the 3ft 6in (1.067m)-gauge Teito Rapid Transit system.

The Tohoku and Joestu Shinkansen schemes, meanwhile, had laboriously hacked through the undergrowth of economic stringency and local environmental protest. Once forecast to open its metals to traffic by 1977, the Tohoku line did not greet its first tracklayers until early that year. And not until mid-1977 were years of niggling argument over the

Right: *The New Tokaido Line, seen here, was laid with concrete-sleeper track. Much of the Sanyo line, however, was constructed of solid-slab concrete trackbed, and this will be the practice in most future construction.* / Japanese Information Centre

line's course into Tokyo resolved. Ever since 1971 the people of Omiya, a satellite town about 20 miles from Tokyo's centre, had striven to drive the Tohoku beneath ground in their neighbourhood. It took five years to win their grudging consent to elevated tracks, but that cost the Shinkansen operators the inconvenience of yielding Omiya its own Shinkansen station and agreement to stop all trains there. In Tokyo itself the JNR was pig-in-the-middle of local trench warfare. The old 3ft 6in-gauge main line from northern Japan has its separate Tokyo terminal at Ueno and when JNR promulgated a logical plan to concentrate all Shinkansen routes converging on the capital in one station elsewhere, shopkeepers in the vicinity of Ueno terminus raised Cain at their threatened loss of casual trade. But just as strident were Ueno's ordinary residents, who refused to be disturbed by an above-ground Shinkansen. The outcome? As you might expect, face-saving but costly Oriental compromise: JNR reluctantly mollified both factions by undertaking to run the Tohoku Shinkansen into an underground terminal at Ueno.

With the Joetsu line's construction making steady progress, JNR moved in late 1977 to order a new six-car prototype train-set as a Tohoku and Joetsu line model; this was to be delivered in the spring of 1979. A vital feature of this prototype would be reinforced protection against wintry conditions, which will be more severe in the northern areas traversed by the Tohoku and Joetsu lines than on the routes south of Tokyo — and on the latter they can be pretty troublesome.

Until mid-1977 there was little optimism of any early start on further Shinkansen projects. True, the extraordinary 33.7 mile Seikan Tunnel under the Tsuguru Strait was half-finished, but there was widespread scepticism that it would ever house a Shinkansen rather than just a link between the 3ft 6in-gauge systems of Honshu and Hokkaido islands. Pessimism had been fuelled by the swingeing 50% fare increase of late 1976, which had savaged New Sanyo line carryings, dropping this route's revenue well below budget, and trimmed Shinkansen traffic as a whole by 3.25 million passenger-miles, or nearly 10%, for the financial year from spring to spring, 1976-7. But in mid-1977 the Government unexpectedly revived the corpses of the Hokkaido, Kyushu and Hokuriku Shinkansen and authorised the start of route surveys.

Sad that a concept which so invincibly demonstrated the viability of a dedicated high-speed passenger railway custom-built to commercial and social demand of the late 20th Century should latterly have been humbled by parish-pump politicking. Sad, too, that its development should to some extent be at risk from the appalling financial situation of JNR overall, which is so largely attributable to the physical constraints from which the Shinkansen concept breaks loose: the narrow gauge that sorely handicaps passenger speed progress and cripples the freight service by its severe limitation of axle loadings and hence of freight vehicle capacity. Freight operations were responsible for nearly 60% of the gargantuan JNR deficit of £2¼ billions in 1976-7.

So far as the narrow-gauge passenger services are concerned, it is worth noting that JNR are, at the time of writing, the most energetic developers of tilt-body apparatus in the world. Following lengthy evaluation of a prototype fleet between Nagoya and Nakano from 1973 onwards, a second squadron was ordered to take up service on the Kisei line from Osaka to the tourist resorts of the Kii peninsula from the autumn of 1978. Completion of the second order would raise the total of these Type 381 tilt-body multiple-units to 167 cars.

One final tribute to the Shinkansen deserves payment. Many of the latter-day high-speed inter-city rail developments in Western Europe and North America might never have been born — certainly would not have been so confidently conceived — had it not been for the gleaming model of the New Tokaido Line.

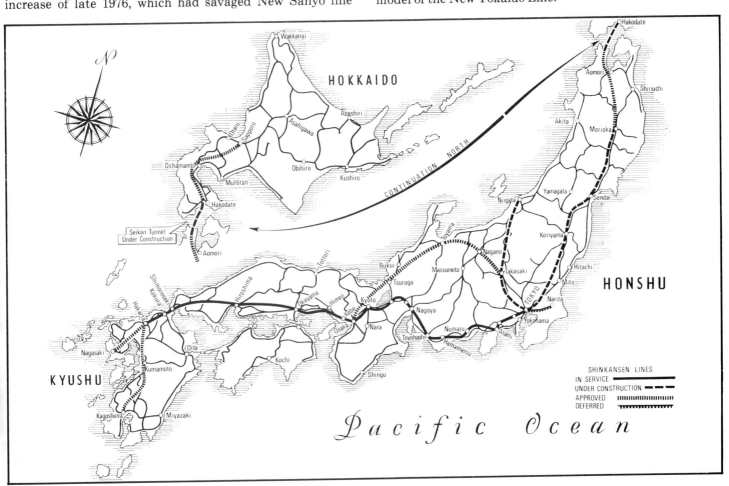

6. Britain's Inter-City Spurts Ahead

In the 1930s Britain's railways had been among the world pace-setters. By the outbreak of the Second World War, however, it was only in maximum speeds, in both daily service and overt record-breaking attempts, that they were holding their own. As for end-to-end speeds, which is what counts commercially, Britain had slumped well down the table. In that department steam could not compete with the new diesel trains of Germany and North America.

For many weary years after the Second World War comparisons grew steadily more damaging. In the first place, the war left Britain's railways in a deplorably run-down condition. Fixed structures had had no more than the minimum maintenance essential to keep them usable. Replacements were limited to renewal of equipment crucial to the war effort. After it was all over one company alone, the London Midland & Scottish, calculated it would have to spend £14 millions (at 1945 money values, mark you) merely to overtake arrears of maintenance on track and signalling, and another £26 millions to return its permanent way to proper peacetime standards. Financially three of the 'Big Four' railways — the exception was the Great Western — had been at a low enough ebb before the war; since the scale of Government payments for wartime traffic handled was grossly inequitable they were still more strapped for cash when peace returned.

If Britain's railways had been as badly savaged by enemy action as those on the European mainland, their post-war recovery might have been quicker. If bombs have made much of your line barely usable, comprehensive rebuilding is inescapable; and if you have to rebuild, it's logical to modernise, not replace like for outdated like — particularly when dollar aid is there to help finance the reconstruction. It is no depreciation of railwaymen's enterprise and knowhow on the other side of the English Channel to observe that that is largely how and why mainland European railways jumped ahead of Britain's in post-war redevelopment.

In Britain the railways had suffered incidental damage, but nowhere so seriously that it could not be patched up. From end to end they were still workable. Successive Governments, Conservative as well as Labour, decided that the railways had very low priority in the industrial queue for scarce raw materials and capital investment. Only a handful of sizeable improvement schemes were conceded and for the most part the railways had either to renovate on the cheap or else make do and mend for the first ten years after the war.

So, by 1951 only two of the 50 most important inter-city rail routes in Britain had had their services restored even to 1939 speed levels, let alone improved. Worse still, only seven major towns and cities — Bradford, York, Newcastle, Edinburgh, Glasgow (by the East Coast Route from London

Right: English Electric's 3,500hp 'Deltic' diesel-electric Co-Co prototype, vividly liveried in light blue with yellow patterning, pulls into Preston during its early trials on British Rail's Euston-Carlisle main line in the late 1950s.

Kings Cross, not the primary West Coast Route from London Euston), Portsmouth and Cardiff — had faster trains from London than before the First World War. Two of the country's most important cities, Birmingham and Sheffield, had not merely no faster trains from the capital than in 1939, but a markedly slower service overall than just before the First World War. Early in 1952 French Railways' timetables were already showing over 30 daily mile-a-minute timings, up to a maximum of 77.1mph (124kmph), on their newly electrified Paris-Dijon main line alone. German Railways were already operating 15 mile-a-minute end-to-end schedules. The by now nationalised British Railways, with just six mile-a-minute timings, all over the favourable Darlington-York stretch of the East Coast main line, were lagging behind even Sweden and Denmark, who could boast twelve and ten respectively. As for the USA, where the inter-city passenger train was still near the apogee of its glory, timetables there were sprinkled with 2,764 daily runs totalling over 150,000 miles (240,000km) scheduled at a mile-a-minute or better; of this massive figure 16,665 miles (26,815km) were being covered daily at over 70mph (112.6kmph) and 3,597 (5,788km) at over 75mph (120kmph), up to a maximum of 86.2mph (138.7kmph).

Mind you, one must not overestimate the difference an earlier opportunity for British Railways to modernise might have made to this stark picture. Two of the major improvements effected on British Railways before, in 1955, they were at last allowed to invest heavily in modernisation were electrifications, certainly. But these were only the delayed fulfilment of pre-war projects. Up to 1955 such money and resources as the railways had been permitted to spend on replacing their most antiquated steam engines had gone on yet more steam power, what time the pilot main-line dieselisation schemes drafted by at least two of the pre-nationalisation 'Big Four' were discarded by the new management of the nationalised British Railways. Sir Nigel Gresley's triumph over the German diesel competition before the war was not all gain. Without it, British Railways might have built up a methodical step-by-step experience of diesel traction which would have greatly accelerated their post-war recovery. Instead they had belatedly to throw themselves into a pell-mell dieselisation, more precipitate than on any other railway of such size, which inevitably and repeatedly fell on its face and wasted literally millions of pounds until designers, builders and operators had sorted the good from the unreliable and were talking a common language.

Hope of an ultimate speed revival in Britain was fortified by the 1955 Modernisation Plan's espousal of electrification for both East and West Coast main lines out of London, the former as far as the West Riding of Yorkshire and York itself, the latter as far as Birmingham, Liverpool and Manchester. It was soon obvious, though, that industrial resources would only run to one scheme at a time. Choice fell on the Euston-Birmingham/Liverpool and Manchester — and also on the 25kV 50Hz ac method, in a reversal of previous British policy motivated by the now patent success of French pioneering in high-voltage ac traction. But the costs of the electrification were soon vastly outrunning estimates. The then Minister of Transport, no champion of railways at any time, halted the scheme after its first provincial stages had been completed and the future of inter-city rail services in Britain looked bleak. On other trunk routes British Railways' first main-line diesels, lumbering machines with a very unimpressive power/weight ratio, were incapable of much improvement on steam's end-to-end schedules. Consequently the railways were steadily losing traffic to the roads. There were those in British Railways who counselled that this be accepted gracefully as the inevitable beginning of the end for the inter-city passenger train. In the late 1950s the rot had set in

across the Atlantic; by 1970, it was confidently predicted, the North American passenger train would be a dodo — and nothing, some said, would stop the British inter-city train going the same way within a decade.

Not so, insisted the management of one sector of British Railways in particular. Even with steam, the Eastern Region had proved the commercial potential of a daylong regular-interval service of comparatively lightweight trains, timed as nearly as possible to a standard schedule and accelerated to the limit of the locomotives' endurance and economy. Now the Eastern Region was determined to lay its hands on power that would make this sort of inter-city service practicable at the 75mph (120kmph) end-to-end averages research showed would keep it fully competitive with road travel over the country's new motorways. If the Eastern couldn't have electrification, then British industry had just unveiled a diesel prototype which looked the next best thing.

That was the English Electric 3,300hp 'Deltic' diesel-electric, so called because it was built around two of the opposed-piston engines of triangular cross-section, resembling an inverted Greek letter *delta*, which English Electric's subsidiary Napier had developed to meet a British Admiralty specification for a high-powered diesel engine to drive fast naval patrol boats. A prototype locomotive, the most powerful single-unit diesel in the world's railways at the time, had demonstrated some phenomenal tractive powers on test with British Railways in the summer of 1956; and it could be happily geared for a maximum speed of 105mph (169kmph). The Eastern pressed for and in 1958 won a production series of 22 to take over the principal inter-city services between London Kings Cross and the West Riding, the North-East and Edinburgh.

The inauguration of the first fully 'Deltic'-powered East Coast Route timetable in the summer of 1962 was the post-war turning point in British Railways' inter-city passenger services. It wasn't just the startling acceleration, with the 'Flying Scotsman's' London-Edinburgh journey time slashed overnight by an hour, to come down to six hours for the 392.7 miles (631.9km), and the opening up of stretches of the route to regular 100mph (160kmph) maximum speeds. Equally significant was the dexterous timetabling and rostering of both 'Deltic' locomotives and train-sets, to extract the maximum possible daily mileage from the equipment and offer an intensive and fast regular-interval service from London to all the major industrial centres on the East Coast Route with strictly limited resources.

Even so, the 'Deltics'' potential was but partially realised. In tightly-knit Britain sizeable towns and cities almost jostle each other by comparison with the distances that separate them in, say, central France. Many of them in Britain are the site of railway junctions, for again Britain has more cross-country routes carrying substantial traffic than France. Many of those junctions were not laid out with a long-term eye to the speed of through traffic. And apart from their curbs on sustained high speed, no British main line was built free of speed-restraining curvature in its open stretches to anything like the extent, for example, of France's main line from Paris to the south-west. Consequently the 'Deltics' were wasting far too much of their considerable energy

Top right: 'Deltic' in a hurry: one of the production series of 22 3,300hp units for BR's East Coast Main Line, No 55.009 Alycidon, speeds from Edinburgh to London Kings Cross. / Peter J. Robinson

Right: Another East Coast route 'Deltic', No 55.021 Argyll & Sutherland Highlander, hums through the rolling Scottish countryside between Grantshouse and Reston with an Edinburgh-London Kings Cross express in November 1977. / Peter J. Robinson

working up to top speed for short spells, then having to slow to 20mph (32kmph) to negotiate the serpentine layout at Peterborough or to 30mph (48kmph) for the sharp bend at Durham (to quote two notorious examples), after which they would be expensively opened up to regain 100mph (160kmph) as quickly as possible, only to be slowed yet again perhaps 20 miles further on: and so on.

Again the Eastern Region went to bat. At comparatively modest cost compared with electrification, they argued, not far short of electric traction performance could be obtained from the 'Deltics' by giving them better ground to work on. They won their case. At the start of the 1970s an extensive programme of track and signalling improvements costing over £60millions was put in hand on the East Coast Route. Tracks were relaid, junction layouts simplified, two-track bottlenecks widened, some of the worst curves ironed out (two of the most awkward, at Peterborough, were treated by rebuilding the whole station), level crossings eliminated and multiple-aspect colour-light signalling controlled from a few strategic centres installed in place of outdated, manually-operated semaphores, to establish much better traffic control and extend braking distances. At the end of the day the route had been made fit for 100mph (160kmph) the whole way from London Kings Cross to Doncaster, 156 miles (251km) and for 85 (136.8) of the 112 miles (180km) on to Newcastle; a good deal of the trackage was in fact fettled up for 125mph (200kmph), with an eye to that coming High Speed Train era to be described later in this chapter. Between Kings Cross and Newcastle the only troublesome speed restrictions which remain are those over the swing bridge at Selby, under the great curving arch roof at York station and over the curved viaduct at Durham, all of them formidably costly to eliminate.

So by 1976 the East Coast Route timetable could show a fastest London-Edinburgh time of 5 hours 27 minutes by the 'Flying Scotsman', representing an end-to-end average speed of 72.1mph (116kmph) for the 392.7 miles (631.9km)

inclusive of an intermediate stop at Newcastle. Over shorter distances there were many timings at 75mph (120kmph) or better from start to stop, up to a best of 80.8mph (130kmph) for the 204.7 miles (329.4km) between Darlington and the outer London railhead at Stevenage.

The travails of the West Coast Main Line electrification ended eventually. Full electric service was opened from Liverpool and Manchester to Euston in the spring of 1966, and Birmingham and the West Midlands were brought into the network a year later. The timetables, needless to say, were transformed, and again in regular-interval frequency at uniformly high speed, maximising the utilisation of locomotives and coaches, as well as in reduced transit times and raised maximum speeds. Electric traction's superior accelerative power, of course, allowed considerably more of the mileage to be run at the permitted maximum of 100mph (160kmph) than on the East Coast Route, so that the newly electrified railway became immediately the fastest in the country.

One should here interpolate that though 100mph (160kmph) has been the official limit with West Coast Main Line electric locomotives, the machines are not in any way governed to that speed; nor are they fitted with self-recording speedometers, as are French locomotives, so that a driver in France is wary of being confronted with evidence of any rush of blood to the head. Consequently it is no extreme rarity to touch at least 110mph (177kmph) behind a British electric locomotive — or, for that matter, behind a 'Deltic' diesel. When that happens one may well cover 75 miles (120km) or more of the West Coast Main Line at a consistent average of 100mph (160kmph).

Below: *British Rail's latest breed of ac electric Bo-Bo, 5,000hp Class 87 No 87.004, takes the Euston-Inverness 'Clansman' through Rugby.* / Philip D. Hawkins

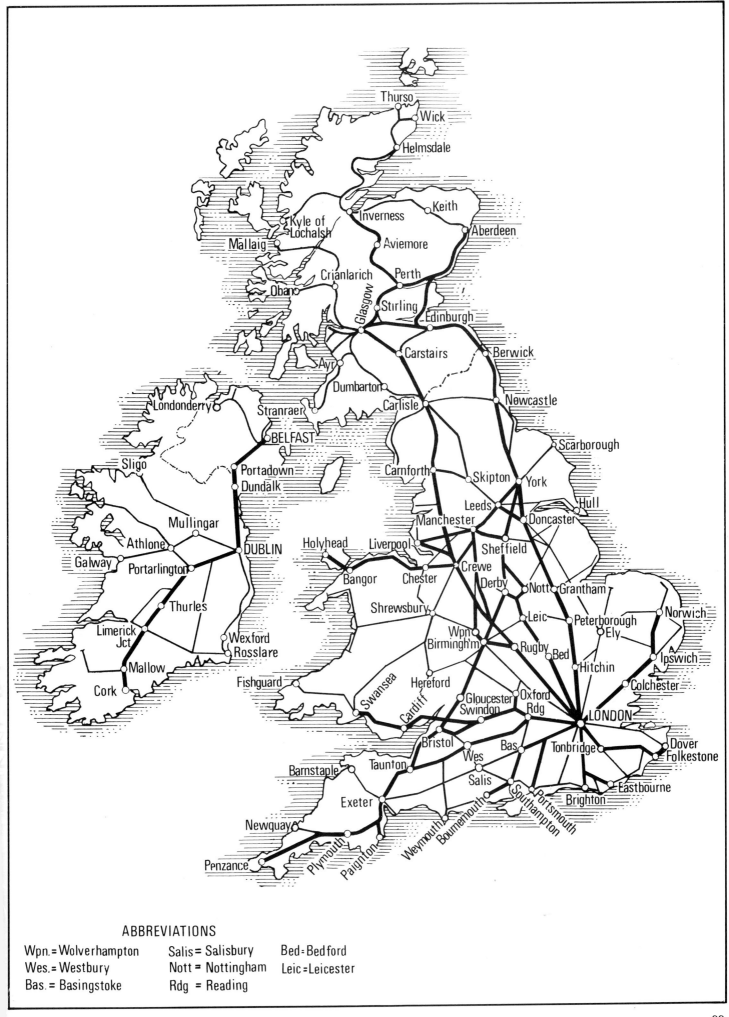

ABBREVIATIONS

Wpn. = Wolverhampton   Salis = Salisbury   Bed = Bedford

Wes. = Westbury   Nott = Nottingham   Leic = Leicester

Bas. = Basingstoke   Rdg = Reading

The commercial impact of that mid-1960s inauguration of revolutionised East Coast and West Coast Main Line timetables, the one with 'Deltic' diesels and the other with electric traction, confounded the sceptics in the corridors of British power as well as within British Railways management. In 1965 British Railways, then under its Beeching regime, had issued a policy document which accepted the eventual eclipse of the inter-city passenger train. The only uncertain factor was how long it could drag out a rearguard action against air and road competition. Given that prognosis, 70mph (112.6kmph) was held to be a reasonable end-to-end average speed for which to budget as far ahead as 1984; in which case, the British Railways Board submitted, several alternative trunk routes could be ripped up or reduced to single track and a mix of up to 200 passenger and freight trains each way daily crowded on to the remainder.

But the cherished freight tonnage drained steadily away, whereas passengers flocked on to the speeded-up and intensified inter-city services. By the end of the 1960s the West Coast electric services had doubled passenger carryings between London and the North-West, cornered three-quarters of the total travel market on the route and driven the domestic airline to a defensive trimming of its flights between London and both Liverpool and Manchester. Between London and Birmingham public response was such that service frequency was soon stepped up to half-hourly each way throughout the day.

The Government as well as British Railways chiefs turned about, the latter smartly, the former with rather less alacrity. First fruit of the changed attitudes was authorisation to extend the electrification beyond Weaver Junction (diverging point of the Liverpool route north of Crewe) to Glasgow, a project over which the Government had dismally dragged its feet for years (some of them, ironically, under a Minister of Transport who was later to become Chairman of the British Railways Board and as such to berate his Ministerial successors for blocking his own electrification programme — Sir Richard Marsh).

Today no electrified railway apart from Japan's Shinkansen operates an inter-city service of such speed and frequency combined as British Rail from London's Euston. Even in the off-peak hours this main line is running six 100mph (160kmph) trains each way every sixty minutes over the first 82.6 miles (133km) between London and Rugby, where the Birmingham trains diverge. With the completion of the catenary into Scotland, Glasgow was brought within five hours of London inclusive of a Preston stop, representing an end-to-end average for the 401.5 miles (646km) of 80.3mph. That schedule could only be achieved with electric traction's ability to romp unconcerned up the famous climbs over England's northern fells and the Scottish lowland hills; to Shap summit with its final four miles (6.4km) of 1 in 75 and to Beattock, where the southern ramp is a near-10 miles (16km) grind at 1 in 74-88. At the time of writing the timetables for the whole 25kV ac inter-city network radiating from London's Euston show 165 daily start-to-stop runs at 80mph (129kmph) or better, totalling just over 15,000 train-miles (24,000km). The fastest are two trains timed to cover the 65.1 miles (104.7km) between Rugby and the outer London railhead at Watford Junction in 44 minutes start-to-stop at a scheduled average of 88.8mph (143kmph).

As soon as the West Coast electrics and the East Coast 'Deltics' had made a nonsense of the Beeching regime's

Left: *Making for the summit of one of the two long and famous banks on the West Coast Main Line from London Euston to Scotland — Shap, between Crewe and Carlisle. Nowadays all that reduces the ac electric locomotives from 100mph to 90mph at the summit is not the long, steep climb but the curvature. No 87.001* Royal Scot *threads the Lune Gorge near Tebay with the 13.45 London Euston-Glasgow.* / Brian Morrison

101

pessimistic outlook, British Railways' passenger management was badgering the mechanical and civil engineers to deliver still higher speed. They had no ready-wrapped answer.

In the first place, they were beginning to get some unexpected bills for intensive operation even at 100mph (160kmph). Like their colleagues on the European mainland, they were finding after the first few months of high-speed electric service out of Euston that conventionally-engineered locomotives and rolling stock were punishing the track pretty severely, despite the fact that it had been comprehensively rebuilt with continuous welded rails on a new and strong foundation. Next, there was the problem of power. Given the characteristics of British main lines, with their comparatively high incidence of enforced checks on maximum speed, it looked as though only electric traction could produce the rapid acceleration that would maximise the limited opportunities for sustained speed in excess of 100mph (160kmph). But the Government was keeping a tight grip on the electrification purse strings. Then there was the safety question. For regular operation at speeds much above 100mph (160kmph) some form of continuous cab signalling looked desirable; and that would be very costly to develop and instal.

It was not the traditional railway engineers who came up with a seemingly triumphant solution to most of these problems, but the covey of brains British Railways had recruited from a contracting aerospace industry to found its Derby research and development centre in 1962. The research centre was established at a time when British Railways' coach riding was under withering fire for its proneness to 'hunting', or vicious lateral oscillation, at

Above: *Several British Rail diesel traction types have run briefly or regularly at 100mph. When first built in 1959 the 2,270hp 'Warship' diesel-hydraulic B-Bs of the Western Region, a design derived from the German Federal Class V200, were allowed to make this speed on the accelerated Bristol-London Paddington 'Bristolian', timed to complete the journey at an average of 71mph (114kmph). Within a few weeks riding problems had the new locomotives restricted to 80mph, however. In this picture a 'Warship' accelerates the London-bound 'Bristolian' out of Bristol past Stapleton Road Junction.* / G. F. Heiron

Centre left: *Anxious for more power and speed than any single unit in its fleet could provide, British Rail's Western Region experimented briefly in the summer of 1966 with pairs of English Electric 1,750hp diesel-electrics regeared for 100mph (160kmph) on some of its London-Bristol and South Wales services. This pair was photographed on the 18.15 from Bristol, forging up the bank to Box Tunnel.* / G. F. Heiron

Bottom left: *The 4,000hp Hawker-Siddeley Kestrel prototype, powered by a single Sulzer V16 engine, was designed for 125mph (200kmph) operation, but British Rail found it too heavy on the axles for such pace. It was never run in Britain at that speed and was eventually sold to Russia. Here it heads BR's 7.55 London Kings Cross-Newcastle through the outer London suburbs in October 1969.* / D. L. Percival

Above: *The ac electric multiple-units built for the short-distance London Liverpool Street-Clacton service in 1962 were proclaimed as an all-line Inter-City model and given official 100mph (160kmph) capability, but this has yet to be fully exploited. On the left is an eight-car formation of these units, Class 309, passing Colchester en route from Clacton to London in May 1977.* / Brian Morrison

Left: *The English Electric-built 2,700hp Class 50 diesel-electric Co-Co has a 100mph (160kmph) rating — and regularly makes that pace on BR's Western Region. No 50.019 hurries out of Brunel's magnificent Box Middle Tunnel portal with the 10.45 Paddington-Bristol in May 1975.* / Philip D. Hawkins

speed, often when vehicles were almost fresh from overhaul. One of the new team's first remits, therefore, was to study the behaviour of flanged wheel on steel rail.

The outcome was 18 months of the most exhaustive research ever carried out in this area. Restarting from first principles, the men at Derby determined not only the fundamental causes of the 'hunting' phenomenon, but also the crucial parameters of track and vehicle suspension design that would guarantee smooth and stable running in the high speed ranges, on curved and slightly imperfect track as well as the straightest and truest of metals. The findings were put to successful proof in an experimental four-wheeled freight vehicle that was tested at up to 100mph (160kmph) on the open track and at up to 140mph (225kmph) on stationary rollers at the Derby research centre.

From that base the Derby team evolved a passenger train concept which, it was claimed, would achieve the commercial speed targets without sacrifice of passenger comfort or extravagant energy consumption on existing track. The outline was unveiled in 1967 as Britain's 155mph (250kmph) Advanced Passenger Train, or APT. The APT, they said, would be no more expensive to run than an orthodox locomotive-hauled train: but it would be capable of a 50% higher speed, would be able to take curvature 40% faster, and all without alteration of existing track or modification of the existing signalling system's braking distances. Far from just avoiding any aggravation of speed wear and tear on track and vehicles, it would actually reduce the problems.

Right: *Another sighting of a Class 50: No 50.016 skirting the Devon coastline with the 08.45 Plymouth-Paddington in April 1977.* / D. Griffiths

Below: *Many systems are contemplating solid slab concrete trackbeds of various types for their high-speed railways. The advantages are greater solidity and strength, plus greatly reduced need of maintenance: disadvantages are much higher first cost and a more cumbersome tracklaying process. This is an experimental BR installation.* / British Rail

The heart of the Derby concept was a suspension system that positively 'steered' the wheels into and through curves, eliminating any juddering contact between flanges and railhead. At the same time an electro-hydraulic servo system on each vehicle would counteract the centrifugal force effect on passengers by a smoothly graduated inward tilt or the coach body; the tilt movement would be automatic, initiated and controlled by sensors continuously measuring the lateral accelerations experienced in the passenger area, and each vehicle would tilt independently of its neighbours, so that throughout the train there would be ideal reaction to a curve's configuration from its start to its finish.

It is not so much safety as passenger comfort which demands this extra, artificially stimulated lean into a curve. For a conventional train the derailment speed on a curve is normally well above the ordained limit, which is set at the mark beyond which the centrifugal force effect on passengers will be unnerving. This latter limit can always be raised by canting the track more sharply inward. But that is only sensible if at the same time you can raise the minimum speed of any trains using the route. Too high a degree of cant in relation to the slowest-moving trains will result in excessive wear on the inner rail of the curve. Thus the degree of a curve's cant, or superelevation, is always a compromise between the ideals for the fastest and slowest trains on the route. Needless to say, if you build new railways for exclusive use by standard high-speed passenger train-sets, as the Japanese and French have done or are doing, you can permit yourself sharper curvature for a given speed than on a mixed-traffic line because you are fixing the degree of cant in relation to a far narrower speed band. It should be added that in the APT the converse risk of undue wear on the outer rail of a curve because the body-tilt allows its passage at above-average speed, is eliminated by the suspension's wheel-steering aptitude.

At the time the wraps were taken off the original APT designs, gas turbine traction using aerospace's new compact, low fuel-cost engines looked the white hope of economical high-speed trains. The APT was to be powered by a single Rolls-Royce Dart turbine of 1,500hp. As for the promise that it could be braked from its intended top speed of 155mph (250kmph) within existing signalling distances, that would be ensured by a multiple-disc system of aircraft type.

Give us the money and the tools and APTs can be in squadron high-speed service by the end of 1972, promised a confident British Railways Board. That, alas, was just the first of many pious hopes to be set at naught by a combination of divided opinion within both Government and British Railways management, technical second and third thoughts, financial stringency and plain over-optimism. The contrast between the coherent, step-by-step advance to higher speed just across the English Channel and the collapse of their own system's attempted 'great leap ahead' into one pitfall after another was painful to many British critics.

For a start, the Government was not anxious to provide a cash-hungry British Railways with the research and development funds. It was uncertain at that stage whether tracked hovercraft, or hovertrains, were not a better investment, particularly since perfection of the British-developed linear electric motor as potential tractive power. Not until 1973 did the Government finally acknowledge the nonsense of investing vast sums in a totally new inter-city passenger movement infrastructure, what time the potential of the existing railway infrastructure had not been fully exploited — and never mind the still considerable scepticism that acceptable ride quality could be achieved in a hovertrain.

Within British Railways the born-and-bred railway engineers scorned the APT as near science-fiction fantasy.

They had little time for the young upstarts from aerospace who had not come up the hard way of coaxing dirty steam-age machinery into good running order. To stake the inter-city train's future on cramming so much practically untried and innovative technology into one package was madness. British Railways, they urged, must first allow conventional engineering another chance.

But now the *parvenu* scientists on the railways found kindred spirits among newly-appointed scientific advisers in Government. The latter were persuaded that APT technology was not merely the sole hope of salvation for British Railways' inter-city traffic, but, near enough, the sign from heaven for which every other railway in the industrialised world had been peering. It would be an export world-beater. So, in 1968, the Government stumped up half the projected research and development cost. Not only that, it actively discouraged any further investment in conventional inter-city passenger equipment, such was its new-found faith in APT. At last, in the summer of 1969, the first orders were placed for prototype APT hardware.

By then more than a year had already been spent waiting for Government endorsement. Just as well, perhaps, for the APT designers were still changing their minds. They had veered from two-axle to bogie running gear and back again; become disaffected with the Dart and attracted to a new range of inexpensive 350-500hp turbines which motor manufacturers Leyland were developing for heavy road freight vehicles; and adopted a hydrokinetic device as the main braking system. Briefly, a hydrokinetic brake achieves its effect by opposing to movement the pressure of a water-glycol fluid; the energy thus created is converted into heat that is dissipated to the atmosphere.

With three years gone by and not even prototype hardware on the track, in 1970 the British Railways Board yielded to mounting pressure from its passenger management and ordered a further development in conventional rolling stock. It was to be a double-ended multiple-unit, capable of 125mph (200kmph), in which seven or eight air-conditioned cars of a new 75ft-long (23m) design would be enclosed by two power cars each equipped with a 12 cylinder Paxman Valenta 2,250hp engine driving through an electric alternator transmission. Two years later a prototype was ready for track testing, in the course of which it was propelled up to a new world speed record for diesel traction of 143mph (230kmph) over near-level track between Darlington and York on 11 June 1973.

The first routes to be allocated production High Speed Trains, or HSTs as the new diesel train-sets are generally known, were those of the Western Region between London's Paddington and Bristol/South Wales. For a number of reasons, mainly beyond the control of British Railways management, the production programme lagged well behind schedule and it was not until the spring of 1977 that the full planned service could be launched, under the brandname of 'Inter-City 125'. That full service took British Railways at a bound up to second place in the world rail speed table, yielding best only to the Japanese Shinkansen for combined speed and frequency. And the overall cost of designing and building all the train-sets, and of the track and signalling work necessary to maximise their speed potential, had been slightly less than the final APT research and development bill was to total — infinitely less than the enormous expense of a brand-new railway.

As on the East Coast Route of British Railways, a great deal of the extra speed was won by ironing out curves and relaying junctions in the course of a thoroughgoing reconstruction of the track from the foundations up to ensure durable quality under intensive 125mph (200kmph) running. The outcome is that HSTs humming out of Paddington can make almost immediate use of their ability to reach 125mph

Above: *British Rail's prototype HST diesel train, No 252.001, makes 100mph through the Thames Valley as it approaches Reading in April 1976 on the 15.15 Bristol-Paddington service.* / Brian Morrison

Left: *One of the production series Class 253 HSTs on British Rail's 'Inter-City 125' service, approaching Paddington on the 09.50 working from Bristol in October 1977.* / Brian Morrison

Below left: *Opening up: a snort of smoke from the Paxman Valenta engine as the driver opens the taps for a smart HST getaway from Bristol.* / P. J. Fowler

Above: *Second-class saloon of British Rail's standard high-speed Mk III coach, incorporated in the HST and used in locomotive-hauled formations on other routes.* / British Rail

Above right: *First-class saloon of a Mk III coach.* / British Rail

(200kmph) within 5½ minutes of a standing start on level track. They can hold that speed for 72 miles (116km) continuously to Swindon, except for an 80mph (129kmph) check through Reading. On the Bristol route curvature rules out further top speed, but South Wales-bound HSTs have about 25 more miles (40km) in which they can make 125mph (200kmph) before they dive into the Severn Tunnel. Little modification of the route's multiple-aspect colour-light signalling was required, since it was a cardinal point of the HST specification that velvet-smooth deceleration from 125mph (200kmph) to a dead stand must be unfailingly possible within the existing minimum braking distance of 6,600ft (2,164m). That requirement was met by fitting each axle with wheel slide detectors that co-act with the electro-pneumatically-operated disc brakes to meter to each wheel sufficient pressure for maximum braking effort without judder or damage to the wheel treads. The only signalling refinement on an HST route is the introduction of flashing single or double yellow aspect ahead of some strategic facing junctions to give drivers earlier warning of a turnout.

In its two power-car, seven-trailer version the HST has a power/weight ratio of 11.8hp/tonne. Advanced lightweight construction technology, including use of aluminium alloy for components like the fuel tanks, has trimmed the weight of each power car to 70 tonnes. Thus its axle-loading, a crucial consideration in limiting high-speed wear and tear on track and train, is little more than 17 tonnes — a remarkable achievement in a diesel power unit, when one reflects that the French could not improve on 16 tonnes in the electric power units of their TGV Paris-Sudest train-sets (see Chapter Ten).

Despite the relative shortness of journey times on the Western Region 'Inter-City 125' routes, British Railways took a different line on train catering from the French in their TGV Paris-Sudest units. Whatever the route, British Railways were convinced that the HSTs must offer full hot meal service as well as buffet fare. But they were just as concerned as the French not to squander revenue-earning seat space in a necessarily limited train formation, so their catering division was given the none-too-easy job of covering both types of food service within the equivalent of one coach length. That necessarily meant no separate restaurant car, but meal service to seats nearest the kitchen, so that on the busiest HST services it's wise to reserve space in advance if you plan to take a full meal. But since the capacious new-style buffets of the HSTs have a refined type of microwave oven that turns out a decent range of over-the-counter hot snacks (not to mention draught beer on tap), it's not such a deprivation if you are crowded out of the dining space. The majority of HSTs have a single catering vehicle combining buffet and kitchen; exceptionally on the East Coast London-Scotland HST service the train-sets have one bigger kitchen adjoining the first-class vehicles, the buffet with its small kitchen in a separate car among the second-class accommodation.

Not the least impressive feature of the HSTs' debut on the Western Region and South Wales routes was the ingenuity with which no fewer than 48 125mph (200kmph) services each way daily were superimposed on the rest of the Western Region main line traffic. By no means all the other inter-city services sharing the fast tracks had power capable of even 100mph (160kmph) top speed. And over the double-track stretch of the combined HST route between Didcot and Swindon the HSTs have to contend for track space with

daylong freight traffic between the industrial areas of South Wales and northern England.

'Flighting' solved most of the off-peak problems. The standard pattern of HST departures from Paddington is three trains in every hour, two of them limited-stop services at five-minute headway to South Wales and Bristol respectively, the third, around the midpoint of the hourly pattern, a 'semi-fast'. (One inserts the quotes because these HSTs serving the intermediate traffic centres have bookings that demand such hot pace as a 96.8mph (155.8kmph) average start to stop for just 24.2 miles (38.9km) faintly downhill from Swindon to Didcot.) This grouping has the two limited-stop HSTs closed up on the tail of the preceding semi-fast by the start of the 24 mile (38km) Didcot-Swindon double-track bottleneck, which they occupy in procession for about 20 minutes of each hour. That leaves a reasonable residue of every hour for the track to be monopolised by slower-moving trains. In the morning and evening peaks, when both HST and other services are augmented, timetabling is very tight indeed, particularly in the London suburban area, since some of the longer-haul commuter trains have then to be found space on the fast tracks over the first 36 miles (58km) out to Reading — and their traction is limited to 90mph (145kmph).

The HSTs have been proved fully capable of 100mph (160kmph) start-to-stop timings on the Western Region. On Queen Elizabeth II's Silver Jubilee day, 7 May 1977, a celebratory HST excursion from Bristol to London was set to run the 117½ miles (189km) each way in 70½ minutes and bettered the time in both directions, averaging 103.3mph (166kmph) eastbound and 104.4mph (168kmph) westbound, both start-to-stop. The official working timetables at the time of writing require several trains to eat up the 41.3 miles (66.5km) from Swindon to Reading at a start-to-stop average of 103.3mph (166kmph), though the public timetables show a slightly easier allowance.

As for city-to-city performance, the standard 'Inter-City 125' non-stop timing over the 133.4 miles (215km) from Paddington to Newport, first major call across the Welsh border, is 86 minutes, which demands a start-to-stop average of 93.1mph (150kmph). Even with two intermediate stops an HST does it in 92 minutes. This highlights a vital advantage of the lightweight high-speed train in the population corridors of a country like Britain: the fact that it can take up so much intermediate business in its end-to-end high-speed stride. And the outcome of that is an astonishing tally of short-distance sprints in the Western Region 'Inter-City 125' timetable: over 70 every day timed start-to-stop at an average of 90mph (145kmph) or more, up to the top mark of 103.3mph (166kmph) mentioned earlier. One must add that the HST's riding at 125mph (200kmph) on the reconstructed track of the route Brunel so superbly engineered in the last century is as near-impeccably smooth and quiet as that of any other rail vehicle in Western Europe. This is due largely to embodiment of APT groundwork in the Mk III coach's running gear.

In their first 1½ years of service the Western Region HSTs pulled in 28% more passenger business. That was in competition primarily with the London-South Wales motorway. Next the HSTs would come up against more exacting opposition — a regular-interval, pay-as-you-board shuttle air service whose centre-to-centre time between cities was just out of competitive reach, even with reasonable allowance for ground travel to and from airports. That was between London and Edinburgh, following full application of the second squadron of HSTs to the East Coast Main Line and its Kings Cross-Newcastle-Edinburgh and Kings Cross-West Riding services in 1978.

Initially the HSTs accelerated the 'Flying Scotsman' to a non-stop timing of 3½ minutes over three hours between London and the train's first stop at Newcastle, representing a start-to-stop average of 87.7mph (141kmph). Then following track improvements north of the English-Scottish border, the overall London-Edinburgh time should come down to at least 4½ hours inclusive of the Newcastle stop. Even this first-stage HST timetable, in which the inaugural batch of East Coast train-sets had to be found paths amongst a preponderance of slower, locomotive-hauled services, showed a start-to-stop timing as fast as 100.9mph (162.3kmph) over the 48.75 miles (78.4km) from Stevenage to Peterborough by the 8.00 Kings Cross-Edinburgh. Before the 1970s are out, however, the 'Flying Scotsman's' schedule end-to-end may well have been squeezed as tight as 4 hours 10 minutes, which would entail averaging 94.2mph (151.6kmph), Newcastle call included, the whole way. Moreover, the 10 other hourly trains each way daily between London and Edinburgh will be on timings almost as fast; and the equally frequent service to other major towns and cities covered from London's Kings Cross, such as Bradford, Leeds, Darlington and York, will be of similar standard. In short, diesel traction will be putting up a standard hourly-interval, non-supplementary fare inter-city service at the same levels of comfort and speed, over similar distances, as the best attempted so far in regular working over existing, conventionally-signalled track by electric traction — the latter on just two exclusively first-class, supplementary-fare trains, the French 'Aquitaine' and 'Etendard'. Quite an achievement.

So what, meantime, of the Advanced Passenger Train?

Eventually a turbine-powered prototype emerged simultaneously with the prototype HST. In outline the articulated four-car unit was a vastly different animal from the models and sketches published at the announcement of the project (and even they then changed shape almost from year to year). Practically all its evaluation was done in private, the road tests on a specially prepared stretch of otherwise disused track in the Midlands. Whereas the French were constantly flourishing the latest speed exploits of their TGV Paris-Sudest prototype train, TGV001, and buttonholing every visiting VIP for a high-speed jaunt in the unit, British Railways treated their prototype, known as APT-E, like a secret weapon. Not until 1975 were its doings declassified.

In August that year APT-E was suddenly brought front of stage for a series of Sunday speed tests on the Western Region's Paddington-Bristol main line, and whipped up to 151mph (243kmph) over a five-mile stretch between Reading and Swindon. Two months later APT-E's competence over typically unregenerated British main line was proved by setting it at the Midland route from London's St Pancras to Leicester. Here conventional trains were at the time limited to 90mph (145kmph) throughout. Held at 125mph (200kmph) most of the way, but unleashed to 135mph (217kmph) between Luton and Bedford, APT-E's riding was exemplary as it sailed through the 99 miles (159km) in 58 minutes at a start-to-stop average of 102.4mph (165kmph). People on the train were particularly impressed with the barely perceptible 75mph (120kmph) negotiation of a curve at Market Harborough which enforces a 50mph (80kmph) on all conventional trains.

Around this time I was offered a ride in APT-E on its Old Dalby test track in the Midlands. No doubt about it, taking bends at high speed was a rare experience — or rather, it was no palpable experience: the automatic control of the counteracting body-tilt was so infinitely adjusted to the changing superelevation as the train took the bend that only by peering each way out of the window could I be sure we were on a curve, or how sharp it was.

But in other respects the trip had me worried. Plainly, a coach body that is going to tilt abnormally cannot have as generous cross-section as a conventional coach body, or it may side-swipe any conventional train it passes on a bend. As a result the interior of the APT is decidedly confined by

comparison with an orthodox Mk III coach in an HST. Reduced body width narrows the centre saloon gangways and the individual seat widths, while the pronounced inward taper on the coach walls up to the roof, coupled with necessarily low ceilings, brings luggage racks down uncomfortably close to the head level of window seats. All this, too, cramps the buffet and kitchen.

I can't help feeling many passengers will question whether the extra speed — and for reasons to follow it won't now be that much higher — is worth the sacrifice of Mk III comfort. I have similar reservations about the French TGV train interiors, though not to the same extent: the French are not providing for body-tilting, and even if they were their problems would not be exacerbated by the more restrictive British loading gauge.

Towards the end of 1974 the Government authorised construction of three more APTs, termed pre-production prototypes and designated APT-P. Unlike the APT-E, they were to be 25kV ac electric. For one thing, there was no longer any practical power plant in view for a non-electric APT. The Leyland gas turbine's early promise had faded even before the 1973 oil crisis wiped out turbine traction's economic advantage, and no high-power diesel engine on the market looked readily adaptable to the APT's configuration. But in addition British Railways were beginning to appreciate the speed gains attainable on a number of key inter-city routes by the partnership of HSTs and not

Far left: *Fresh angle on the HST: another view of a Class 253 unit entering London's Paddington after the sprint up from Bristol.* / Brian Morrison

Left: *In 1978 the HSTs made their regular service debut on the London Kings Cross-Newcastle-Edinburgh service. This shot is of a Class 253 set, borrowed from the Western Region, leaving Edinburgh Waverley for London on a special excursion in July 1977.* / G. A. Watt

Below: *Third route to acquire HSTs will be the Western Region's from Paddington to Devon and Cornwall, to which this unit paid a visit on a special excursion in April 1977; bound from London to Plymouth, it had just reached the Devon coastline at Dawlish Warren.* / L. Bertram

impossibly expensive track works. The sensible route on which to blood the APT was therefore the electrified West Coast main line between London's Euston and Scotland. And there the three APT-Ps took on their first passengers in the spring of 1979. However, though they have been tested up to their design speed of 150mph (240kmph) on the open line, in public service they are limited to 125mph (200kmph). And that maximum is unlikely to be raised for some years to come.

Why the caution? First, while you can design a train to work at up to 150mph (240kmph) within the limits and distances of existing lineside signalling — and APT-E's hydrokinetic brake fulfilled that specification during its Western Region road tests — you can't bulldoze reluctant railwaymen into driving it without the benefit of more sophisticated aids to judgement. British Railways came to realise that they could not introduce regular operation at speeds in excess of 125mph (200kmph) without some form of continuous cab signalling. British Railways had — and still have — a system in readiness, but they could not cope financially with the costs of its widespread application.

The British system is inductive loop, similar in essentials to the German Federal apparatus that was fully described in Chapter Seven. As in the German system, the use of looped cable laid between the running rails for the transmission and receipt of data greatly extends the variety of information that can be channelled between control point and train by

comparison with coded track circuit methods. That is a vital consideration where high-speed trains are mingling with other conventional traffic on an existing main line; build a new railway almost bare of junctions and stations, then dedicate it exlusively to high-speed trains, and coded track circuits will amply cover the more limited message requirement, as French Railways' new TGV Paris-Sudest line arrangements demonstrate (see Chapter Ten).

The British Railways system provides four communication channels, including ordinary speech, from track to train, and two in reverse from train to track. Its superior characteristic is that it is modular, which broadens even further the range of data that can be transmitted either way. The data-processing unit on the train can be fed such comprehensive and continuous information, not only on signal aspects but on route characteristics — gradients, imminence of junctions and speed restrictions, etc — that automatic driving becomes feasible. And of course, given the capacity of the system to report back automatically and continuously an equivalent amount of data on the train's speed, progress and position, not merely automatic driving but computer-controlled working as a whole main line from one strategic centre is the ultimate objective of this development. In brief, automatic train operation, or ATO as it is generally known these days.

Meantime British Railways have contented themselves with a much simpler supplementary device on the APT's first regular route. Even with a 125mph (200kmph) ceiling some additional driving aid was felt essential because of the relaxed APT speed limits round curves. Just possibly a driver manning an APT one day and a conventional locomotive the next might momentarily forget which he was on. Throughout the fast tracks of the APT route, therefore, every stretch of line over which an APT must come below 125mph (200kmph) is denoted by transponders laid between the running rails. These are passive circuitry devices, activated by apparatus on the passing train, which consequently need no external power supply and are inexpensive by comparison even with coded track circuitry. But because they are passive they can transmit one unvariable message only; they cannot, for instance, relay changing signal aspects. On the APT route they are installed at every point where the permissible speed varies, either up or down. Their effect on the complementary trainborne

apparatus is to vary appropriately a display on the driving desk, so that the driver has continuously in front of him the maximum speed at which he should be travelling.

Another reason for the APT's restraint to 125mph (200kmph) for the foreseeable future has already been alluded to in the discussion of French high-speed development on already electrified routes. It is now obvious that the power demands of a number of APTs at simultaneous full bore in the same electrification section cannot be satisfactorily met without substantial and very expensive modification of both trackside current feeder gear and catenary (for reasons that are nothing to do with efficient contact between pantograph and conductor wire at maximum speed; that problem has been overcome).

APT is visualised in two basic formats. For ultimate 155mph (250kmph) operation the layout is two power cars and 12 trailers, the greatest train-length the generality of British main line platforms can accept, though the power cars could comfortably sustain their maximum performance with two more trailers. All three APT-Ps are of this type, so that maximum potential can be evaluated. Until the bill for full-speed operation in regular service can be faced, most production units are likely to be of the alternative one power car-and-ten trailer layout, which is not designed for operation above 125mph (200kmph).

The APT-Ps have their power units sandwiched in the middle of the formation. This arrangement has several advantages. It avoids adding the weight of orthodox buffers and drawgear to the axle loading of the power car and in the two-power-car trains allows both of them to take current from one pantograph, which would be impossible if they were separated: test running at high speed has proved the superior efficiency of current collection through the one pantograph. But the reverse of the coin is lack of room alongside the power plant for more than a pencil-slim emergency walkway to connect the two articulated trailer units on either side of the power cars. Passengers cannot roam freely between the two sets of passenger accommodation; and that means each must have its own catering. Future one-power-car units will have the traction moved to a redesigned driving car at one end of the formation to eliminate this handicap.

The APT-P coaches are exceptionally lightweight. The aircraft-style, semi-monocoque constructional techniques

Top left: *The driving desk of the APT-P. In the centre of the console, showing '125', is the transponder-activated display which keeps the driver continuously advised of the maximum speed he must observe.* / British Rail

Top: *The prototype APT-E gas turbine-powered unit on a test run down the Midland main line in the London suburbs, pacing traffic on the M1 London-West Midlands motorway, in 1974.* / British Rail

Above: *The camera freezes the turbine-powered APT-E making 149mph (240kmph) near Steventon during its high-speed trials on the Western Region Paddington-Swindon main line in the summer of 1975.*

applied to APT-E were discarded as too expensive for mass production, and each trailer car body is now welded up from aluminium extrusions running the full vehicle length. Combined with weight-saving through articulation and in many components, notably a special low-energy air-conditioning plant, this brings the APT-P trailer out at only 23 tonnes, less than three-quarters the weight of a Mk III coach, but with near-identical seating capacity.

Although steel-built, a 4,000hp APT-P power car turns the scales at only 69 tonnes. Like the rest of the set, it has an automatically tilting body, but the pantograph has to be mounted on an anti-tilt device that stabilises it under the overhead current wire whatever the posture of the power car body. The layout of the drive from the power plant to the road wheels is decidedly unusual. The higher the speed in

mind, the lower the unsprung mass of a vehicle needs to be to contain track wear and tear, above all the impact in railjoints and crossing components. On APT-P the unsprung mass had to be reduced well below that of an HST, which debarred conventional bogie-mounting of the traction motors. The motors, therefore, are in the car body in a mounting that incorporates the hydrokinetic brake; from the brake a transfer gearbox takes the drive to a cardan shaft that leads to a final drive gearbox mounted on the bogie frame, whence there is quill drive to the road wheels. The thyristor-controlled traction motors, incidentally, are Swedish-built by ASEA, the firm generally acknowledged to have perfected the thyristor control system; nevertheless, the decision to import traction gear for such a front-runner in British rail industry's export effort raised many a pained eyebrow.

After about a year's bedding down in existing timetable paths the prototype APT-Ps were due in 1980 to open up 100mph (160kmph) average journeying between London and Glasgow on a 4 hours 10 minutes timing for the 401.5 miles (646km), inclusive of a single intermediate stop at Preston. That would represent an end-to-end average of 96.4 mph (161.5kmph). In the current state of the route, a four-hour schedule would be beyond the capacity of a one-power car-ten-trailer production APT, the optimum timing for which has been computed as five minutes over the four hours. The hope is that sufficient signalling modification and track works can be executed to ease permanent speed restrictions and wipe out the five-minute discrepancy resulting from a poorer power/weight ratio by the time series APT production starts, hopefully in 1981. Even if it were free to run at up to 150mph (250kmph), however, the computers calculate that the two-power-car version would not better 3 hours 46 minutes for the London-Glasgow distance. That underlines the limited high-speed scope of the West Coast main line's alignment.

On the more amenable East Coast Route from London to Scotland the two-power-car APT's full speed range would pay more substantial dividends. As against the diesel-powered HST's probable inability to improve on 4 hours 5 minutes as a London Kings Cross-Edinburgh schedule, including a Newcastle stop, as a remotely practical operating proposition without hitherto intimidating infrastructure improvements — for example, the cutting of a straighter path through York — the computers say an electric two-power-car HST could manage 3 hours 28 minutes. That would entail 113.3mph (182.3kmph) end-to-end, the Newcastle call notwithstanding.

No doubt about it, then, that the APT promises the fastest inter-city services obtainable in the current state of world rail technology without embarking on new railway building. To attain average speed levels the same or not immeasurably superior, the French, West Germans, Italians and Japanese have been or are laying out more than ten times as much, mile for inter-city mile, as British Rail has sunk in its APT research and development.

The pity is that APT has taken so long over its halting translation from theory to hardware that at the emergence of the first APT-P no squadron production orders were as yet in the pipeline, and that APT's future on British Rail seems now to hinge on authority for more electrification. Already it is certain that the interlinked Inter-City services from London Euston to Birmingham, Liverpool, Manchester and Glasgow cannot be fully taken over by APTs before 1985. Meanwhile, HSTs should be raising the inter-city speeds of Britain high enough to hold Britain's place around the top of the world table as they spread to the London-Plymouth route and the vital complex of cross-country services linking Newcastle, Leeds, Manchester, Sheffield and Liverpool via Birmingham with South Wales and South-West England.

7. West Germany's Speed Hopes Checked

Reparation of appalling damage was not the only Herculean task confronting the new West German railway system, Deutsche Bundesbahn, after the Second World War. Another was geographical reorientation. The pre-war Deutsche Reichsbahn had been built up to serve the mainly lateral traffic flows of a united Germany, but the post-war partition turned the natural commercial axis of West Germany north-to-south. That thrust the main weight of passenger and freight traffic on to lines which for much of their distance either lacked track capacity to handle it or were physically unsuited to high speed. In some cases the handicaps were combined.

For instance, on what was now a key trunk route from the northern port of Hamburg to the heart of West Germany, a stretch of 23 miles (37km) between Celle and Hannover was single track. Further south, between Hannover and Würzburg, this crucial north-south artery has few scenic superiors outside the Alps as it threads the ranges that make up West Germany's *Mittelgebirge;* all that disfigures a glorious panorama of wooded and castle-specked hills is the obscene apparatus of the East German border, which almost fences the railway for a mile or so south of Göttingen. But the contours force the line to curve this way and that for miles on end; rare are the short stretches of straight track where a driver can open up to the normal inter-city speeds of the 1970s. The same applies to the long Rhine Valley section of the trunk route from the Ruhr and Cologne to Frankfurt or to Mainz and Switzerland, and to the eastern end of the main line between Stuttgart and Munich.

Until the early 1960s the maximum speed limit anywhere on the Deutsche Bundesbahn, or German Federal Railway, was 87.5mph (140kmph). Electrification had been pushed ahead rapidly after the war, however, and by 1960 many trains were being timed to the hilt that the speed ceiling conceded. Over the speed-conducive Mannheim-Karlsruhe-Freiburg stretch of the trunk route to the Swiss border at Basle, for example, the timetable showed several start-to-stop bookings demanding averages of around 75mph (120kmph) by trains like the 'Rheingold', 'Helvetia' and the Hamburg-Basle 'Komet', this last an improbable eight-car articulated diesel multiple-unit composed entirely of sleeping accommodation that was built in 1953 but did not survive long into the 1960s.

Whatever its place in the world inter-city speed table at this juncture, the German Federal was unarguably ahead of all comers on comfort. In the late 1950s its new standard 86ft 7in (26.4m) coach body on heavy Minden-Deutz bogies, very efficiently soundproofed though as yet not fully air-conditioned, set parameters of size and ride quality that were to be adopted by every major railway on the mainland of Europe; even today's standard European coach is still plainly inspired by the German Federal model of two decades back. The major innovation of the Minden-Deutz bogie — so-called because it was the collaborative product of German Federal coach designers at Minden and the private coachbuilders Klöckner-Humboldt-Deutz (also known as Westwaggon) — was its replacement of conventional axlebox

Below: *West Germany's first post-World War II train-sets built new with 100mph (160kmph) capability were a pair of one-off streamlined diesel multiple-units that attracted a lot of attention when they were exhibited at the Munich Transport Exhibition of 1953. One was a seven-car, 135-seater day-train unit articulated throughout over a single axle between cars, the other an eight-car all-sleeper unit — uniquely in diesel multiple-unit history — with berths for just 40 in its 29 sleeping compartments; this set was also articulated, but on two-axle bogies. Both sets made extensive use of light alloy in their construction to achieve very light weight. After lengthy testing to eliminate teething problems the day train saw several years' service as the 'Senator' between Frankfurt and Hamburg from 1954. The night train, which was owned by the West German sleeping and restaurant car company, DSG, and wore the DSG emblem on its nose (illustrated), operated as the 'Komet' between Basle, Switzerland, and Hamburg. Each unit was eventually fitted with four 210hp engines and transmissions were hydro-mechanical. The German Federal Railway's classification was VT10.5.*

Top: *The German Federal's first contribution to Western Europe's 'Trans-Europ Express' rolling stock pool was the Class VT11.5, later 601, seven-car diesel-hydraulic multiple-unit introduced in 1957. Speed did not quite match up to the impression enforced by the aggressive streamlining, for the units were limited to the then all-line maximum of 87.5mph (140kmph). /* J. L. McIvor

Above: *A pair of German Federal Class VT11.5 units, by this time displaced from TEE service, finish their career on domestic West German Inter-City work; they are near Hannover on the Frankfurt-Cologne 'Sachsenross' service. /* 'Railphot' Y. Broncard

Left: *The southbound 'Rheingold' streams away from Cologne, making the most of the straight stretches to Bonn before it enters the speed-limiting curves of the Rhine valley. Up front is 8,100hp Co-Co electric No 103.122. /* 'Railphot' Y. Broncard

guides by spring-steel guiding leaves, which absorbed all fore-and-aft and lateral forces. For frictionless damping, the axleboxes were given helical instead of laminated springs with hydraulic damping, while articulated swing links and hydraulic shock absorbers between the bolster and bogie frame prevented lateral motion of the bogie imparting sympathetic side-sway to the coach body. Coupled with its advance in this area, the German Federal was extending continuous welded rail more rapidly than any other European system at the time. Coaching technology and cwr in conjunction set a German Federal inter-city trip of the 1950s apart from any other European rail experience for serenity and silence of ride.

The German Federal stepped up to its first post-war 100mph (160kmph) running in May 1962. Standardbearer was one of the most charismatic of the pre-war international luxury trains, the 'Rheingold' from Holland through Germany to Switzerland and Italy, now reborn with the magnificent new coaching stock that was to become — and at the time of writing still is — the standard pattern for all German Federal 'Trans-Europ Express' and supplementary-fare internal 'Inter-City' services. Back in 1962 the 'Rheingold' was not in the TEE fleet, as it is now, and the new train-sets and the Class 112 (E10.12 at the time) locomotives which hauled them initially prefigured today's standard German Federal blue-and-cream livery.

The new 'Rheingold' shamed most of the equipment in TEE service in the early 1960s, even the Germans' own bulbous-nosed diesel-hydraulic multiple-units. It was the most luxurious train Europe had yet seen. The cars which particularly caught the eye, of course, were the kitchen-diner-buffet, with its double-deck service area, kitchen upstairs and scullery below; and the observation car, bar at one end, train secretary's and train telephone room at the other, and in the centre the raised vista-dome saloon above a mails/baggage room. I can still remember marvelling at my

first summer's-day ride in the vista-dome, astonished that the air-conditioning and tinted glass made one impervious to the sun beating down on the overall glass roof and lost in admiration at the tranquillity of the ride: that high above the track, given the riding quality of the new stock as a whole, 'gliding' was for once the *mot juste* and not a journalistic *cliché*. You can't ride those observation cars in the 'Rheingold' or its companion 'Rheinpfeil' any more unfortunately. Though the vista-dome had been carefully shaped to shoehorn through all the bridges and tunnels of the 'Rheingold's' normal route, clearance problems could arise if emergency forced a detour. In the 1970s the DB discarded the cars and in 1977 sold them to one of the German travel agencies which does big business in charter holiday trains; the new owners have trimmed the domes' contours and now use the cars in their holiday specials to all corners of Western Europe.

Elsewhere in its formation the 'Rheingold' premiered, besides spacious compartment firsts, those superb German Federal open saloon firsts with individual semi-reclining and rotating armchairs, for my money still the most comfortably-seated and relaxing rail coaches in all Europe. Another innovation of the 1962 'Rheingold' that is now quite common practice was its automatically closing, air-assisted vestibule doors. Nowadays every railway, the German included, takes care to placard the doors with advice to passengers that they are self-closing. Strangely, the Germans neglected this at first and I remember wondering on my first 1962 trip how long the apparatus would stand the mayhem as passenger after passenger — even Customs officials — tried to manhandle the doors to behind them.

The equipment which allowed the German Federal to push the 'Rheingold' up to 100mph (160kmph) over suitable trackage was the electro-magnetic track brakes fitted to every vehicle. That safeguarded braking within existing signalling distances. As a result the train could be given a

Far left: *Close-up of the glass-domed observation car that used to run in the 'Rheingold' (there was another in the 'Rheinpfeil').* / J. L. McIvor

Above: *On the upper floor of the 'Rheingold' observation car.* / Deutsche Bundesbahn

Left: *Inside one of the spacious reclining-seat air-conditioned saloons with which the German Federal set new European rail comfort standard in 1962; they are now a standard first-class alternative to compartments on all West German TEE and Inter-City services.* / Deutsche Bundesbahn

Right: *Close-up of individual reclining-seats in a first-class saloon.* / Deutsche Bundesbahn

Below: *Stenography at speed: train secretary at work in a German Inter-City flier.* / Deutsche Bundesbahn

timing as fast as 62 minutes for the 83.1 miles (127km) from Freiburg to Karlsruhe, average 80.4mph (129.4kmph), and one almost as tight in the southbound direction. The following year the Dortmund-Munich 'Rheinpfeil', which exchanged through coaches with the 'Rheingold' at Duisburg, was refurbished with a similar train-set and similarly allowed to run at up to 100mph (160kmph).

Even before the new 'Rheingold' took the tracks the German Federal was set on speeds higher than 100mph (160kmph). At the start of the 1960s it had invited the major West German traction builders to submit their designs for a 125mph (200kmph) locomotive, on six axles all motored to keep the axle loadings in check. The chosen design, a joint project by Henschel and Siemens-Schuckert, materialised in early 1965 as the first four prototypes of Class E03, now Class 103. After four years of evaluation, this handsome and extremely powerful 108 tonne design, continuously rated at 8,100hp but boasting a one-hour rating of 8,750hp at its 125mph (200kmph) top speed, was adopted as standard. Deliveries of a production series began in 1970 and the fleet, numbering 148 by the middle of the decade, became the staple power of the German Federal's inter-city expresses. On 13 September 1973 No 103 118 of the class, hauling three research department vehicles, was tested with specially modified gearing up to a new German electric locomotive speed peak of 157.2mph (252.9kmph).

The first four E03s emerged in time for the German Federal to lay on a public high-speed demonstration concurrently with a big international transport exhibition that was staged at Munich in the summer of 1965. The 38.5 miles (62km) of track between Munich and Augsburg were fettled up and throughout the exhibition period a special train of 'Rheingold' stock shuttled between the two cities in 26 minutes start to stop, average 88mph (140.8kmph), inclusive of a crawl over the long curving exit from the Munich exhibition station, a 50mph (80kmph) slowing for a curve en route and a final decorous entry to Augsburg.

Apart from track preparation, the racing stretch had been fitted up with the German Federal's version of continuous cab signalling and train speed control. The railway already had an effective and widely-applied automatic warning system, the Indusi. In the Indusi system, track-mounted oscillating circuitry devices ahead of each signal, one ahead of a warning signal and two spaced ahead of a stop signal, emit individually tuned codes if the signals are not clear. Apparatus on the traction unit picks up the warnings and, if the driver does not respond by touching his vigilance switch and taking appropriate braking action, activates the necessary braking automatically.

The combination of the E03's rheostatic braking and the 'Rheingold' stock's electro-magnetic track brakes were not deemed adequate for deceleration from 125mph (200kmph) within existing signalling distances, however. The new locomotives were therefore fitted up to work with a new inductive loop system of continuous cab signalling, which would give advance information on signal aspects and provide automatic speed control.

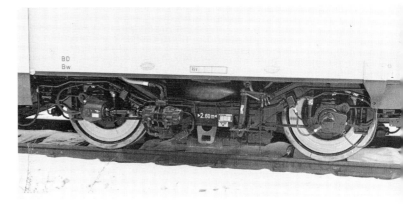

Right: *Close-up of an electro-magnetic track brake, in this application on a German Federal Class ET403 electric multiple-unit: the flat shoe can be seen, raised out of use, below the centre of the bogie frame* / Deutsche Bundesbahn

Below: *A typically immaculate 100mph 'Inter-City' express of the German Federal: the Hamburg-Munich 'Schwabenpfeil' with Co-Co No 103.182-2 at Essen.* / A. W. Hobson

Above: *The driving cab visual display of the 'target speed' prescribed by the German Federal's continuous cab signalling and automatic speed control system for 125mph (200kmph) operation can be seen just above the driver's left hand in this view of the control desk in an ET 403 electric multiple-unit.* / Deutsche Bundesbahn

The inductive cable loop, laid on the sleepers, is crossed over every 100m (328ft), which changes the magnetic field. This serves to identify the location of a passing train. Trainborne apparatus can work out the train's position on the route by keeping count of the magnetic field changes from the start of a loop, which can be as long as a mile. This system can automatically report this data to the control centre, where the location of every train in the area is thus continuously recorded.

The system has all the basic control and reporting elements for full automated railway operation. Apparatus at the relevant signalling interlocking is continuously 'addressing' every train within a loop at split-second intervals in electronically coded messages, requesting automatic return of data on each train's speed and position from the trainborne apparatus, which includes data-processing devices to originate the coded signals back. These outgoing signals are introduced to the loop at a higher frequency than the incoming commands, to segregate the two coded streams.

Minimum braking distance from 125kmph (200mph) is set in the German Federal rubrics at 3,000m (9,843ft). The basic principle of the automatic system is to monitor continuously that a train making top speed is never less than that distance from a signal or other situation demanding a full stop, or the appropriately reduced distance from a graded speed restriction. Continuously scrutinising the state of the line in its controlled area, the lineside apparatus is transmitting its commands to a train as 'target speed', to which the driver of an E03, or Class 103 nowadays, must adjust his automatic speed regulator upward or downward. The lineside control's data-processor also advises the distance ahead, up to 5,000m (16,400ft) over which the 'target speed' should be maintained. The data-processor on the locomotive reproduces this data visually on a driving desk dial. At the same time it is comparing actual with dictated speed and will activate emergency braking if it detects serious wrong-side descrepancy.

When I rode the demonstration Munich-Augsburg train at the end of June 1965 there was one ominous moment.

Rounding a long curve between Nannhofen and Haspelmoor at 127mph (204kmph), our coach wheel flanges bit really hard into the outer rail and centrifugal force imparted some pretty violent lateral judders to the usually battleship-steady 'Rheingold' coach bodies. We weren't at safety risk, of course, but it was obvious the curve had not had its cant adjusted to the amount necessary for reasonable passenger comfort at that speed. Or, one was certain, for the track's health under continuous pounding at 125mph. And so it was to prove.

From May 1966 the German Federal substantially accelerated its Munich-Hamburg 'Blauer Enzian' and allowed the train up to 125mph (200kmph) over the Munich-Augsburg stretch and to 112mph (180kmph) over the newly-doubled and resignalled track between Hannover and Celle. This was Europe's first public service operation at that speed, the Munich-Augsburg demonstrations apart. But within a couple of years or so a limit of 100mph (160kmph) was reimposed.

A German Federal civil engineer had complained to me at the 1965 Munich exhibition that even 100mph (160kmph) running was punishing track upkeep costs with an extra 20%. Still higher speed was now threatening to load the usual bill with an extra 50 or 60%. The continuous signalling system was pretty costly too, but it was the wear and tear on track that chiefly decided the German Federal to cry halt while they re-examined their track and vehicle technology.

Weight of engineering opinion on the German Federal now was that the only economical tool for higher speed was a multiple-unit which spread the weight of traction gear throughout the train and reduced axle-loadings. The double-

Left: *The striking outline of a Class ET403 electric multiple-unit is emphasised in this action shot.* / Deutsche Bundesbahn

Below: *Interior of a first-class saloon in an ET403 unit.* / Deutsche Bundesbahn

Bottom: *Traction contrast: purring into Bebra on the 'Hermes' Inter-City service from Bremen to Munich, an ET403 unit passes the plinth-mounted steam Pacific No 012.102 that has been put on display outside the station as a testimonial to the type's service from the local depot until 1973.* / Y. Broncard

ended format also looked to have some operational point, considering the number of major stations that were termini involving reversal in inter-city itineraries — Frankfurt, Stuttgart and Munich, for example.

So, in 1973, there appeared the three sleek Class ET403 electric multiple-units, smoothly streamlined four-car articulated units with every axle motored so that maximum axle-loading was only 14.7 tonnes, but with installed power of 5,150hp. They were built by Linke-Hoffmann-Busch and Messerschmitt-Bölkow-Blohm, with electrical equipment by AEG, Brown Boveri and Siemens-Schuckert, and the air-suspension bogies were by MAN. The four cars seated 183 (and incorporated a restaurant and a train secretarial room) in a setting as elegant as that of the railway's locomotive-hauled inter-city stock, but a trifle less roomily, for the units' bodies were fitted with automatic tilting devices and hence were of more constricted cross-section.

The ET403s were based at Munich and went into regular inter-city service over the main line thence to North Germany. But even they were kept to the 100mph (160kmph) limit until the spring of 1977, when the German Federal once again cleared the Munich-Augsburg route for 125mph (200kmph). The following spring the speed ceiling was raised to 125mph (200kmph) over four more stretches — Munich-Augsburg, 38.5 miles (62km); Augsburg-Donauwörth, 26 miles (42km); Hannover-Uelzen, 58 miles (93km); and parts of Hamburg-Bremen, 76 miles (122km). By then, though, the multiple-unit format had been discarded as too inflexible operationally, and the three ET403s were never to give birth to a fleet. The 74 trains retimed at 125mph over these sections were almost entirely locomotive-hauled by Class 103 electrics.

Choice of high-speed equipment, however, was very much a secondary consideration compared with finding the scope to exploit its potential over a considerable distance. Only in the plains of North Germany and in the Upper Rhine Valley are German Federal main lines reasonably aligned for speed. Here and over isolated stretches elsewhere the German Federal was in the 1970s carrying out track and signalling

improvements to enlarge significantly the route mileage passed for 125mph (200kmph) when it launched in the spring of 1978 the first phase of its planned system-wide timetable redraft, with an hourly two-class service of interconnecting Inter-City trains on every trunk route. Even so, the saving in end-to-end transit time forecast over a previously four-hour journey was not much more than 20 minutes — not a startling amount set against the high cost, particularly, of continuous cab signalling for just intermittent 125mph (200kmph) running.

Outside the topographically speed-suited areas the German Federal confronted another limitation. Some of their most curve-harassed routes were so heavily occupied by freight, the average speed of which could not be raised without massive expenditure on more sophisticated freight vehicle braking, that tinkering with curve superelevation would be counter-productive: extra speed without detriment to passenger comfort would only be bought at the cost of aggravated track wear by the freight traffic.

The only practical course was to move for brand-new, well-aligned bypasses of the most constricting trunk route sections — though some of those would be very costly exercises, as we shall see. So, in 1970, the German Federal had presented to its Government a plan for seven new railways, totalling 590 route-miles (950km), which would be laid out for an ultimate top speed of 186mph (300kmph). Additionally, the railway wanted to upgrade and resignal a further 775 miles (1250km) or so of main line for operation at 125mph (200kmph). The Government accepted the plan as part of its developing national transport strategy and the railway was optimistic of opening by 1985 the first four of the new lines — from Hannover over the Mittelgebirge ranges to Gemünden; from Cologne through the hills east of the Rhine Valley to Gross Gerau, on the outskirts of Frankfurt; from Würzburg to Aschaffenburg, opening up a new approach to Frankfurt from the north-south route; and from Mannheim to Stuttgart. The cost of those four lines alone was reckoned to be nearly £3 billions, at 1970 prices, but at the end of the day the German Federal expected them to win inter-city end-to-end transit gains of the order of 1½ hours between Hamburg and Munich, with the 513 miles (825km) between the two cities being covered in 5¾ hours, intermediate stops included, at an average of 89.2mph (143.5kmph) throughout. An hour would be cut from the Cologne-Frankfurt run, bringing the cities within 1¼ hours of each other, and from the Hannover-Frankfurt transit, cutting that to 2¼ hours; and so on.

The Hannover-Würzburg line was started in the summer of 1973, but only for a few tentative miles to the south. The project was not finally endorsed throughout until 1977, when the Mannheim-Stuttgart line at last got the green light. At that date the other two routes in the priority quartet were still short of authorisation and at best only the two schemes actually under way still looked capable of completion by 1985.

Part-cause of the delay was environmental haggling. Though West Germany's *autobahn* builders were carving swathes out of the countryside without much let or hindrance, one community after another rushed to the barricades to keep the far less land-hungry and environmentally destructive railway from their doors.

Left: Scenically a delight, but a severe handicap to economical rail operation: the winding Rhine Valley, one of the speed-restricted trunk route sections to be bypassed in the German Federal's plan for new railways. A southbound TEE, with a Class 103 electric in charge, passes Die Pfalz, the ancient mid-river toll house of the 14th Century, between Koblenz and Bingen. / S. Rickard

123

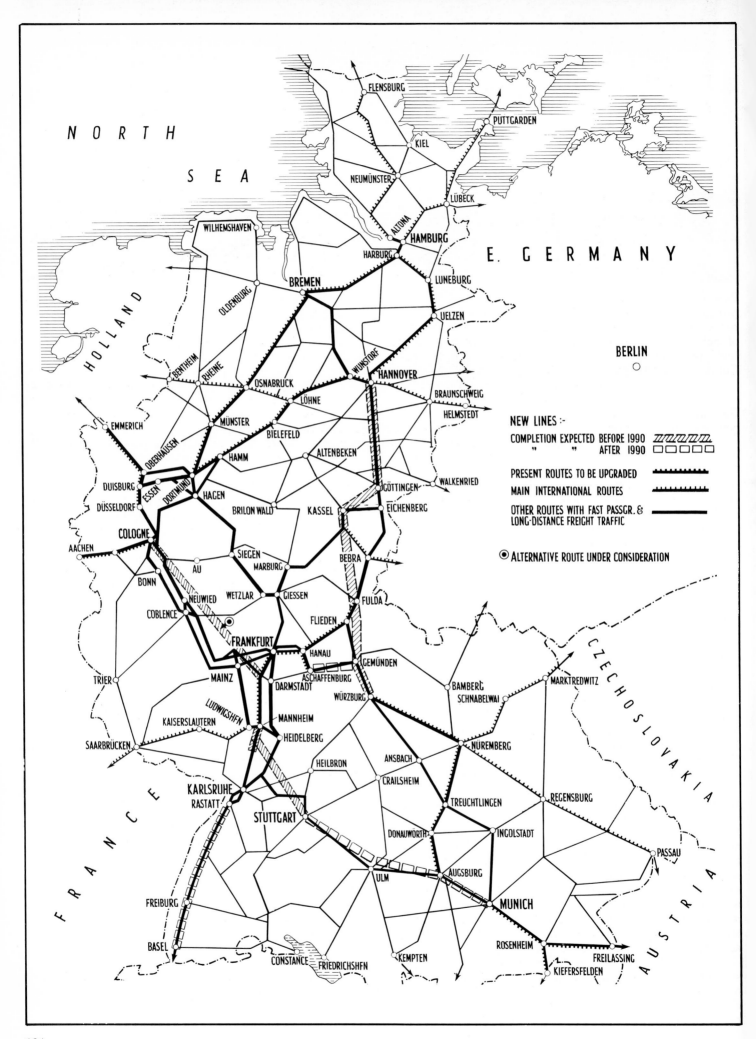

NORTH SEA

E. GERMANY

HOLLAND

FRANCE

CZECHOSLOVAKIA

AUSTRIA

BERLIN
○

NEW LINES :-
COMPLETION EXPECTED BEFORE 1990
    "   "   AFTER 1990

PRESENT ROUTES TO BE UPGRADED
MAIN INTERNATIONAL ROUTES
OTHER ROUTES WITH FAST PASSGR. &
LONG-DISTANCE FREIGHT TRAFFIC

⊚ ALTERNATIVE ROUTE UNDER CONSIDERATION

FLENSBURG
PUTTGARDEN
KIEL
NEUMÜNSTER
LÜBECK
ALTONA
HAMBURG
HARBURG
WILHELMSHAVEN
LUNEBURG
BREMEN
UELZEN
OLDENBURG
WUNSTORF
BENTHEIM
RHEINE
OSNABRUCK
HANNOVER
BRAUNSCHWEIG
LÖHNE
HELMSTEDT
EMMERICH
MÜNSTER
BIELEFELD
ALTENBEKEN
OBERHAUSEN
HAMM
WALKENRIED
DUISBURG
ESSEN
DORTMUND
GÖTTINGEN
DÜSSELDORF
HAGEN
BRILON WALD
KASSEL
EICHENBERG
COLOGNE
AACHEN
SIEGEN
BEBRA
AU
MARBURG
BONN
WETZLAR
GIESSEN
FULDA
NEUWIED
COBLENCE
FLIEDEN
⊚
FRANKFURT
HANAU
GEMÜNDEN
TRIER
MAINZ
ASCHAFFENBURG
DARMSTADT
BAMBERG
MARKTREDWITZ
WÜRZBURG
SCHNABELWAI
LUDWIGSHFN
MANNHEIM
KAISERSLAUTERN
HEIDELBERG
SAARBRÜCKEN
NÜREMBERG
HEILBRON
ANSBACH
KARLSRUHE
CRAILSHEIM
REGENSBURG
RASTATT
TREUCHTLINGEN
STUTTGART
DONAUWÖRTH
INGOLSTADT
PASSAU
FREIBURG
ULM
AUGSBURG
BASEL
MUNICH
CONSTANCE
FRIEDRICHSHFN
KEMPTEN
ROSENHEIM
FREILASSING
KIEFERSFELDEN

Above: *Start of the new Hannover-Würzburg line: an early stage of the project was the 1977 completion of massive flyover on the outskirts of Hannover to keep the heavy freight traffic making for local yards clear of the Inter-City tracks.*
/ Deutsche Bundesbahn

Pettifogging litigation over lines of route was absurdly protracted. Along the path of the Mannheim-Stuttgart route, for instance, seven inhabitants of the little community of Schwetzingen protested the expected noise level of the high-speed trains as intolerable all the way up to the High Court at Karlsruhe. Other little pockets of resistance managed to halve the programmed rate of investment in the new railway. As for the Cologne-Gross Gerau line, the German Federal was eventually compelled to rethink its course virtually from scratch.

More significant factors, however, were the influence of worldwise economic recession and its impact on West Germany's heavy industry, plus the country's heavy investment in its inter-city road network and the benefit of that to road transport's efficiency, particularly as neither road users nor inland water transport, rail's other powerful competitor in West Germany, pay anything like the same share of their track costs as the German Federal. Heavily dependant on bulk minerals for its freight tonnage, the railway lost volume which it could not replace adequately in the still buoyant merchandise freight market because it was unable to match the economy, efficiency and quality of road transport, eagerly exploiting to the full the ever-improving road network on which the West Germans have lavished such huge resources in the past two or three decades.

Throughout the 1970s the cost of the railway to the country escalated frighteningly through a combination of remorselessly rising compensations, supports, grants and deficits — some of it, one must stress, entirely the result of political decision: for instance, the enforced maintenance of local passenger fare scales that are now grossly uneconomic. By 1977 money actually taken over the counter from the German Federal's customers was falling short of the railway's total expenditure by around £4 billions a year.

Two years earlier, in late 1975, the railway directorate and the Federal Government had agreed that the haemorrhage could only be stopped, and must be, by a drastic physical trimming of the system coupled with competitive strengthening of its business core in a thoroughgoing technological modernisation. More important now than a steady increase of passenger train speed was rejuvenation and re-equipment of the whole merchandise freight apparatus, to fit the railway for successful assault on that market with a network of tightly-timed, interconnecting train services. The new railways were now a strictly bread-and-butter component of this new framework.

The new railways were never conceived as purely high-speed passenger lines, but today one hears no talk whatever of a revolutionary passenger role. German Federal officers rhapsodise more over the vast reduction of staff that will result from simplified operation and modern traffic control systems. They accent firmly the mixed traffic purpose of the projects, which of course strengthens the investment case in the context of the railway's sorry financial state. The objective now is to exploit the new and upgraded railways as much for a more efficiently and operationally less costly trunk freight service as for an enhanced passenger service. The capacity of their modern track and signalling is to be maximised by channelling through them the most intensive mix of passenger and freight traffic practicable. And that means 125mph (200kmph) will likely remain the German Federal inter-city speed ceiling until the 1990s. However, although the German Federal seems to be devoting a large part of its investment to cost reduction, especially through automation of administrative functions as well as operational systems, it is not abandoning research into higher speeds. In 1977, for instance electric locomotive No 103.118 was taken up to 155mph (250kmph) well over 100 times in tests of track and vehicle behaviour on the German Federal's specially prepared high-speed trial stretch between Gütersloh and Neubeckum, on the Bielefeld-Hamm line.

Terrain that forced the railway builders of old to take serpentine, heavily graded courses doesn't make life easy for the engineers of today seeking a more speed-conducive path. That stands out from only a cursory study of the engineering involved in one of the more difficult sections of the Hannover-Würzburg line, the 37 miles (59.5km) from the borders of the Hessische and Bavarian Länder, or provinces, into Würzburg, which strikes through the mountainous region of the Mittelgebirge. Even though 38% of this mileage will be in 17 tunnels and 13% of it on bridges or viaducts, some grading as steep as 1 in 80 — the maximum on the existing route — has been found unavoidable. In one tight topographical corner, too, the engineers have had to tighten the otherwise standard curvature radius of 7,000m to 5,300m. The worst stretch of 1 in 80 will extend for no less than 4½ miles (7.3km) continuously, where the line climbs away from its bridging of the Main valley near Gemünden, tunnelling its way through the Mühlberg mountain up to the highest point of the new railway in the midst of Bavaria's nature reserve at Rohrbach. In this area, understandably, the planners were compelled to have above-average care for the environment, which aggravated their problems in coping with the terrain. Speed and efficiency apart, the new Hannover-Würzburg will clearly be a line to travel purely for spectacular experience when it is complete.

8. Italy's New Rome– Florence Railway

Italy was probably the first country in Europe to set about expensive construction of new railways to supersede 19th Century lines that were hopelessly unsuited to the competitive speed market of the 20th Century. As far back as 1913 the Italians had embarked on a new *Direttissima* to shorten the distance between Bologna and Florence and eliminate some appalling gradients of the existing railway over the Apennine Mountains. The First World War interrupted the work but under Mussolini it was pressed to completion in 1934.

A second *Direttissima* was begun after the First World War and finished by the autumn of 1927. This was the coastal route from Rome to Naples. It shortened the run between the two cities from the old inland route's 154.4 miles (248.7km) to 134 miles (215.8km), reduced the maximum altitude to be surmounted by 676ft (206m) and presented trains with a vastly better alignment. As soon as it was commissioned the Rome-Naples tranist time tumbled overnight from 4 hours 25 minutes to 2 hours 50 minutes. By the outbreak of the Second World War electric traction was yielding a fastest Rome-Naples schedule of 1 hour 48 minutes, positing a start-to-stop average of 72.5mph (118.2kmph).

The Bologna-Florence *Direttissima*, part of the Italian State Railways' spinal trunk route from Milan to Rome, was a titanic engineering operation. The old line had heaved itself up a weary succession of severe curves and gradients as sharp as 1 in 45 to a summit 2,021ft (616m) up in the Apennine Mountains at Pracchia. The new line all but halved this climb and markedly flattened the gradients by burrowing the railway under the mountains in the 11.5 mile (18.5km) Apennine Tunnel, then second longest in the world, and 29 other tunnels aggregating 23 miles (37km) in length. The fastest Bologna-Florence time over the old line had been 2 hours 26 minutes; in the final months before the Second World War electric trains were coursing through the mountains to link the two cities in a mere 51 minutes for a start-to-stop average of 70.8mph (114kmph). But there was also the hair-raising prestige run staged with a three-car ETR200 electric multiple-unit for the glory of Il Duce in July 1939 which I have described in Chapter Three.

Pre-war public service speed standards were gradually recovered after 1945, but not significantly improved. For two decades Italian State Railways made inter-city passenger news chiefly for the elegance of their de-luxe Milan-Rome flagship, the electric multiple-unit 'Settebello', or 'Lucky Seven', which took the rails in 1953.

The three seven-car green-and-grey Class ETR300 electric multiple-units built for the 'Settebello' immediately caught the eye with their novel nose-end layout that I mentioned in an earlier chapter: the panoramic passenger .observation

Left: *A sample of the rugged country traversed by the Bologna-Florence* Direttissima *in its passage of the Apennine Mountains.* / Italian State Railways

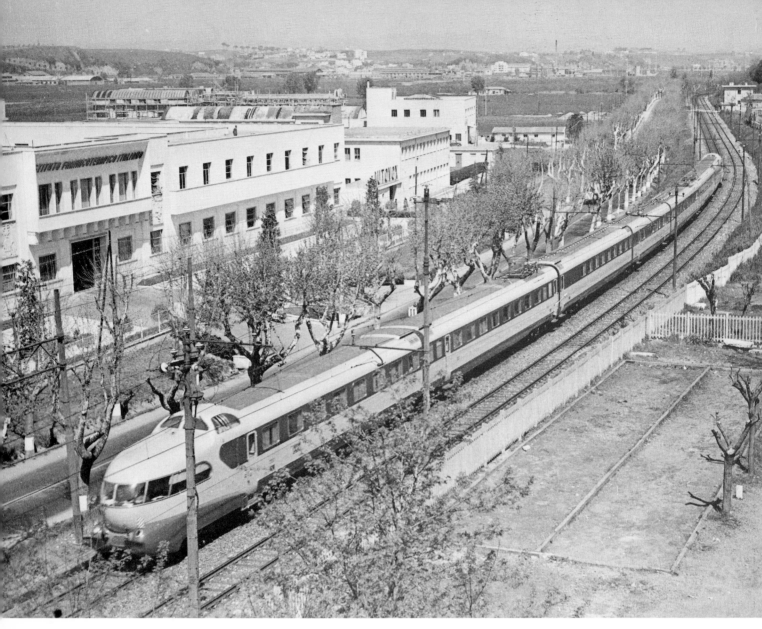

Above: *This shot of an ETR300 'Settebello' train-set on its Rome-Milan run also highlights the curvature typical of so much of the old route until it reaches the Po Valley.* / Italian State Railways

Right: *Front-end of an ETR300 train-set, showing the passengers' observation lounge with the cab protruding above the roof.* / Italian State Railways

Far right: *One of an ETR300's ten-seater lounges.* / Italian State Railways

128

lounge occupying the floor area where one normally expects to find the driving cab, and the driving crew perched in an eyrie of a cab set back from the nose and protruding above the roof like a cockpit. But the inside of the exclusively first-class 'Settebello' was strikingly designed too. The two outer articulated twin-sets that housed the passenger seating were neither orthodox compartment nor orthodox saloon, but laid out entirely in 10-seater lounges. Each room, an aesthetic delight in contemporary Italian decor, sat six passengers on two settees against the lateral walls and four more on loose armchairs in the centre of the floor area. The centre articulated triplet of the set was made up of a baggage room, bookstall and souvenir shop (since replaced by extra seating), radio and telephone office, handsome restaurant and bar, and kitchen. A four-coach variant of the design, the ETR250, appeared in 1960 and four of these were built.

The ETR300s were built with 100mph (160kmph) capability, but at first they had scant opportunity to exploit it. For the southern section of the Rome-Milan trunk route pursued such a sinuous course through the hills north of the country that in the first 90 miles or so (145km) speed was nowhere permitted to exceed 110kmph (68mph). Thereafter, though the alignment was more friendly, signal spacing and braking power fixed the ceiling at 87.5mph (140kmph) except over tracts of the broad Po valley beyond Bologna, where the 'Settebello' could briefly kick up its heels. At first, therefore, its end-to-end Rome-Milan timing was six hours for the 393.5 miles (633km) inclusive of intermediate stops at Florence (involving reversal), Bologna and Piacenza.

By 1962 the Italian State Railways, or FS, knew they had to overcome the handicaps imposed by nature if their long-haul passenger traffic (a bigger component of their revenue than of most Western European railways) was to withstand air and road competition. A ten-year plan tabled that year set sights on average speeds of over 90mph (150kmph) as essential to hold off air transport over the longer runs, up to about 625 miles (1,000km). As far as possible, it submitted, that standard should be sought without vastly expensive modification of the infrastructure, but rather by an integrated development of track, traction, rolling stock, braking, signalling and train control. Regular and extensive

125mph (200kmph) operation on the existing tracks was the immediate objective; for the longer term, though, the target must be a speed ceiling of 155mph (250kmph).

Most conspicuous material evidence of the railways' intentions in the early 1960s was the widespread main-line application of coded track circuitry to prepare the ground for a continuous cab signalling system. From the end of the 1960s several hundred locomotives and multiple-units were equipped with cab apparatus and inductive pick-ups. Because of its expense, the full system has so far been confined to the key FS main lines where alignments are conducive to higher-speed working. For less heavily-trafficked or physically speed-limited routes the FS developed concurrently an intermittent cab signalling system employing track-mounted transponders. This was applied experimentally to parts of the Brenner main line in 1969 and has since been installed throughout that route from Verona to the Austrian frontier. In the Italian system the transponders are more sophisticated than the elementary single-message transponders which British Rail have economically adopted for the Advanced Passenger Train route, as described in an earlier chapter. The Italian appliance provides for a variable coding that defines the signal aspect reflected back when the transponder's inert circuitry is activated by apparatus on a passing traction unit.

For the 100mph (160kmph) operation envisaged over most suitably aligned sections as continuous cab signalling became operational there was no need to elaborate the conventional signalling. On reasonably straight and level track the orthodox warning and stop aspects were reckoned adequate to brake a train from top speed to a stand within two sections of standard 1350m signal spacing. But over some 50 miles (80km) of the Rome-Naples *Direttissima* the speed limit was to be raised a notch to 112mph (180kmph) and here earlier warning of adverse signals was essential. Over these higher-speed stretches the track-circuitry was arranged to transmit an additional coded warning 1,350m ahead of a signal at caution; that set up a milk-white light on the driving desk display, whereat the driver must start braking if he was making more than 100mph (160kmph), or

emergency braking would be automatically applied. A further step-up in speed to 125mph (200kmph), however, was felt likely to require alteration of signal spacing.

In special tests the FS was getting the feel of the higher speed ranges during the 1960s. Favoured test vehicle was usually the pleasingly-styled lightweight inter-city electric multiple-unit that was premiered in 1961. These 60 tonne, 87ft 8in (26.7m)-long motor coaches, classified ALe601, had all axles powered for a total continuous output of 1,000hp. First-class only, they were designed to associate with a choice of six different trailer types — the Le601 first-class, the Le640 first and second-class composite, the Le680 or Le700 second-class, the Le480 kitchen-restaurant and the Le360 kitchen-restaurant-bar. The whole compatible fleet was air-conditioned and each vehicle was cabbed at each end, trailers as well as power cars, for supreme operational flexibility. Not only could the power component of a multiple-unit be varied at will to suit the demands of a specific service, but the possible permutations of train format were limitless; there was nothing to stop a set being fronted by a kitchen to suit some arcane operational requirement.

As early as 1962 one of the first batches of Ale601 power cars was being worked up to 140mph (225kmph) in pantograph tests near Grosseto, on the Rome-Genoa main line. In 1968-70 five of the series were fitted up with rheostatic braking and had their gearing modified and power stepped up to 1,420hp to extend their practicable speed range. It was the first pair of this quintet to be altered, Nos ALe601.008 and 010, which at the end of 1968 were opened up to a maximum of 155mph (250kmph) under the reinforced catenary of the Rome-Naples line. For eight continuous minutes the two railcars were held at 150mph (241kmph) or better. In 1970 21 new ALe601s were delivered with the same characteristics as the rebuilds and these units were handed the crown of Italy's fastest daily services, two *rapidi* each way between Rome and Naples via the *Direttissima* that were timed to cover the 130.5 miles (210km) in 1½ hours non-stop at an average of 87mph (140kmph). The schedules were eased out by five minutes later in the decade, however.

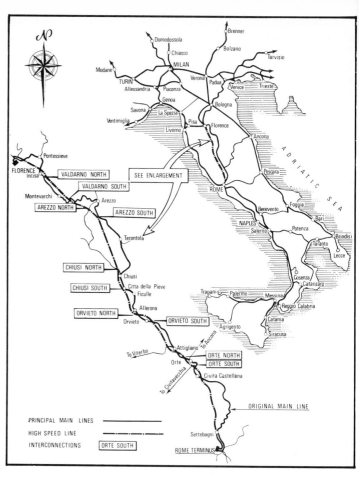

Right: *An Ale 601 electric motor coach; one of these has been tested up to a maximum of 155mph (250kmph).* / Italian State Railways

Below: *An electric multiple-unit train-set forming the 'Peloritano' from Rome to Sicily via the Messina Ferry, and including ALe 601s, heads across the Mingardo viaduct on its way from Battipaglia to Reggio Calabria.* / Italian State Railways

Although the FS was steadily adding 125mph (200kmph)-capability locomotives and multiple-units to its traction fleet in the 1970s, the ceiling over most of the system was held at 93mph (150kmph). Off the Rome-Naples *Direttissima* the only units with a dispensation to run at 100mph (160kmph), over stretches of the Bologna-Milan main line, were the Class ETR300 electric multiple-units. Apart from refurbishing to fit them for the prospective 125mph (200kmph) ceiling, the ETR300s had been uniquely equipped in 1970 with automatic braking programmers to work in conjunction with the coded track circuitry and continuous cab signalling.

Like the devices on the German Federal Class 103 electric locomotives, the Italian programmer comes into play as soon as a warning code is picked up inductively from the track circuitry. From then on it is continuously comparing the train's distance from the danger signal ahead and its speed with a predetermined deceleration curve. At the same time the apparatus takes full automatic control of the braking, so long as it is still detecting warning codes. The initial warning will be succeeded at the start of the next track circuit section by a new code instructing either that deceleration must continue to a full stop, or that the following signal has to be passed at restricted speed. The apparatus will react to the first of these two codes by braking down to 25mph (40kmph), to the second by decelerating only to 40mph (65kmph), after which control of the train will be entirely with the driver. The final stages of deceleration are left to the driver's discretion because — as the Japanese too have concluded — provision for automatic judgement of the precise point along a station platform or in advance of a signal at which to halt the train is intolerably expensive. The cost of the automatic braking programmers as fitted to the ETR300s so daunted the FS that their application to other traction units was deferred until regular 125mph (200kmph) working became a practical possibility.

The crippling effect on end-to-end train speed of central Italy's otherwise entrancingly mountainous terrain was patent when the 'Settebello' was accelerated to a 5¾ hour Rome-Milan timing following the revamping of the ETR300s. Across the broad Po Valley the southbound 'Settebello' timing was screwed up to 1 hour 38 minutes for the 135.5 miles (218m) from Milan to Bologna, average 83mph (133.5kmph), while northbound, when a Piacenza stop was inserted in the itinerary, the 91.2 miles (146.7km) from Bologna to that point were booked in 65 minutes for an average of 84.2mph (135.5kmph). But in sharp contrast the curvature and gradients prevented any better start-to-stop average than 63.7mph (102.5kmph) over the 196.3 miles (316km) from Florence to Rome.

The main line from Milan through Florence to Rome, and the continuation to Naples and Reggio Calabria for the ferry crossing of the Messina Strait, to Sicily, is the Italian State Railways' spinal chord in every sense, for it bears nearly a third of the system's entire traffic. From the 1950s onward the FS had already laid out huge sums to increase its capacity. Apart from comprehensive resignalling and track-circuiting on modern principles, and relaying with heavy continuous welded rail, the whole distance from Battipaglia, south of Naples and Salerno, to the Straits of Messina was double-tracked. Millions of pounds, too, had been spent on eliminating some of the countless level-crossings between Milan and Florence and between Rome and Naples. On the Rome-Florence core, however, no half-measure would close the glaring gap in speed potential between the outer and central sections of the Milan-Naples route. The incessant curvature and gradients inherited from the original builders must be bypassed. Thus, in 1969, with the financial support of a consortium of Italian industry in the shape of ten-year low-interest loans, the FS launched construction of its third major *Direttissima* from Rome to Florence.

Although the new infrastructure was to be expensively engineered throughout for maximum speeds of 155mph (250kmph), even 186mph (300kmph), the highest rates were becoming a longer-term dream by the month. Before the 1970s were very old, FS executives were stressing that they were concerned primarily to enlarge track capacity by creating, in conjunction with the old route, a four-track main line from Rome to Florence. At the peak of the summer holiday season parts of that inter-city stretch were groaning under more than 100 trains each way daily and, given the mixed character of the traffic, strangulation was threatening. Any rise of maximum speed ceiling would therefore be limited to the possibilities created by a segregation of traffic between old and new lines in such a way as to narrow each route's speed band as straitly as possible.

The Rome-Florence *Direttissima* was, in fact, a component of planned four-tracking the whole way from Milan to Salerno, south of Naples, either by widening or improving existing infrastructure or by building new. By the late 1970s the FS had already quadrupled from Milan to Piacenza and the short distance from Prato into Florence, and had drafted schemes to enlarge the intervening Piacenza-Prato section that would include a stretch aligned for really high-speed between Piacenza and Bologna. The original inland Rome-Naples route had been modernised and electrified. And from Caserta, on this last route, an

Left: *One of the remarkable bi-directional flying and burrowing junctions between the old Rome-Florence route and the new* Direttissima; *this one is at Orte North.*
/ Italian State Railways

alternative electrified route of modern standards to the south was being created by upgrading more inland byways and constructing a new link with the existing route in the Salerno area; this section would bypass the centre of Naples.

The original time-scale issued for completion of the Rome-Florence *Direttissima* was far too rosily optimistic. It was euphorically predicted that the whole line would be in service by 1974. That, however, allowed neither for post-oil crisis financial stringency, nor for severe geological problems in some areas. Besides these uncovenanted difficulties, the line of route aroused fierce controversy in some places, above all Florence.

It was early 1977 before even a section of the new line was ready for use — and even that not in its entirety — from Rome to Citta della Pieve, between Orvieto and Chiusi. I rode the special train that ceremonially inaugurated this stretch on 24 February that year.

The *Direttissima* diverges from the old route 10 miles (16.9km) out from Rome Termini station at Settibagni. Almost immediately one got the measure of the engineering involved in hewing out of the unhelpful terrain a railway with curvature of minimum 3,000m (9,840ft) radius and a ruling gradient of 1 in 125 (relaxed to 1 in 330 in some tunnels). In the 75.8 miles of route between Settibagni and Citta della Pieve 34% of the distance is in tunnel, 15% elevated on bridges of viaducts and 49% on embankment or in cutting. On this stretch alone the railway threads 17 tunnels, topped in length by Orte (5.8 miles or 9.3km) and by that under Monte Sorate, between Settebagni and Gallese (3.5 miles or 5.7km). Underestimated geological resistance to tunnelling had disastrously compromised the Orte operation — and swamped its budgeted costs — so that the inaugural train had to detour through Orte town on the old line. After some heady pace over the straight and true alignment of the first stage of new railway beyond Sittibagni, it was an abrupt translation to a 19th Century railway world as the suddenly hobbled train, flanges squealing, bent gracefully this way and that on the seemingly relentless curvature. One could well understand the FS wanting a new railway at almost any price.

Orte, junction for the line from Rome over the Apennine Mountains to Ancona, is one of the eight points of interconnection between the new and old routes. All are bi-directional, an elegant tracery of burrowing and flying junctions that minimises conflict between different streams of traffic and nowhere restricts a diverging train to a lower speed than 62mph (100kmph).

The next junction to the north is Orvieto, before which town the new railway sweeps over the Paglia River on a civil engineering showpiece, the 3.3 mile (5.4km) Allerona Viaduct, one of the longest in the world to date. From Orvieto to Chiusi the new route generally parallels the old, but the new line burrows under Chiusi town to strike a route well clear of the old to Arezzo, where it avoids the town. That detour was one of the major factors delaying completion of the route's central sector. Arezzo howled that commercial extinction loomed if it were relegated to service by second-division trains on the old line and took weary months to mollify. More extensive tunnelling (the San Donato alone is 6.8 miles or 11km long) was involved in the approach to Florence, which was another fiercely argued issue. Conservationists protested that the railway must be brought into the city underground to avoid pollution and desecration of Florence's precious buildings and treasures, but were ultimately defeated on grounds of exorbitant cost.

Besides its vastly superior alignment for speed, the Rome-Florence *Direttissima* shortens the route-mileage between the two cities from 195.1 miles (313.9km) to 157.8 miles (253.9km). The proclaimed objective upon completion had been a Rome-Florence transit time of 1½ hours, involving a non-stop average speed of 105mph (169kmph), but fulfilment of this before the late 1980s at the earliest looks an increasingly sanguine hope in the fading 1970s. All else apart, the whole of the *Direttissima* is not expected, as I write, to be ready for traffic before 1982; and for the present 112mph (180kmph) is the maximum permitted on the section in traffic. With the commissioning of the Settibagni-Citta della Pieve stretch the FS ventured only a modest acceleration of the 'Settebello' that cut its Milan-Rome time to 5 hours 35 minutes inclusive of Bologna and Florence stops; but as the Italian press scathingly remarked, up to 1970 *superrapidi* were publicly timed to link Milan and Rome non-stop in a best time of 5½ hours, the old line's severe handicaps notwithstanding.

From what was said at the press conference that prefaced inauguration of the Settibagni-Citta della Pieve section one gained the impression that the Italians were more determined than ever to treat the *Direttissima* as essentially a gain of sorely needed track capacity rather than an encouragement to much higher speed, despite the vast sums spent to create a very high speed infrastructure. There was reiterated emphasis on the flexibility now placed at the operators' disposal, particularly as old and new routes had been brought under a single operational control, and the ease with which freight as well as passenger trains could be switched from one route to another through the eight interconnections.

One drawback to a substantial rise in the speed ceiling we have encountered in earlier chapters — the limitations of the traction current supply apparatus. Surprisingly to my mind,

Top left: *The central section of the 5,878yd (5,357m)-long Paglia River viaduct north of Orvieto on the Rome-Florence* Direttissima. / Italian State Railways

Top: *A 5,600hp Class E444 electric locomotive and a train of the Italian State Railways' latest first-class inter-city* rapido *stock en route from Naples to Rome.* / Italian State Railways

Above: *Fiat's tilt-body test car, the Y.0160, on tangent track and demonstrating its suspension round a curve.* / Italian State Railways

considering their thought for the long-term speed horizon in engineering the infrastructure, the Italians have not installed on the *Direttissima* a current feeder system that could cope with the simultaneous demands of two or three trains hitting top speed with the loads customary on many of the route's expresses. As it is, operation in excess of 125mph (200kmph) would be impracticable unless formations were confined to a single locomotive and eight coaches, whereas even in the off-peak seasons one or two trains making up to 15 coaches or more characterise everyday working on the Rome-Florence route. Double-heading is no solution: that merely aggravates the current supply overload problem. Either the timetable must be drastically re-written, dividing the heaviest trains, or really high speed can only be bought, it would seem, at the cost of sub-optimum *Direttissima* productivity by restricting its use to lightly-loaded fliers in the peak traffic periods. Another possible solution is a doubling of the *Direttissima's* traction current voltage from

3,000 to 6,000V dc, which the FS is seriously considering, though a tricky problem or two is envisaged in conversion of the traction units to dual-voltage operation; however, preliminary experiments have been conducted with a shunting locomotive.

At the time of writing, moreover, the FS has only some 150 electric locomotives and multiple-units with 125mph (200kmph) capability. Spearheading this fleet are the 80 tonne, 5,600hp Class E444 electric locomotives introduced in 1967 and skittishly brand-named *Tartaruga*, or 'Tortoise' — which is no enthusiast's laboured whimsy, incidentally: with elephantine humour the FS has actually painted a small tortoise on the bodyside of every E444. These days the predominant image of a front-rank, first-class-only Italian *rapido* is much less a grey-green multiple-unit formation than it was a decade ago, much more an E444 fronting a homogenous rake of the stately red-lined cream and blue-grey luxury *Gran Conforts* coaches which the FS has standardised for its key internal services from the Fiat creation for Italy's locomotive-hauled TEE services.

Prospective power unit for the forecast 1½ hour timing between Rome and Florence is a stretched version of the E444, a six-axle, 8,500hp design denominated E666. As I write, though, the world has still to greet a prototype both of this and of the projected ALe541 electric multiple-unit motorcoach with 155mph (250kmph) potential.

Pending emergence of the ALe541s, Italy's one train-set officially credited with an operational maximum speed of 155mph (250kmph) is an experimental four-car electric multiple-unit with tilting coach bodies built by Fiat in 1975. In 1972 Fiat constructed a single test vehicle, designated the Y.0160, as a private venture and it was the encouraging results of two years' evaluation of this car on the FS that prompted production of a full-scale passenger unit. A similar four-car set was built simultaneously for exhaustive trials by the Spanish National Railways, RENFE.

Body-tilting apart, these Fiat train-sets display a highly unusual method of equalising axle-loading in an electric multiple-unit: the two 400hp traction motors on each of the four cars are mounted under the carbody frame, each driving one axle of their adjacent bogie through a cardan shaft. The bodies are built of light alloy and the total weight of the unit is 156 tonnes, so that it has a very healthy power/weight ratio of 20.5hp/tonne, well above the figure essential to maintain 155mph (250kmph) on straight and level track. Braking is primarily rheostatic, with air-operated discs in support for final deceleration to a stand or supplementary force in an emergency, when electromagnetic track brakes can also be brought into play. The current-collecting pantographs are mounted on a structure built up from the bogie bolster so that they do not tilt with the coach body. The tilting apparatus is reasonably simple; tilting is actuated by hydraulic servo-motors under the combined control of accelerometers and gyroscopes, the former to measure constantly the lateral forces to which a car is being subjected, the latter the changing superelevation of the track, so as to ensure the accelerometers do not spuriously initiate a tilt as a result of some track irregularity.

The *Pendolino*, as the Italians dub the tilt-body unit, went into public service on the Apennine Mountain route from Rome to Ancona in the spring of 1976. On that line, of course, it has no scope whatever to exploit its maximum speed potential, but even within the normal speed ceiling of the route the *Pendolino's* ability to curve 25% faster than orthodox stock without discomforting its passengers enabled an immediate 45 minute cut in the end-to-end timing for the 185.5 miles (298.5km). That, given the hostile characteristics of so much Italian main-line alignment, is obviously the tilt-body's *métier* on the FS rather than service of extreme speed.

9. The Tide Turns in North America

Howard Hosmer may be no name to conjure with outside North America, but it has a niche in US railroad lore. Hosmer was the Interstate Commerce Commission functionary who in 1958 scandalised the railroad buffs with a public prediction that within a decade the rail passenger coach would 'take its place in the transportation museum along with the stagecoach and the steam locomotive.'

In the event it did come dangerously near to kinship with the dodo. Immediately after the Second World War, North American railroads had enjoyed a deceptive boom in their passenger business. That encouraged them to spend big on still more sumptuous and still more extravagantly staffed passenger equipment. But very quickly the airlines got a grip on the medium- and long-haul market, which with the onset of jetliners quickly expanded to a 75% domination. Long-distance road coaches were in there battling, too, but they were puny competitors by comparison. Over the shorter hauls, of course, it was express highway development, an even more rapid growth of automobile ownership and cheap gasoline that haemorrhaged the railroads' traffic.

Through the 1950s and 1960s the timetables were progressively thinned of the great inter-city trains as managements gloomily totted up the red-ink difference between dwindling revenues and huge running costs that were escalating rather than abating. Some railroads were opting out of the passenger business altogether. Others, principally in the East, vainly sought the answer in an assortment of unconventional lightweight trains, imported Spanish Talgos amongst them; but the customers promptly showed with their feet what they thought of single-axle riding and cramped, plasticised coach interiors compared with the stateliness and solidity of orthodox US passenger equipment. By the end of the 1960s nationwide timetables that had offered upwards of 15,000 passenger trains daily in the 1930s were down to a limp listing of under 500; and rail's share of the US passenger market had collapsed to a miserable 7.2%.

The first glimmer of hope was the city of Philadelphia's unprecedented 1958 undertaking to subsidise the improvement of local railroads' commuter services as a more economic proposition than yielding yet more highway expenditure to automobiles crowding the city's approaches. From that germ was to flower the Federal Government's Urban Mass Transit Act of 1965 and the subsequent Federal aid for approved public transport development in the conurbations.

But at the same time lobbyists were mounting ever stronger pressure for action to stave off genocide of the inter-city passenger train. Most respected of the voices crying halt was that of the Democratic Senator for Rhode Island, Claiborne Pell, who had been devoting considerable time and energy to what he termed from the Greek word for a large city the 'megalopolis' problem. Focus of Pell's attention was the increasingly crowded communication lanes, in the air as much as on the ground, in the so-called North-East Corridor of teeming cities that runs from Boston through New York, Philadelphia and Baltimore to Washington: but he was also concerned with 21 other corridors linking large cities 200-400 miles (320-640km) apart that he could define around the country. He wanted the now sadly decaying passenger railways in these corridors refurbished for 100mph (160kmph) trains.

Pell's work was the inspiration of the High Speed Ground Transportation Act signed by President Johnson at the end

Below: One of the abortive lightweight essays of the 1950s, the 'Train X' that captivated Robert R. Young and was built by Pullman-Standard. This is New Haven's push-pull version, with a locomotive at each end, that ran between New York and Boston as the 'Dan'l Webster'. / Cecil J. Allen collection

of September 1965. The value of the Act was the principle of Federal support for rail revival that it established rather than its munificence. In hard cash it offered only $90 millions towards refurbishing the North-East Corridor trunk route — a paltry figure set against the huge Federal investment in air and road facilities: what's more, the operating Pennsylvania Railroad was bidden to hand over to the Federal coffers any profits attributable to the Government share of the improved service.

Three years earlier, shortly before Johnson's advisers had recommended he take revival of tracked transport seriously and set up an Office of High Speed Ground Transportation, the Pennsylvania Railroad had embarked on an exhaustive study of the economics and practicalities of upgrading its sector of the North-East Corridor, the stretch from New York to Washington. Its findings were complete by the passage of the Johnson administration's Act. They were negotiated with Washington and the outcome, in April 1966, was agreement to a Federally-sponsored two-year demonstration project to assess public reaction to an intensive high-speed New York-Washington high-speed passenger service with new equipment, improved passenger facilities both on the ground and on the move, and the backing of market-oriented fares. At the same time a second demonstration project was agreed on the New York-Boston main line of the New York, New Haven & Hartford RR: this was to employ the United Aircraft Turbotrain that had taken the fancy of Canadian National, of which more anon. Before long both projects were to come within the same operating orbit following the New Haven's curtain-raiser to the general financial collapse of major railroads in the North-East. By the time the New York-Washington project came to fruition the whole North-East Corridor route was under the suzerainty of the shortlived Penn-Central conglomerate.

There was not too much to complain of in the existing speed-compatibility of the New York-Washington main line. Four-tracked for most of its 226.1 mile (364km) length, it was straight or curved no more seriously than to 1,870yds (1,700m) radius for 174 miles (280km) of the 180 miles (290km) of route lying outside the major metropolitan areas. Computer calculations suggested that with due allowance

for permanent speed restrictions, modern rolling stock working off the existing 11kV ac overhead current supply could cover the New York-Washington distance non-stop in a minute or two over 2½ hours given a maximum speed limit of 120mph (193kmph). Making the likely six intermediate stops, that suggested the contemporary fastest schedule of 3 hours 35 minutes by the 'Afternoon Congressional' could be cut to under three hours.

The Pennsylvania main line was already equipped for intermittent cab signalling, which was considered adaptable to safe operation at up to 125mph (200kmph). Another operational feature of the route for much of its distance was bi-directional signalling in association with frequent crossovers, to give the operators a great deal of scope to loop slow-moving trains and allow faster services to overtake: these facilities were now increased. The track was comprehensively relaid with continuously welded rail and new motorists' railhead stations were set up athwart important roadways on the outskirts of New York and Washington, at Metropark and Beltway respectively (Metropark, however, has never been a regular call of inter-city trains, only of commuter services).

Pending delivery of new train-sets the Pennsylvania decided to exploit the completed trackwork for a yard or two more pace from its existing equipment. Some of the beloved 4,620hp GG1 electric locomotives were regeared for a maximum of 100mph (160kmph) — years back, in its development stage, a GG1 had been pushed up to 115mph (185kmph) in tests — and conventional coaches refined for the same speed. About 15 minutes were cut from New York-Washington schedules and for the first time the route was graced with some schedules timed at over 80mph (130kmph) start to stop, up to a high point of 85.5mph (137.6kmph) between Baltimore and Wilmington, 68.4 miles (110km) in 48 minutes. But the venerable GG1s did not take to this 1968 rejuvenation, nor did the old-fashioned Pennsy catenary.

Below: *The North-East Corridor in Pennsylvania days: a GG-1 electric crosses the Delaware at Trenton, NJ, with the New York-Florida 'Silver Meteor'.* / W. R. Osborne

After a succession of breakdowns, chiefly the result of flashovers, the accelerated schedules were discreetly withdrawn.

Worse woes were brewing in the high-speed train sets to come, however. Trouble had been virtually guaranteed from the start by the Federal Government's insistence on design by committee — a grouping of Pennsylvania men, representatives of the Office of High Speed Ground Transportation and consulting engineers. Then, with no recent native experience of designing high-performance electrified railroad equipment, the committee unwisely essayed an overnight leap ahead to a concept which hopefully would look the Japanese Shinkansen technology proudly in the face. Far too little of the resultant Metroliners' components had been put through the essential preliminary mill of practical evaluation in the tough railroad environment. Above all, it was soon obvious that the Metroliners had been pointlessly over-designed; such infrastructure improvements as the budget would cover were insufficient to accommodate the Metroliners' maximum performance, even if that had been available troublefree.

By 1965, when the design committee was appointed, the whole railway world was genuflecting towards Tokyo and Osaka, and the New Tokaido line model — which a Pennsy delegation had studied at first-hand — must have strongly influenced the choice of multiple-unit format for the Metroliners. Another plus for the concept was that US law allowed a multiple-unit to be single-manned, but not a locomotive-hauled train. To spread the bulk of the electric traction equipment and allow its underfloor mounting to maximum extent, each car would be motored; and each would have a driving cab, for maximum operational flexibility in train make-up.

The performance specification set for the Metroliner design was staggering. The initial acceleration rate demanded was 1mph/sec (1.6kmph/sec), to hustle a train up to 125mph (200kmph) in two minutes or less and to 150mph (240kmph) in three minutes or less on straight and level track; maximum speed capability was to be 160mph (257kmph) and a train should be able to maintain 150mph (240kmph) up a 1 in 100 gradient. Dynamic braking was

required which, with electro-pneumatic disc braking below 70mph (113kmph), would bring a train from 160mph (257kmph) down to rest within 2,580yds (2,360m). To cope with that specification every axle of each 85ft (25.9m) Metroliner coach was fitted with a 300hp (continuous rating) traction motor, capable of a one-hour output of 640hp at 100mph (160kmph), so that every car in a train would have a short-term punch of 2,560hp. Such installed power had never before been imagined for a US traction unit of some 75 tonnes all-up weight. Suspension was by a combination of coil and air springs.

One complex component that was to figure conspicuously in the protracted teething troubles of the 'Metroliners' was the inter-car coupler. To allow instantaneous coupling and uncoupling cars by remote control from a motorman's cab, the flat-face, hook-type tight-lock couplers at each vehicle end had built into it no fewer than 126 electrical contacts plus three air lines, covering a wide range of controls and communications from the door-operating mechanisms and power control lines to the public address and crew communication systems.

When he signed the High Speed Ground Transportation Act in 1965 President Johnson had gaily forecast the debut of 125mph (200kmph) trains within about a year. At the end of that year the target date receded to October 1967. But came the fall of 1968 and there was still no Metroliner in public use. As a Republican Senator put it scathingly to the Transportation Secretary, the North-East Corridor still had 'nothing to show but a fleet of cars that won't run and a flock of potential passengers who no longer take the project seriously.'

Since the original two-year demonstration project contract had legally expired in March 1968 without a revenue-earning passenger being carried, a joint Government-railroad-supplier task force had been deputed to determine the reasons the failure-plagued Metroliners were not fit to begin public service. Most serious of the troubles were failures of the traction control and braking systems — in fact, neither Government nor railroad would accept delivery of cars with the original Westinghouse dynamic braking, on the grounds that it fell short of performance specification. There was

Above left: *In Penn-Central livery a 'Metroliner' hums down the North-East Corridor.*

Above: *'The ultimate in luxury for ground travel' claimed Penn-Central when they issued this publicity photo of the Pullman-equivalent, revolving-armchair Metroclub accommodation in a Metroliner.*

some unedifying infighting amongst the protagonists, too: for instance, when Metroliner coachbuilders Budd blamed the start-up delays on allegedly unsatisfactory traction motors and control gear by the firms who shared this equipment contract, General Electric and Westinghouse, the latter promptly slammed the ball back into the Budd court with a counter-charge that it had been contracted to design for cars over 20% lighter than Budd had managed to build.

The tripartite task force took refuge in a blanket defence that the project managements had been 'overly optimistic with respect to the planning and scheduling requirements of a project of this magnitude and complexity.' But, it consoled, the major problems remaining of electronic component fallibility, wheel overheating under the airbrakes, pantograph bounce at speed and poor riding would soon be unravelled and the trains would be rolling by end-1968.

In the event they started creeping into service early in 1969 as the GE-equipped cars were gradually passed fit for service. In January a six-car formation began with a single New York-Washington return journey timed in a minute under three hours for six stops en route. A second followed in February and a third in April, this last on something like the original schedule prospectus: New York-Washington each way in 2½ hours non-stop, average 89.8mph (144.5kmph) for the 224.6 miles (361.4km). And in March, on private test, a Metroliner was coaxed up to 165mph (265.5kmph) between Trenton and New Brunswick, NJ, over a stretch of now Penn-Central main line (the merger of Pennsylvania and New York Central had been consummated just before the

Metroliners' long-delayed debut) which had had its current supply arrangements specially stepped up. But all this was still a far cry from the hourly New York-Washington high-speed service billed in the demonstration project, which was not yet deemed to have begun. Though the GE-equipped cars were trickling into service, no one was then prepared to put a date on admission of the Westinghouse-equipped vehicles to complete the 61 car fleet. A Senate committee censured the Department of Transportation for failure to control the project effectively: despite the lateness of the hour and the loss of face that might be suffered, the Department was urged to take counsel from overseas railroad managements that plainly knew better what they were doing in the high speed rail field.

But such service as they had in 1969 the public quickly took to. Taking their cue from Washington luminaries like Senator Edward Kennedy and wife Joan, enough people forsook Eastern Airlines New York-Washington shuttle to build a load factor of 75% or thereabout in 1969. The prefabricated catering of the snack cars serving coach-class passengers and of the Metroclubcar Pullman equivalents miffed some with nostalgic yearning for the expansive (and as a rule catastrophically uneconomic) dining car menus of yore, but most were appreciative of the seating comfort. And for the first time in years Americans were running on rails at 100mph (160kmph) and more. Generally top speed was in the region of 115mph (185kmph), but although the Metroliners' governors were supposed to cut off at 125mph (200kmph), some claimed they had touched as much as 140mph (225kmph). Incredibly, the driving cab was left open house to passengers as well as curious train staff at this speed. Wrote one traveller: 'I simply joined the troupe, walked through the sliding door and watched over the engineer's shoulder. What is the rationale? Even in streetcar days you weren't supposed to talk to the motorman. I think I'd like to ride up there with the pilot next time I'm aboard a 727!'

By 1971 the availability of cars permitted a seven-train service each way daily and the Department of Transportation was prepared to concede that the demonstration had officially started. Requirement to serve the Capital Beltway automobile railhead on the outskirts of Washington and griping from Baltimore and Philadelphia had by now compelled abandonment of the New York-Washington non-stop run. All northbound Metroliners were on the five-stop, 2 hours 59 minutes schedule and the best southbound timing was 2 hours 50 minutes, but the intermediate running called for some of the fastest point-to-point timings in the world at that time. All seven trains had to cover the 68.4 miles (110km) from Baltimore to Wilmington in 43 minutes, average 95.4mph (153.5kmph) and five the same distance in the reverse direction in a minute more, average 93.3mph (150kmph).

Meanwhile, what of the other leg of the North-East Corridor demonstration project, from New York to Boston? To sketch the background there, steps in time must be retraced to developments across the 49th Parallel in Canada.

In the 1950s and 1960s Canadian attitudes to inter-city passenger traffic had been marked by a remarkable reversal of roles as between the country's two major systems. In the middle 1950s the private-enterprise Canadian Pacific, to judge by the level of its equipment investment, seemed to have some faith in the future of the business, whereas the Federal Government-owned Canadian National was echoing US pessimism that the erosion of passengers by road and air could never be stemmed. The CN view was back in 1961 by the report of a Government-ordered Royal Commission on Transportation, known as the McPherson Commission after its chairman, which expressed strong fears that freight shippers were being penalised with overloaded rates to offset

passenger traffic losses. It recommended subsidisation of lossmaking services deemed essential to the public good, but at a steadily reducing level that would eventually slim Canada's rail passenger services down to an indispensable minimum. Between 1960 and 1963 CN did in fact trim its annual passenger train mileage and its passenger car fleet by around a quarter.

Then, suddenly, CN and CP exchanged pulpits. It was CP's chairman, Norman Crump, who in 1965 was bluntly declaring that he saw no future in the passenger business, while CN President Donald Gordon was saluting the passenger as 'the most precious and perishable commodity the railways carry.' CN passenger management had been reorganised and was eagerly applying itself to a new market-oriented strategy.

Visually, the changed CN attitude was dramatised by a new corporate identity styling of every CN service under a distinctive CN logo — the 'rampant tapeworm' to traditionalists, but an international prizewinner among the cognoscenti. Locomotives and cars were decked out in new livery and staff in new uniforms; propaganda material revitalised; customer relations training given high priority. Some 700 inter-city coaches were given an interior revamp and 174 high-quality long-haul cars, such as ex-Milwaukee 'Hiawatha' Super-Domes, bought or leased from US railroads that had discarded them in the contraction of passenger service. And passenger fares were re-written in a 'Red-White-and-Blue' plan that heavily discounted off-peak rates as an inducement to fill empty seats out of season.

Its preparations complete, in the fall of 1965 CN withdrew from its mid-1930s arrangement with CP to pool services and revenue in the key Montreal-Toronto corridor. CP's irritation at the move was intensified when, on 1 November that year, CN sharply intensified and accelerated its Montreal-Toronto service with four trains each way daily plus a fifth at peak periods. With the benefit of speed ceiling raised from 83 to 90mph (133 to 145kmph), the fastest of these expresses, the 'Rapido', lopped 1 hour 16 minutes from the previous best timing to make the 335.3 miles (540km) in a minute under five hours with two intermediate stops for crew-changes. Its tightest point-to-point timing was one of 87 minutes for the 115.3 miles (185.7km) from Dorval, on the Montreal outskirts, to Brockville, for an average of 79.5mph (128.0kmph). Before long demand encouraged CN to double the 'Rapido' service.

Speed wasn't the only new characteristic of the CN service, incidentally. CN passenger management garlanded it with promotional gimmickry, from free coffee service, child care facilities and stereo music over the PA system to post-prandial Bingo sessions in the diner and, on the evening 'Rapido', some fustian kitsch described in the railroad's promotion as 'a Gay Nineties Bistro Car with authentic brass gaslight fittings, prints and posters of the period, waiters in bright yellow waistcoats and a honky-tonk pianist.'

By 1966 CN had boosted its passenger carryings almost 39% compared with 1961 and the average passenger journey was almost the same amount longer. Time, alas, was to justify the sceptics who pointed out that as a result of the discounted fare scheme the revenue from the increased business was a long, long way from overtaking expenses, but in those heady mid-1960s CN was euphorically confident of closing the gap by the early 1970s. To do that, though, demanded more speed. Market research showed, it was said, that this was the only superior quality that kept many

Left: *A Canadian National 'Rapido' at Cedars, Quebec, in May 1975.*
/ Kenneth A. W. Gansel

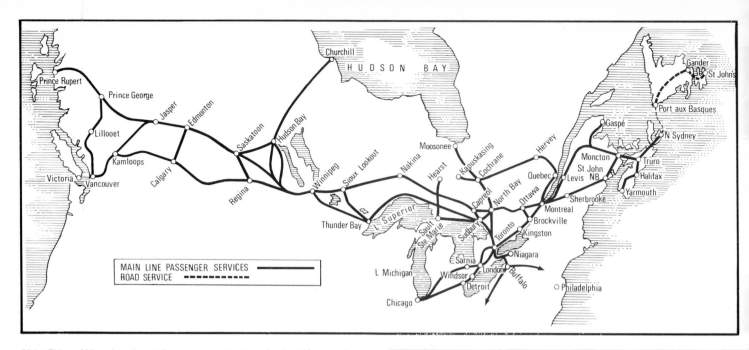

MAIN LINE PASSENGER SERVICES ————
ROAD SERVICE - - - - - - - -

Right: This ex-Milwaukee observation car was among the redundant US streamliner cars taken over by Canadian National: it was run between Halifax and Montreal. / Canadian National

Below right: A UAC Turbo-train in its original Canadian National livery sets out from Montreal. / Canadian National

travellers wedded to the Montreal-Toronto air service; if city centre-to-centre times were competitive, such people might well be prepared to pay more to ride the train, given its superiority under so many other heads.

Since 13.5% of the Montreal-Toronto route-mileage was curved, some of it quite sharply, CN understandably balked at the cost of trying to extract signficantly higher speed from orthodox equipment. Happily, it seemed at the time, an unorthodox answer was in the wings right on cue.

With defence expenditure contracting, several North American aerospace firms had been prompted by Lyndon Johnson's High Speed Ground Transportation programme to dabble in adapting their technology to surface transport. One was the United Aircraft Corporation, which had entered a turbine-powered train-set derived structurally from airframe technology in a design contest sponsored by the US Department of Commerce as a result of the Act. This concept United Aircraft now offered to Canadian National.

UAC's Turbo-train design was based on the premise that reduced resistance was the economical way to gain speed: extra power should be used only to make good what aerodynamics could not achieve. Vital features, therefore, were reduction of weight, aerodynamic drag and mechanical resistance, plus a low centre of gravity and a pendular suspension which would win so much pace over curves that there would be no need to aim for extravagantly high speed on straight track. In tests a three-car unit of Turbotrain vehicles was said to have negotiated at 140mph (225kmph), with reasonable smoothness, a curve that limited conventional equipment to 79mph (127kmph); on a straight jointed track it was worked up to 157mph (253kmph); on straight continuously welded track to 171mph (275kmph).

The Turbotrain version adopted by CN was a seven-car unit, with power concentrated on two four-wheel bogies, one at each end of the set, and the rest of the unit articulated in single-axle junctions between cars (a close-coupled arrangement that usefully eliminated inter-car vestibules). Each single-axle bogie was guided by telescopic arms which were in essence ball-bearing screw actuators; these were to position the bogie, so that theoretically it should always

Left: *Close-up of a UAC Turbo-train's single-axle articulation.* / P. J. Howard

Below: *Tray meal service in the 'Turboclub' accommodation of a Canadian National Turbo-train.* / Canadian National

bisect the angle between adjoining cars on a curve. To ensure proper tracking and stop the cars hunting the ends of the actuator rods were connected to the carbodies through resilient rubber mountings. Especially complex was the suspension of the highly unusual inside-bearing powered bogies, to which the drive from a cluster of very compact, UAC-modified, Pratt & Whitney 400hp ST-6B turbines in each power car was a formidably intricate web of mechanical couplings and shafts. The low-slung design had the roofs of the articulate trailers, at 11ft, as much as 2½ft lower than those of conventional cars without loss of passenger headroom. The power car domes, which at roof level were 13ft above the track, were fronted by driving cabs but mostly occupied by passenger space: a small saloon with revolving chairs for premium-class 'Turboclub' clients at one end of the unit, a less roomy saloon with fixed seats and tables for 'Turboluxe' patrons at the other. A glass partition between dome saloon and cab gave one a grandstand view of the driving console and the unfolding road ahead. Turboclub passengers were blessed with hostess meal service at their seats; for the rest it was self-service from a Turboluxe cafe counter.

The weight economy of the Turbotrains' aluminium, tubular steel-strengthened bodywork was certainly remarkable. Set against 13 cars of orthodox 'Rapido' stock, a twin-Turbo formation of 14 cars had room for 36 fewer passengers, 604 against 640, but at 317.5 tonnes the Turbo ran out at only 30.4% per cent of the 'Rapido's' tare train weight including traction!

UAC built five seven-car Turbotrains for CN at its own expense and agreed to lease them to CN for eight years. Under the contract UAC also undertook maintenance for the first five years and gave CN an option for subsequent three- and two-year renewals of the deal. For those generous terms, motivated no doubt by eagerness to get in on the ground floor of reborn high-speed railroading, UAC was to pay heavily.

CN had spent a fair amount of money on track strengthening and modification of superelevation on curves — even some modest realignments — before the Turbotrains' public service debut on 12 December 1968. Nevertheless the newcomers had to be limited to a top speed of 95mph (153kmph) instead of their potential 120mph (193kmph) out of deference to the Montreal-Toronto route's 240 or so public highway crossings and 700 agricultural or private crossings. Even so, riding did not impress journalists on an inaugural press trip. One US writer found it sadly reminiscent of the repudiated US lightweight essays of the mid-1950s. 'Rail noise considerably exceeds that of standard equipment', he wrote, complaining that 'wheel bounce over rail joints is highly preceptible.' As for the ingenious suspension, he found curves a 'major problem ... the many cups of coffee splashing testified to the rough-riding characteristics. The single-axle articulation in practice negotiates curves in a series of short jerks rather than the smooth flowing motion promised in the press releases.'

The Turbotrains had already slipped their intended introduction date of the 1967 summer, to coincide with Canada's Centennial, when they finally took on CN passengers in the winter of 1969. But it was soon dismally clear that even that delay had not been enough to solve all the development problems.

The inaugural Turbotrain schedule was sparklingly attractive — well-nigh an hour slashed from the Montreal-Toronto timing to clip it to four hours flat for an end-to-end average of 83.8mph (134.8kmph). And it was on offer by a seven-car set midday and evening each way on weekdays, though as soon as the new equipment had bedded down CN aimed to have two twin-unit 14 car formations making a three-leg daily tour of just over 1,000 miles (1,610km), with the remaining seven-car unit in reverse. Fond hope, it soon transpired.

Within just weeks of their launch the Turbotrains had been so persistently lamed by failures, principally of their auxiliary equipment, which plunged the trains into heatless dark, that CN withdrew them and despatched them to UAC for attention. For the rest of 1969 there was no Turbo service. At last the trains resumed operation in May 1970, but yet again CN found them fault-prone and in mid-February 1971 all five sets were sidetracked once more.

By now UAC, obliged to foot the bills for every alteration sought by CN, was getting nettled. It wasn't having anything like the same bother with the two three-car sets it had been contracted to supply for trial to the US Department of Transportation, and which had been in demonstration public service (not on very exacting schedules) between New York and Boston since the spring of 1969. The aerospace men

Below: *A Turbo-train leaves Ottawa Union station on a morning run to Montreal in October 1974.* / P. J. Howard

Below right: *Amtrak's American-built (by Rohr Industries) version of French Railways' RTG gas turbine train-set.* / Amtrak

had a mounting suspicion that CN was ordering its Turbotrains off the road every time a hinge creaked or an engine coughed. And they said so, publicly. To which a CN vice-president retorted crisply that 'the trains never did measure up to the original contract and they haven't yet.'

As with the Metroliners, but probably more so, the root of all the problems was inexperience in a rugged railroad operating environment. A great deal of ingenuity and derived technology had been packed into the Turbotrain without extended practical evaluation in railroad conditions; from transmission to suspension and auxiliaries, far too many vital components seemed to have been translated straight from the drawing board to the series production line.

Eventually, after some substantial modification of the gearbox drive and the pendular suspension, plus reinforcement of the sound insulation, CN were pacified and their Turbotrains at last took up untroubled service from the start of 1974. But the schedules they were fulfilling in the late 1970s were well short of the 1960s promise — at best 4½ hours between Montreal and Toronto with three intermediate stops, the fastest intermediate booking a start-to-stop time of 102 minutes for the 145.2 miles from Kingston to Guildwood, average 85.4mph (137.4kmph).

As for the two Turbotrains in the US, favourable public reaction persuaded the Department of Transportation to retain them on the New York-Boston route beyond the original October 1970 terminal date of the demonstration project. But nobody hereafter was writing turbine traction into their visions of a full-scale revival of US inter-city rail speed. Though the French-built Turboliners which were imported in 1973, then proliferated in 1975-6 by a combination of further orders from France and domestic building under licence, impressed with the reliability, the post Arab-Israeli 1973 war explosion of fuel prices had destroyed overnight one of gas turbine traction's prime advantages, fuel cost economy.

Meanwhile, the Metroliners and Turbotrains in the US were under new management. Confronting a real risk of the inter-city passenger train's extinction, public opinion had mobilised sufficiently to arouse a tremor or two in Washington. After two years of Congressional deliberation and stalling by powerful factions within the Nixon administration, a Federally-financed takeover of all inter-city rail services by a quasi-Governmental operating agency on an approved network was finally ordered by the Rail Passenger Service Act of 30 October 1971. Thus was Amtrak born.

For a while the Amtrak management sounded uncertain whether its remit was just to hold a saline drip over the passenger train or to set about transplant surgery. From 1972 onwards, however, it set about positive redevelopment; and an immediate candidate for attention was the North-East Corridor where Amtrak was ringing up more than half its revenue, and particularly the New York-Washington Metroliners.

The whole fleet was now serviceable — or theoretically so: availability was reported to be no better than 75%, in-service car failures to average one every 3,000-4,000 miles (4,800-6,400km) or so and maintenance costs to be running at a swingeing 77 UScents a car-mile. Despite such traumas, the Metroliners had built up a solid and generally enthusiastic clientele, even if the trains might have been running on another planet for all that the great majority of New York-Washington business commuters seemed to know of the service (the total unawareness of Metroliners amongst almost all the publishers I was dealing with in New York in the mid-1970s used to astonish me). So the service was augmented to 14 trains each way daily.

Moreover the Department of Transportation had shown that the cars could be perfected. In 1973 it had paid for two of each type to be returned to their respective equipment suppliers, General Electric and Westinghouse, for a long list of nearly 100 modifications. The four rebuilds, distinguishable by new rooftop excrescences housing dynamic brake heat vents and air intakes that were originally underfloor-mounted (with resultant overheating), were shown off to the press in July 1974 on the 22 mile (35km) demonstration stretch of Penn-Central main line in New Jersey between Trenton and New Brunswick. If the riding was still something less than blissful, the rest of the equipment functioned immaculately. Braking from 125mph (200kmph) was as smooth and rapid as the specification predicated, while the cars had no trouble in making a top speed of 152mph (245kmph).

The only cloud on the day was the bill. First cost of a Metroliner car had been $450,000, or around £250,000; the revamping totted up to $550,000, or over £300,000. The vehicles were already halfway through a front-rank service life put at little more than a decade because of their intensive use; could the enormous outlay on refurbishing the whole fleet be justified so late in the day?

That apart, there was the $64,000 question of how long the New York-Washington tracks could stand up to high-speed pounding. The Metroliners were very much the minority

users, for of the near-1000 trains travelling the North-East Corridor tracks daily two-thirds were commuter, nearly 200 freight and a mere 100 or so Amtrak services. Following its official bankruptcy in 1970 Penn-Central had been still more strapped for cash to keep the track in order and within a year or so a 100mph (160kmph) had to be clamped on the 'Metroliners', enforcing some schedule deceleration and compromising punctuality quite seriously.

Amtrak had always hankered after a thoroughgoing reconstruction of the North-East Corridor into a super-speed railway in the 150mph (240kmph) class. By the mid-1970s, however, the prospective costs were so astronomical that the idea had scant chance of endorsement — still less so from a Ford administration with a Secretary of Transportation plainly antipathetic to the whole Amtrak concept: to him, for instance, supported rail passenger service other than in the populated Corridors was akin to keeping up an outside privy — 'At one time it made a lot of sense, but once you get plumbing...'

A new approach of some kind to the North-East Corridor issue was inescapable following the brushfire bankruptcies of almost all the major railroads in the North-East in the early 1970s. To save the situation another quasi-governmental organisation, Consolidated Rail Corporation, or Conrail for short, was born in the Railroad Revitalisation and Regulatory Reform Act, the so-called '4R' Act, of 1975, with a mandate to rationalise a heavily duplicated network down to a sensible, economical core.

The '4R' Act's draughtsmen solved the North-East Corridor dilemma by proposing a reversal of roles. Amtrak should buy the route lock, stock and barrel and become the managing operator, leasing out the tracks to Conrail's freight trains and the various regional transport authorities' commuter services. The Ford administration doggedly resisted the idea and fought for the retention of Conrail as landlord, but Amtrak eventually won too powerful a support from Congress for the White House to prevail. So the track, 107 stations and an assortment of maintenance facilities were knocked down to Amtrak for an all-in price of about £50 millions, to the anguish of Penn-Central's creditors and stockholders, who howled that the figure was the grossest undervaluation of the assets.

The Ford administration flatly refused to countenance super-railway rebuilding of the North-East Corridor. But it did agree the grant of an additional £900 millions, 10% to be stumped up by States along the line, to upgrade the whole Boston-New York-Washington route for 125mph (200kmph). Added to cash already advanced, that topped Amtrak's coffers up to some £1.65 billions for Corridor modernisation.

The work began in 1977. Over 1,000 track-miles are being rebuilt to overtake years of skimped maintenance (to the outrage of the US wooden sleeper industry, reconstruction features the first major North American installation of concrete sleepers) and 50 curves are undergoing extensive realignment. Of the 855 bridges along the route, 770 need substantial attention; 150 built before 1895 must be completely rebuilt and half the remainder erected since 1895 need reinforcement. Four tunnels in New York and Baltimore, the maintenance of which was being sadly neglected, cannot now escape rebuilding, since their clearances have to be enlarged to accommodate the 25kV 60Hz ac traction current system which it has been agreed will generally supersede the old Pennsylvania 11kV 25Hz in a complete modernisation of the route's catenary and current supply. But between New York and New Haven the principal user, New York's Metropolitan Transport Authority, has successfully insisted on a 12.5kV 60Hz traction current system for its commuter trains. That obliges Amtrak expensively to fit its new equipment for triple-voltage operation, since it will also have to cope with the

remains of the old 11kV network should emergency dictate diversion of Amtrak trains. The final section of the Corridor route from New Haven to Boston is being electrified for the first time.

Another blow to the project has been the reluctance of any of the affected States except Massachusetts to stump up their financial contribution, which was to help cover substantial station improvements and continuous fencing of the route; as a result, much of the station modernisation will probably be scratched. The other major component of the reconstruction is comprehensive resignalling for control of the whole route from just three centres.

The ultimate objective is said to be a New York-Washington transit time of 2 hours 40 minutes inclusive of stops, and of 3 hours 40 minutes from New York to Boston, again inclusive of stops. For the size of the investment that does not sound a particularly mind-blowing advance on the 1977 New York-Washington best of a minute under three hours. Projected service frequencies are: 19 hourly-interval trains each way daily between Boston and New York, with four short-haul trains each way superimposed on this timetable between Springfield and New York; no less than 65 trains each way daily between New York and Philadelphia, at headways of only 17 minutes in the peak periods; and 53 each way daily between Philadelphia and Washington, at peak headways of 22 minutes. In addition six night trains each way are planned. By 1990 passenger journeys by all modes in the North-East Corridor are forecast to reach 131 millions per annum, compared with 80 millions in the mid-1970s. The commercial target set for the revitalised railroad is a near trebling of its present carryings by 1990, which will mean an increase in its market share to 20% compared with today's 12%. Of this gain the planners expect the greater part to be an abstraction from road, with a 12.8% reduction in automobile and a 28.4% cut in bus traffic; air transport is seen as surrendering 10.7% of its business.

As for the tools to do the job, Amtrak seems a mite schizophrenic. On the one hand its five-year capital investment plan submitted to Wahington at the end of 1977 called for a the rest of the Metroliner fleet to be given the same expensive treatment as the four samples refurbished at Government expense. On the other, after testing a French

Left: *A 'Metroliner' at work for Amtrak in the New York-Washington corridor.* / Amtrak

Right: *The Swedish demonstrator, an ASEA-built Type Rc4 Bo-Bo, leaves New York while under Amtrak evaluation. Amtrak's new electric locomotives for the North-East Corridor are being based on this model*

Below: *VIA RAIL takes over: a former Canadian National 'Rapido' decked out in the new blue and yellow livery.* / Canadian National

multi-voltage CC21000-class Co-Co and a Swedish ASEA-built Type Rc4 Bo-Bo against its own rather ill-starred GE-built E60CP Co-Cos (which it might sell off to Conrail as freight power) Amtrak ordered the first of a projected squadron of 53 triple-voltage lightweight locomotives with 130mph (219kmph) capability based on the ASEA model. General Motors are building the locomotives around ASEA electric traction equipment.

To pinch more speed from its schedules in other areas of the US, Amtrak was looking at a new contender in the high-speed train stakes developed in Canada. There, too, the stage was being set for another attempt to rejuvenate the passenger train in the busy corridors of the country's eastern provinces.

While Amtrak had been finding its feet in the US, Canadian National had been fast losing confidence in its ability to salvage the inter-city passenger train economically. Soon CN was sounding as pessimistic as CP had done a decade earlier and pressing for Federal relief from annual passenger business losses of £50 millions. Without some more potent Government intervention than hitherto, the Canadian long-haul passenger train seemed locked irretrievably in the dismal spiral of crumbling quality and dwindling patronage. But in 1974 Pierre Trudeau's Liberal Government was elected on promises, amongst other things, to stabilise the country's rail passenger services within a new transport policy framework.

In 1976 the Government was ready with its intentions. There was to be an Amtrak-style handover of both CN and CP passenger services to a single agency. CN and CP had already anticipated this by agreeing to pool their passenger service marketing and launch a new offensive, coupled with a fresh corporate identity that featured bold new royal blue-and-yellow train liveries, under the brand-name VIA which CN had devised for its own passenger marketing in 1976. This initiative was made the foundation of the new order and from the spring of 1978 VIA Rail Canada Inc, to give the agency its full title, assumed the management of all the country's inter-city passenger services on behalf of the Federal Government.

The Federal Government also offered full financial support for upgraded passenger services. So far as major routes were concerned, it accepted that upgrading meant thoroughgoing rehabilitation of the track — by now just as rundown as so much in Amtrak territory — curvature realignment, resignalling and elimination of as many level crossings as was practicable; it wasn't enough to modernise passenger equipment. And as an earnest of its intentions it

Left: *The prototype LRC power car thrashes up the snow at 129mph (207.6kmph) on its high-speed test run over Canadian Pacific tracks between Montreal and Quebec City on 10 March 1976.*

Right: *The Bombardier-MLW prototype LRC power car and trailer.* / Bombardier-MLW

Below: *Close-up of the LRC power car.* / Canadian National

Bottom: *Furnishing of the prototype LRC trailer.* / Bombardier-MLW

offered about £19 millions to upgrade the CP line in the Montreal-Quebec corridor for a demonstration project to start about 1980 (though the sum was a pittance set against Federal outlay on other forms of transport: for instance, more than £100 millions had been frittered away on an abortive STOL aircraft service between Ottawa and Montreal). A further $90 millions was promised to extend the scheme from Montreal to Windsor if the pilot exercise went well.

For its demonstration train-sets, the Canadian Government accepted the VIA men's preference and bought a Canadian product. This is the tilting-body LRC — for 'Light, Rapid, Comfortable' or *'Léger, Rapide, Confortable'* according to your stance on Canada's linguistic issues. LRC is the 1971 brainchild of Alcan Canada Products, part of Aluminum Company of Canada, which was subsequently developed, with financial aid from the Canadian Government, by a consortium of Canadian firms and is now built by Bombardier-MLW Industries. The initial Canadian order is for 22 power cars and 50 passenger trailers; two of the power cars are reserves, leaving the rest to be operated as either single power car-five trailer or twin-power car-ten trailer units. The first four trains were programmed to enter Quebec City-Montreal service in the spring of 1980, the remainder to set up revamped service in other Canadian inter-city corridors. Apart from Amtrak, a number of other foreign operators have been keenly eyeing the LRC, notably the Portuguese, but also railways in Australia, Brazil and the Middle East.

Like British Rail's HST, the Canadian LRC is designed to extract up to 125mph (200kmph) from existing track and signal spacing — though at this writing VIA is mum on the prospective LRC ceiling in Canada: local opinion tends to the view that the Canadian LRCs will be restricted to a lower maximum, considering the power car's heavy 25 tonne axle-

146

loading and the lateral track stresses set up by tilt-body coaches taking curves at above-average pace.

Like Britain's HST, Canada's LRC is fitted with diesel-alternator power plant in locomotives which can be marshalled outside a rake of passenger trailers for double-ended push-pull operation; in the case of the LRC, the power cars, each fitted with an MLW Series 251 engine, are 2,900hp. But as already indicated, unlike the HST the LRC has tilt-body apparatus to increase its speed potential in unfavourable track conditions. Each LRC vehicle has its independent two-axle bogies, of conventional design characteristics except that each is fitted with a servo-controlled roll bolster which acts as an independent, stable platform that banks the carbody to the appropriate angle for passenger comfort; a sensor in each bogie reacts to centrifugal force and activates the servo mechanism so that it rotates the bolster appropriately to reduce the centrifugal force on passengers to near-equilibrium. The power car bogies are not fitted with the tilt device. The 84ft (25.6m) passenger carbody is a stressed-skin creation of aluminium alloy without a centre sill, and with its centre of gravity reduced to the limit; and each passenger car turns the scales at 42 tonnes. The power car, however, comes out at 83.8 tonnes, compared with a 2,500hp British HST power car's 70 tonnes. The LRC is not sold as a fixed-formation train-set like Britain's HST; its makers envisage operation of single power-car sets as well as two power-car push-pull units with variable trailer make-up, and the two units so far acquired by Amtrak are in fact one power car-and-five trailer sets.

After tests on their respective home grounds both Canadian and US customers for the LRC pronounced themselves well content with the tilt-body's suspension and speed-raising potential on curved track. As for its pace on open track, during the bleak February and March on 1976

CP put that to proof with the prototype LRC power car and trailer in a four weeks' trial of daily round trips between Montreal and Quebec City. On 10 March, lashing up a minor blizzard from the thickly-lying snow, the unit notched a new Canadian rail speed record of 129mph (207.6kmph) east of Montreal.

That evidently roused the old Adam in CN. CN was then fleshing out the bones of the new passenger service campaign which it was soon to share with CP and which was to shape the new VIA structure (VIA's blue-and-yellow livery originated with CN), as I have just described. Fronting CN's offensive for the 1976 summer was a reinvigorated Montreal-Windsor service, featuring amongst other things the luckless Turbos. Despite all their misfortunes, the Turbos, now reorganised as nine-car sets, had amassed over 1¼ million miles of revenue-earning service since 1968; CN clearly thought they had earned a little lustre to efface their chequered early history. Maybe the CP exploit goaded CN to more bravado than they originally intended; be that as it may, on a preview trip from Kingston to Montreal staged later in March 1976 a Turbo-load of 100 guests was whipped up to 140.6mph (226kmph) on a 20 mile (32km) stretch of continuous welded rail.

Whereat Ottawa, too, stirred and both CN and CP had their hands smacked by the Canadian Transport Commission. In future, they were ordered, any high-speed 'tests' must be cleared in advance with the Commission. There was serious point to the rebuke, however. Although CN had actually closed five highway crossings prior to its exploit, because their road traffic warning signals could not be retimed to suit the speeds planned for the Turbo, the Commission was concerned to see that level crossing traffic was properly protected. It was yet another reminder of the severe handicaps a multitude of inherited level crossings present to so many speed-hungry railways in modern times.

10. France's 160mph Railway–The TGV Paris-Sudest

By the mid-1980s world rail speed supremacy will again be Europe's on every count. By then the French will have fully operational a new railway easily outstripping all comers both in its maximum speeds and in the average end-to-end speed of its frequent daylong service.

Chapter Four recounted the French ventures of the 1950s which established that the practical speed ceiling of conventional steel-wheeled trains on steel rail was at least as high as 200mph (320kmph). But I went on to tell how further consideration of the operational practicalities had convinced French Railways that 125mph (200kmph) was economically the sensible limit of speed ambition on existing railways: and moreover that the limitations of existing traction current supply equipment and the disbenefits of widened speed bands on routes heavily occupied by both *rapides* and slower-moving passenger and freight trains have restricted 125mph (200kmph) operation to a handul of trains on two main lines out of Paris. By the late 1960s the French were persuaded that a significant leap ahead in speed demanded the construction of a new railway reserved exclusively to passenger trains linking main population centres. And there was one trunk route where the growth of traffic would justify the investment in this increased track capacity.

That was the former PLM main line from Paris south-eastwards to Dijon and Lyons, which debouches into lines to Marseilles, the Riviera, Switzerland and Italy. This artery links 40% of the entire French population. Since 1960 the traffic it carries, both passenger and freight, has increased at an annual rate of about 3½%; passenger traffic has been going up at an annual rate of 4.2%, more than twice the average for the rest of French Railways, and the expansion of freight volume has been 50% greater than in the rest of the system. Although long sections of the route are four-track, it also has double-track bottlenecks in terrain where enlargement of capacity would be formidably expensive; to have quadrupled the line throughout, in fact, would have cost as much 45% of the bill to build a new railway.

French Railways calculated that if the Paris-Dijon-Lyons route continued to accumulate traffic at the same steady rate, by 1980 those double-track bottlenecks would be near choking by a daily average of almost 150 through trains each way, nearly half of them passenger. Such intensity would severely handicap timetable 'flighting' and thereby frustrate further acceleration of inter-city and international expresses on a route of prime commercial importance, and one exposed to severe *autoroute* and domestic air service competition. Extended *banalisation* — that is, bi-directional signalling of each running line in association with frequent crossovers so that it can be used by trains either way according to relative directional strengths of traffic flow in a given hour — would not create sufficient operational flexibility to solve the problems. In any event, the Paris-Dijon-Lyons main line was

Left: *The main double-track bottleneck on the old Paris-Lyons route, through the Burgundy hills at the approach to Dijon; an 8,000hp CC6500 heads train 5009, the 17.00 Paris-Marseilles.* / Y. Broncard

not so well contoured throughout as some other French main lines for extensive adaptation to 125mph (200kmph) running. The limits of its potential were therefore in sight on more than one count.

So, in December 1969, French Railways laid before their Government a plan for a new high-speed, exclusively passenger railway almost the whole way from Paris to Lyons. The 'almost' was important. The TGV Paris-Sudest scheme (TGV standing for *Train Grande Vitesse*), as it is now known, was to be no Japanese-style Shinkansen, isolated from the rest of French Railways. Once the over-extended Paris-Lyons stretch had been bypassed, the new line's trains must be able to join the existing network and carry smoothly on with no operational complications to the Riviera, the French Alps, Switzerland and all the principal destinations now served by conventional trains over the Paris-Dijon-Lyons main line.

Compatibility with the rest of the system had another vital economic point. The new line's trains would run on existing tracks to the outskirts of Paris and Lyons, so that the horrendous costs — not to mention the aggravation of local communities — incurred in carving a new railway out of an urban environment would be avoided. Once at the outskirts of Paris and Lyons, it would be comparatively easy to plot a line of route through the great expanses of French countryside that would steer clear not just of towns but even of sizeable villages. As for this last, the claim has in the event been justified up to the hilt; the TGV Sud-Est's final line route comes no closer even to a tiny hamlet, let alone towns and villages, than about 800ft (240m), and gives every historic monument and scenic beauty a wide berth. That did not, however, mollify the ecologists and agricultural interests touched by the line's projected path, who mounted a campaign against the scheme even more implacable, virulent and protracted than the predictable offensive from domestic air and automobile industry lobbyists. Eventually the highest council of the French state had to sit on judgement on the arguments.

Unobtrusive projection of a new railway through the heart of France was greatly simplified by the ability of modern electric traction to romp up gradients and by the capacity of low-slung rolling stock to sustain very high speed in comfort even through the curvature of modern track, thanks to latter-day science in vehicle and running gear design. As a result, provided the speed range of traffic using the route is near constant, new railway planners can, without calling for automatic tilt-body train-sets, work to almost the same parameters of ruling gradient and curvature radius as motorway builders. The French recognised this back in 1969, when the railways and the *autoroute* interests came together in a study group to consider the economics and practicalities of combining new railways and *autoroutes* in a common infrastructure.

Had the Channel Tunnel scheme been pursued, the partnership would have come to grand-scale fruition in Northern France. The prospective Channel Tunnel traffic flows topped off justification for another high-speed line, the TGV Nord, from Paris to Lille and the Belgian and German borders, which would have thrown off a branch to the Channel coast and, given a comparable new high-speed British Rail link from the English shore to London, brought London and Paris within 2¾ hours' rail travel of each other by through Tunnel service. The French authorities were simultaneously planning a new *autoroute* from Paris to Lille, and the idea was to combine new railway and new *autoroute* in a single new infrastructure some 240ft (730m) wide for most of the distance. That, it was reckoned, would cut the construction costs of each medium by at least 10%.

The *autoroute* planners would have had to make their curves a little more generous in radius than usual for the

railway's benefit, but they would not have had to give much ground on gradients. The railway engineers were ready to come as close as 1 in 28½ to the normal *autoroute* maximum grade of 1 in 25. By and large, therefore, the *autoroute* could have hugged the terrain almost as closely as if there had been no parallel railway. Where track and roadway were at the same level they would be segregated by a median strip about 100ft (30m) wide, so as to keep train drivers well clear of road vehicles' headlight glare on one side and to protect road traffic from the turbulence set up by high-speed trains on the other. However, both parties were prepared to narrow the median strip very substantially where road and rail were on different levels, provided the ground between them was trenched, or that they were protected from each other by massive concrete terracing.

The concept is being exploited to a more limited extent in the TGV Paris-Sudest scheme. In Seine-et-Marne and Yonne the railway is being built on a common infrastructure with the new A5 *autoroute* from Paris to Troyes for some 35 miles (56km) over the lush plain of Brie between Melun and Sens. The arrangement valuably limits disturbance of the many villages in this rich agricultural area and also reduces the combined cost of carrying both routes across the Seine valley east of Montereau. Another stretch of dual infrastructure is to pair the railway with a new express road from the Franco-Swiss border to the Atlantic coast for nearly nine miles (14km) between Cluny and Mâcon, in Saône-et-Loire. These new roads will not necessarily be completed at the same time as the railway, however.

Construction of the TGV Paris-Sud-Est started at the end of 1976. The new railway itself takes off from the existing tracks out of Paris Gare de Lyon at Combs-la-Ville, 18.6 miles (300km) from the terminus, and from that point 254 miles (409km) of new line head south-eastwards. Throughout the whole extent of the new route there are only two intermediate stations and three junctions, a mark of the railway's quintessential purpose as an exclusive carrier of long-distance, high-speed passenger traffic. The first junction, at Saint-Florentin, is primarily an emergency link with the existing PLM route, which the new line crosses at that point. The flying junction at Pasilly, 100 miles (161km) from Combs-la-Ville, on the other hand, is where trains for Dijon, the eastern French territory around Belfort and Mulhouse, and for Pontarlier or Lausanne, diverge to join the existing Paris-Lyons main line at Aisy, 9.3 miles (15km) away, and complete their journeys over traditional routes. The first of the new line's stations is at Montchanin, to serve the industrial complex of Le Creusot-Montceau-les-Mines, the other 209.4 miles (337km) out at Mâcon, in the heart of the Burgundy vineyards, where the new line makes a flying junction with the old route to segregate trains making for Geneva, Annecy and the Haute Savoie alps, or Italy via Modane and the Mont Cenis. The new route finally rejoins the existing network at Sathonay, 241.1 miles (308km) from Combs-la-Ville, for the entry into Lyons. From there onwards trains follow the traditional routes to Grenoble, to Marseilles, to the Côte d'Azur, and to Languedoc and the Spanish frontier.

The ultimate aim is to work the new line from end to end between Combs-la-Ville and Sathonay at a continuous speed of at least 162mph (260kmph), interrupted only by a solitary permanent speed restriction — and that for a reason unprecedented in railway operation, of which more in a moment. This objective looks the more remarkable when you compare gradient profiles of the existing and the new route. For its first 125 miles (200km) or so the former PLM line climbs almost imperceptibly up the Seine valley, never more steeply than 1 in 200, until the profile shapes into its one pronounced peak as the line makes the long ascent of the Burgundy hills that gradually steepens to 1 in 125 before

Above: *French Railways' first gas turbine traction experiment, a converted RGP425 diesel unit that was tested up to 149mph (240kmph).*

Blaisy-Bas summit, then descends as abruptly through Dijon to resume a more or less level course down the Saone valley to Macon and Lyons. In sharp contrast the profile of the TGV Paris-Sudest is a jagged range of alpine *aiguilles* almost the whole way, dotted frequently with snatches of gradients as steep as the permissible maximum of 1 in 28½, the first of them as the railway dips down to bridge the Seine. Here the TGV Paris-Sudest has been taken much lower than the old line, while in the Burgundy hills it has been taken at least 915ft (300m) higher up the ridges than the old line's Blaisy-Bas summit.

All this, of course, is graphic evidence of the way modern traction and rail vehicle technology allows a new railway reserved to high-speed passenger trains to be constructed far more economically through open country than the conventional mixed-traffic lines of old. No longer do the civil engineers have to wind their lines through valleys, erect massive embankments, carve out deep cuttings or hew tunnels to keep gradients manageable by the heaviest trains. They can take the changing contours in their stride with almost the same nonchalence as motorway builders. Not only can they save on earthworks, they can strike a more direct line of route: thus the distance from Paris Gare de Lyon to Lyons by TGV Paris-Sudest is 264.1 miles (425km), as against 318.2 miles (512km) by the old PLM line.

The one permanent speed restriction is at a summit, not on a lateral curve. There is a ridge in the Burgundy hills approached from each side by a stretch of 1 in 28½ gradient and in that situation there is some risk of a train momentarily taking off as it goes over the top, so a limit of 137mph (220kmph) has been imposed.

In the late 1960s choice of traction for the TGV Paris-Sudest was in doubt. One school of French Railways thought argued vehemently for gas turbine power. Quite apart from the problems of efficient current collection by very high-speed units that were still vexing the electric traction engineers, developments in turbine technology were adding a new dimension to rail power thought. Previously electrification had looked the sensible means to high speed. Diesel traction lacked the accelerative and hill-climbing ability to sustain high end-to-end averages, unless one built into locomotives an extravagant, weight and space-consuming, reserve of power that would be fully used only in spasms. The trouble was, it needed such a volume of traffic to exploit economically the work availability of electric traction and to pay a respectable dividend on the heavy installation costs of the fixed equipment. Then the aerospace industry came up with a range of lightweight gas turbines that promised the same power output as a given diesel engine at around a third of the latter's weight and up to three-quarters of its bulk. The implications for development of a high-speed, lightweight passenger unit were obvious.

The French first evaluated the concept exhaustively by fitting up one end of a standard Type RGP425 two-car diesel multiple-unit with a 1,150hp turbine and hydro-mechanical transmission. In normal secondary passenger service use the RGP425s are limited to 75mph (120kmph). It is one more testimony to French Railways' vehicle design that during the experimental set's protracted test programme it was driven up to 125mph (200kmph) and more nearly 300 times — the peak speed attained was 149mph (240kmph) — and rode as sweetly as a latter-day inter-city coach specifically designed for that pace.

The immediate outcome was a production series of four-car Type ETG gas turbine multiple-units, capable of 112mph (180kmph) maximum speed, which the French applied first to the Paris-Caen-Cherbourg line. With the

151

Above: *A four-car Type ETG gas turbine unit skirting the Normandy coast near Cabourg on a Paris-Deauville service.* / Y. Broncard

Right: *First-class saloon of an RTG gas turbine unit.*

Far right: *An RTG gas turbine train-set on a Nantes-Lyons service near Amplepuis (Rhône).* / Y. Broncard

benefit of 100mph (160kmph) authorisation over half the route, the ETGs transformed the timetable and scored outstanding commercial success. They were followed by a higher-powered RTG series and around 1970 the French announced production of two five-car experimental sets to probe the 185mph (300kmph) barrier with an eye to their TGV Paris-Sudest project.

But then came the Arab-Israeli war and the explosion of oil prices. One of turbine traction's prime advantages, its economical consumption of the cheaper low-grade fuel, was nullified overnight. Soon tests of dual-frequency locomotive No CC21001 at speeds up to 176mph (283kmph) in Alsace were to show that the current collection problems could be surmounted. The final blow to turbine traction came with realisation that its main operational advantage had been destroyed by changes in cost levels. Even when majority opinion was veering to electrification of the new line, it was still proposed to build some train-sets with gas turbines as their main propulsion for through running beyond the TGV Paris-Sudest to Grenoble, as yet not reached by catenary, and into Switzerland, in this case to avoid the complication and expense of providing multi-voltage electrical equipment on the trains to cope with the Swiss 15kV $16\frac{2}{3}$Hz ac electrification. These projected turbine sets would have had the main turbine plant in one power car and a comparatively low-power 1.5kV dc electric plant in the other to move them under catenary on the existing PLM main line. But when industry tendered to build the gas turbine sets their cost was so high compared with the electric version that the French calculated it would pay them better to electrify to Grenoble. As for the Swiss problem, it was now clear that, provided everyone was content with a modest power output under 15kV $16\frac{2}{3}$Hz ac, the disadvantages of providing for three voltages in the electric traction apparatus had been substantially mitigated; in particular, the designers had so shrewdly reduced the weight of the design that there was scope to take in a little more traction equipment without detriment to specified performance. That clinched the debate. The TGV Paris-Sudest would be all-electric.

French Railways still operate their ETGs and RTGs contentedly, and are happy to see their expertise exported. A batch of French-built RTGs, supplemented by a series constructed by Rohr Industries of California under licence, serves Amtrak in the US and more are running in Iran, which had a brief and wildly over ambitious fling at operating the world's fastest non-electric train service with them. On single track and amid all the rigours of desert operation, the Iranians essayed a start-to-stop timing as adventurous as 26 minutes for the 43.5 miles (70km) between Sabzevar and Azadvar when they put their first imported Turbotrain into Teheran-Mashbad service in 1975. That represented a start-to-stop average of 100.4mph (161.5kmph), but some pretty breathless sprints must have been scheduled over the rest of the itinerary. The train made seven intermediate stops — one spun out to 20 minutes — yet the end-to-end timing for the whole 606.6 miles (926km) was initially set at only 8 hours 20 minutes in one direction. The Iranians soon came to earth, however, and today both the Teheran-Mashbad and Teheran-Arak routes, the latter assumed by a second Turbotrain delivered in 1976, are operated to more decorous schedules.

On their home ground the French are now very unlikely to extend gas turbine traction short of some unimaginable transformation of relative energy prices. One of the prospective high-speed gas turbine train-sets was built, however, and this, TGV001, together with a single-unit electric vehicle, Z7001, became the principal test-bed for the proving in action of every design facet and component of the high-speed train-sets to come. TGV001 was a streamlined, low-slung 192 tonne unit of five comparatively short cars, articulated throughout and packing 6,500hp in four turbines supplying current to traction motors on every axle through an electric alternator transmission. Outshopped in March 1972, it had been run up to 182mph (300kmph) in the Landes as early as the following July. When it was retired late in January 1978, in view of the impending delivery of the first pre-production train-sets proper, it had run 15,138 miles (24,358km), at between 161.6mph (260kmph) and 186mph

Above: *The single-unit high-speed electric test car that helped develop TGV technology, No Z7001.* / French Railways

(300kmph), reached a top speed of 198mph (318kmph) in the course of 1,155 miles (1,859km) covered at more than 185mph (300kmph) and reeled off more than 34,000 miles (54,700km) at a pace higher than 125mph (200kmph). Amongst the sheaves of findings from this test programme was the conclusion that 185mph (300kmph) trains could safely pass each other at full tilt, even in a tunnel, given the minimum distance of 8ft 1¼in between the inner rails of adjacent running lines that prevails throughout the new track of the TGV Paris-Sudest.

Two pre-production prototypes and 85 production series train-sets for TGV Paris-Sudest were ordered concurrently with the start of the route's civil engineering in late 1976. In their striking outline, with its smoothly raked, somewhat Citroen automobile-reminiscent bonnet sweeping up to the cab windows, the trains are very closely related to TGV001.

Each train-set consists of two streamlined power cars, each on its own pair of bogies, enclosing a unit of eight passenger cars that is articulated from end to end. This high degree of articulation was adopted to save weight and thus energy, to enhance passenger comfort by keeping seats clear of the bogie area, and to create better inter-car communication. Between the very closely-coupled ends of cars over an articulating bogie the French have in fact been able to mount a very spacious vestibule, tightly sealed to preserve the fullest sound insulation and consistent air-conditioning, and also ingeniously mounted and sprung to maintain stability on the move, so that even at 150mph the passenger will experience little sensation in moving from one car to another. The length of the inner cars of the set is short by mainland European standards at only 57ft (18.7m); the outermost cars, of course, are slightly longer by virtue of the overhang above the independent bogies at each end of the set.

Perhaps surprisingly, in view of the high operational speeds, the coach bodies have no automatic tilting mechanism. As mentioned in an earlier chapter, France was a pioneer of this technology, which has also been pursued in North America, West Germany, Italy, Sweden, Switzerland, Sweden, Japan and Britain. But many of these countries' railways have grown disenchanted with the idea and since the mid-1970s it has been dropped from a number of high-speed train studies. As described earlier, French Railways provided for its application to all 90 of their *Grand Confort* coaches, but never went beyond fitting up two of them experimentally. Technically, most of the body-tilting devices are complex, adding to maintenance worries and expenses, and they also step up vehicle cost and weight significantly. Finally, on most of the routes where their contribution to speed-raising once looked valuable railwaymen now realise that their potential cannot be realised and a dividend won from the cost of their installation without much greater expense in signalling for higher speeds, or even really high investment to raise the average pace of the slowest-moving traffic on the same route.

The weight of each power car has been methodically trimmed to 64.2 tonnes, despite the fact that together they deliver the equivalent of 8,570hp for traction to the train-set's six motor bogies, a pair under each power car and one at each end of the articulated passenger unit. (Talking of the bogies, some will be surprised that the French have adopted heliocoidal springing for their secondary suspension, rather than the air-springing of TGV001 and of many other latter-day high-speed rail vehicles.) The first batch of TGV Paris-Sudest train-sets are mostly dual-voltage, 1.5kV dc for the exit from Gare de Lyon to Combs-la-Ville, the entrance to Lyons and the continuation of most journeys thereafter, 25kV ac for the new trackage of the TGV Paris-Sudest. As already mentioned, through running to Switzerland demands three-voltage adaptability to cope with the Swiss standard 15kV 16⅔Hz ac electrification system and six of the production series are being thus equipped. At one time it was thought these six units would have to be fashioned in

Left: *The high-speed turbine-electric test train-set, TGV001, near Belfort during trials on the Eastern Region main line in the spring of 1972.* / Y. Broncard

Below: *Close-up of one of TGV001's articulating bogies.* / Y. Broncard

Bottom: *The TGV001 power car fitted up with a pantograph for current collection test in Alsace.* / French Railways

aluminium bodywork to compensate for the extra two tonnes weight of transformer, but in the event the latter has proved capable of accommodation without exceeding the specified maximum axle-loading of 17 tonnes. At the time of writing there is no word of provision for operation under the Italians' 3kV dc catenary. French companies primarily involved in construction of the train-sets are Alsthom-Atlantique and Francorail-MTE.

Total weight of a single TGV Paris-Sudest train-set (units can be coupled for multiple-unit operation) is 380 tonnes. Under the line's 25kV ac catenary, therefore, the trains dispose of a formidable power/weight ratio of 22.5hp/tonne. Available power output when a unit is working under 1.5kV dc is halved — an ample provision for the much lower speed ceilings that rule when the unit is working off the new line. A final point of interest on the traction: the French have calculated that the energy consumption of a gas turbine unit on the standard Paris-Lyons schedule proposed for the TGV Paris-Sudest would be 70% greater than that of the electric train-set.

The French thought of pioneering a linear induction braking system on the TGV Paris-Sudest train-sets. The apparatus was attractively simple: coils mounted in a shoe, which would be lowered to close proximity with the rail — but not contact with it — at the moment of braking, whereupon the coils would be energised by current taken from the traction motors to set up a magnetic resistance to relative movement between shoe and rail surface. A prototype was exhaustively tested in the electric railcar Z7001 and proved perfectly effective. But there was a decisive drawback; heating not merely of the shoes on the car but, more importantly, of the rail, to an extent that might set off deformities. Rails would have to be allowed time to cool down between trains and the safe interval was set at 20 minutes. That was far too constricting to the operators, who envisaged need of headways as tight as six minutes in peak traffic periods.

So the TGV Paris-Sudest trains have a unique triple combination of rheostatic brakes on their motored bogies,

Right: *A driving desk of TGV001.* / French Railways

Below: *A high-speed turnout of the type to be installed on the TGV Paris-Sudest.*

double disc brakes on their trailing bogies and electro-pneumatically leather shoe brakes on all axles. Quite apart from their braking purposes, the shoe brakes valuably keep the wheel-rims dry and free of other pollutants that might affect adhesion; consequently they are brought at least lightly into play in every brake application, even at top line speed.

Normal braking from top speed relies mainly on the rheostatic system down to the very low speed range when the other two systems take over; the discs are applied at no more than half pressure, but they are the principal reserve in an emergency, since full on they can exert almost as much restraint as the rheostatic equipment. The normal braking distance from 160mph (260kmph) to a stand is 4,046yds (3,700m) on the level, 6,125yds on the maximum downgrades of 1 in 28½, which nowhere extend for more than 3,825yds; full emergency braking cuts these distance by 220 and 545yds respectively.

The track of the TGV Paris-Sudest is of standard but heavyish rail on concrete sleepers, spaced a little more closely than normal and firmly embedded in ballast as deep as 14in (35cm). The minimum radius of curvature is 4,375yds (4,000m). The most striking pieces of trackwork, undoubtedly, are the unique turnouts of the diverging lines at Pasilly and Macon, which can be taken as fast as 137mph (220kmph) by trains heading away to the old main line. New pointwork has also been laid in at Aisy, where the link from Pasilly meets the existing Paris-Lyons route, so that trains coming off or making for the TGV Paris-Sudest can take these junctions at the old route's ruling speed limit of 100mph (160kmph).

The TGV Paris-Sudest is the professional railway operator's Nirvana. With just three junctions and a couple of very simply laid-out stations in the whole of the new mileage the number of possible routings for trains once they have entered the new railway proper barely reaches double figures. Moreover the whole train service is provided by train-sets of standard power, weight and performance. Nothing could lend itself more obviously to signalling from a single control centre. Moreover, because of the standard characteristics of the trains and the simplicity of the track layout the system transmitting commands from the control centre to the trains need cope with no more than ten or a dozen different coded signals. And they can be comfortably accommodated by a range of low-frequency impulses passed through the running rails and picked up by train-mounted receivers. There is no need of a costly, separately wired system that allows a wide variety of 'messages' to be transmitted both ways, from command post to train and vice versa.

Needless by now to say, the signalling at such speeds has to be in the form of a continuous driver's desk display. There are no lineside signals whatsoever on the Paris-Sudest, though in their absence, and since drivers on the TGV Sud-Est still have full control of their trains, the block sections have to be delineated by lineside markers so that the drivers can accurately judge their deceleration. Although 185mph (300kmph) is the designed maximum speed of the line and its vehicles, initially and for some time to come the operating limit is set at 162mph (260kmph). The higher ceiling would demand a four-block headway between trains, but at the lower limit the TGV Paris-Sudest can be operated on a three-block headway, the length of block depending on the uphill or downhill grading of the line in the area; research proved that the maximum length of block, on a 1 in 28½ downgrade, should be set at about 6,385ft (2.093m). In normal circumstances a train receiving advance warning of a stop has one block in which to decelerate from 162mph (260kmph) to 137mph (220kmph), the next to come down to 160kmph (100mph) and a third in which to come to a stand. Automatic monitoring and overriding devices on the train, naturally, take over braking if the driver does not conform to the commands he is receiving on his driving-desk display panel.

So much for the technicalities of the new railway's track, trains and equipment. What's it like to be inside the trains?

French Railways stress that they have not set out to make the TGV Paris-Sudest a luxury service (though six of the train-sets are being laid out for first-class only). The unquestioned commercial success of their high-speed, first class-only, supplementary fare *rapides* like the 'Aquitaine' and 'Capitôle' has been to a degree double-edged: a lot of Frenchmen seem to have been persuaded that the railway is out of the average white- and blue-collar worker's class. In the 1970s rail certainly became the 'in' travel medium for the upper levels of French society, but that seemed to be wedding more and more of the middle class to the automobile. While the premium *rapides* had few seats to spare, occupancy of the common run of long-distance trains was averaging no better than 50%, and French Railways were more than a little disconcerted by a mid-1970s market research finding that half their passengers only took the train once a year, and that a fifth of all French families never saw the inside of a train from one year's end to another.

Unsurprisingly, then, the TGV Paris Sud-Est is visualised as something of an inter-city Metro — a long-distance, people-moving conveyor-belt. Consequently the interior comfort of the trains does not vie with that of modern TEE stock or French Railways' own *Grand Confort* vehicles. Its closest kinship is with the style of their latest 'Corail' coaches for domestic inter-city service on the traditional system. But because of the low-slung, slender body shape of the TGV Paris-Sudest coach, and the comparatively shallow windows that predicates, there's a less spacious, indefinably more spartan ambience inside the high-speed train. As with British Rail's Advanced Passenger Train, though not so markedly, one feels a little like being in a ground-hugging, air-conditioned airliner.

That sensation is reinforced by the TGV Paris-Sudest catering arrangements. Most Western European railways are trimming their full restaurant car services as grossly uneconomical and running a higher proportion of buffet or self-service cafeterias. The French are not only going further than most, gradually limiting the old-style, multi-course full meal service to TEEs and a few top-rank, heavily business-patronised *rapides*, but are first to adopt airline-style galley service very widely. All their latest 'Corail' train-sets are equipped solely for it. And so it is on the TGV Paris-Sudest trains. There is no hot food service whatsoever, only hot drinks. The only meals available are in the form of pre-prepared airliner-style trays, bought either over the bar in the centre of the train-set or from trolleys perambulated by train-staff from galleys in each half of the unit. It's ironic that the French of all people are taking the lead in such degradation of train catering.

No standing passengers, incidentally, are to be allowed on the Paris-Sudest trains. Seat reservation is obligatory, but it has been made a comparatively easy business; and it doesn't cost the passenger so much as one centime extra. It's a do-it-yourself procedure, so that there is no infuriating queueing for service at a reservation counter. On all stations served by TGV Paris-Sudest trains some 150 machines are installed that supply reservation tickets free of charge at the touch of a button, up to a central computer's calculation of each train service's seating capacity. Without a reservation as well as a travel ticket you cannot board a TGV train.

Below: *A car of TGV001 laid out with second-class seating.*

Maybe the spectacular, world-record-beating standard schedule of the TGV Paris-Sudest trains between Paris and Lyons is so short that the attenuated catering service is justified. End-to-end time for the 265.5 miles (425km) between the two cities is two hours flat, for an average start-to-stop of 132.3mph; that compares with a best of 3 hours 44 minutes by the old route at the time of writing. Predictions of end-to-end times from Paris to cities off the limits of the TGV Paris-Sudest by the new trains include (with best schedules by conventional train at the time of writing in brackets): Avignon 3 hours 49 minutes (5 hours 40 minutes); Lausanne 3 hours 29 minutes (4 hours 39 minutes); Geneva 3 hours 14 minutes (5 hours 40 minutes) and Marseilles 4 hours 43 minutes (6 hours 35 minutes). In all, the timetable of the new line is likely to show around 50 trains each way daily when it is fully operational; outside the morning and evening peaks, frequency will probably range from 15 to 30 minutes, but in the peaks, with some trains at only six minutes' headway, the new railway may well be moving some 12,000 long-distance passengers an hour.

The first of the two pre-production train-sets was delivered in the summer of 1978 to begin another exhaustive test programme. For the first ten months the unit was unlikely to be run at more than 125mph (200kmph) as its complex electronics and other components, especially the braking systems, were put to rigorous test; a gradient equivalent to the steepest on the new railway had been located between Montréjeau and Tarbes, near the Pyrenees, as a proving-ground for the braking systems. A further ten weeks would probably be taken up with proof of the dual-voltage current collection equipment. This first unit was then scheduled to re-enter works around the middle of 1979 to have its laboratory equipment almost entirely removed and undergo fitting-out with full passenger accommodation. The second pre-production train-set, however, was to be delivered ready for passenger service. That was to go into operation on the old Paris-Lyons main line for some months

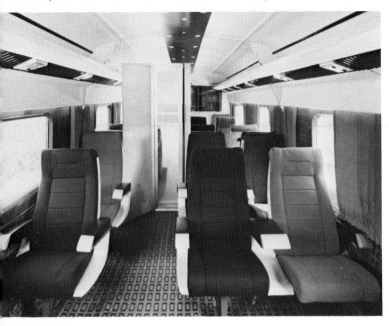

Left: *Mock-up of first-class saloon furnishing planned for the TGV Sudest train-sets.*
/ Alsthom-Atlantique

Below: *The first vehicles of one of the pre-production series of TGV Sud-Est train-sets emerge from the Alsthom-Atlantique works in June 1978.*
/ Y. Broncard, courtesy La Vie du Rail

Below right: *Designer's impression of the look of a TGV Sudest power car.*
/ Jacques Cooper

to assess reaction to its passenger facilities. Finally, and before readiness of the first completed stretches of the new railway, the re-modelled first pre-production set was likely to be put to really high-speed endurance tests of nearly a thousand miles a day on a Paris-Dijon-Strasbourg-Paris circuit as a preliminary to full service commissioning of the St Florentin-Lyons section of the new railway in late 1981. The whole TGV Sud-Est was expected to be ready for full high-speed public service by October 1983.

Meanwhile a feasibility study of a second TGV scheme, the TGV Atlantique, began in late 1977. When Britain opted out of the Channel Tunnel and knocked a number of props from the economic case for the TGV Nord, the high-speed line planned to parallel the *Autoroute du Nord*, French Railways planners switched their attention to the west and south-west of Paris. A dossier of preliminary data on high-speed service to this half of France had already been compiled when the French Government formally proposed a feasibility study in the closing months of 1977.

From the political viewpoint the north-western Breton peninsula has been a thorn in the flesh these past few years, with its aggressive and sometimes violent pressure for at least a measure of autonomy. Bestowal of a TGV could be an emollient. From the railways' viewpoint it would logically integrate with forward traction planning. The main lines to the important ports of Brest, St Nazaire and La Rochelle are not electrified, but electrification of these and other second-rank main lines had in the 1970s become not just practical but essential politics with oil resources looking more finite by the year and oil's price rise potential seemingly infinite.

So the TGV Atlantique project marries extensive upgrading of existing railway with considerably less new railway construction than TGV Paris-Sudest. In the draft map new line would be built only so far out of Paris as is necessary to steer clear of the area now densely occupied by short-haul inter-city and suburban trains. For some of the way the makings of an infrastructure already exist in the trackbed of an abortive commuter railway scheme from Paris Montparnasse to Chartres. At Chateaudun, some 80 miles (130km) south-west of Paris, the new line would split in a flying junction thrusting one fork westwards towards Le Mans, the other south-westwards towards Tours. The westward arm would bypass Le Mans to the south, but throw off a loop to serve that city, then fork again to feed into the existing route to Rennes, Quimper and Brest at Laval, and into the present route to Nantes at Sablé, north of Angers. The southern arm of the TGV Atlantique would bypass Tours, catering for that city by a connection at St Pierre-des-Corps, and merge with the existing main line to Bordeaux and the Spanish border at Monts, nearly nine miles (14km) south of Tours. Beyond the extremities of new railway the TGV trains would stream over existing track comprehensively rebuilt and resignalled for higher speeds, and electrified where necessary. In this scheme, incidentally, there would be further combination of new road and railway on the same infrastructure in conjunction with construction of the express road from the Franco-Swiss border to the Atlantic that figures in the TGV Paris-Sudest scheme.

This project would benefit two groups of trunk routes covering the whole of France's Atlantic coast, from Brittany down through Brest, Lorient, St Nazaire and La Baule to La Rochelle, Bordeaux and the Spanish frontier at Hendaye. Specimen journey times envisaged after completion would represent massive cuts in current schedules, such as (fastest timing as I write in brackets): Paris to Brest 4 hours 2 minutes (5½ hours), to St Nazaire 2½ hours (3 hours 44 minutes), to Bordeaux 3 hours (3 hours 50 minutes) and to Hendaye 4 hours 36 minutes (6 hours 19 minutes). However, these figures suggest that no higher speeds than 125mph (200kmph) are in mind beyond the limits of the new track, no doubt because of the disbenefits of excessively widening the speed band of the mixed traffic that will, one presumes, still be using the existing railway involved in the project.

385.22
Allen

Allen, Geoffrey
Freeman.

The fastest
trains in the world

SHELVED JUL 1980

DATE	ISSUED TO
	AUG 1963 JUN - - '91
	MAR 1981 MAR '90
MAR - - '98	APR - - '94

FREE PUBLIC LIBRARY
Phillipsburg, New Jersey 08865